What Leaders Are Saying About *Parent Fuel*

"I have known and appreciated Barry St. Clair for years. He has a clear and resounding record of good, helpful, and faithful ministry. His new book will greatly help parents (and grandparents) in stirring the potential with the next generation. I know of no one who can do this any better."

—DR. HENRY BLACKABY, founder and president emeritus,
Blackaby Ministries International

"For those of us who operate in the world of professional ministry, Barry St. Clair is an icon. He has spent his life coaching and equipping men and women who wake up every morning with a burden for middle and high school students. In *Parent Fuel*, Barry draws from his experience, both in ministry and as a parent, to equip moms and dads to fuel a fire for righteousness in the hearts of their kids. Thanks, Barry!"

—ANDY STANLEY, pastor, North Point Community Church

"Barry goes to the heart of connecting parents to their kids. Parents of this disconnected generation need the biblical and practical solutions *Parent Fuel* offers. Each chapter is worth the price of the book."

—JOSH AND DOTTIE MCDOWELL, author of
Evidence That Demands a Verdict

"In *Parent Fuel* Barry St. Clair is not just offering nice principles about parenting. He has lived this message, and he has the fruit to prove it. I watched Barry raise his four children to be godly men and women. This practical book will equip you to do the same."

—J. LEE AND DEBORAH GRADY, editor, *Charisma* magazine

"Having kept a foot in the youth world for nearly thirty-five years, I'm convinced that today there's a far greater quest among many for deeper encounters with God's Son. Throughout this groundswell of spiritual passion, Barry St. Clair has been at the forefront, fanning Christ-focused zeal within thousands of young people in every part of the church. Now in this one-of-a-kind, must-have resource Barry equips us parents to serve our teens in the most strategic way possible—not so much as 'fire-starters' because in many cases God has already lit the flames, but more as 'fire-fuelers,' helping our kids become consumed with Christ for all that He is. This book is hot. It puts a lifetime of youth ministry wisdom at the disposal of those whose primary calling is to disciple the next generation of sold-out servants of Christ: their parents."

—DAVID AND ROBYNE BRYANT, Proclaim Hope!

"*Parent Fuel* evaporates the fog around parenting and youth ministry to reveal parenting as youth ministry. It paints a clear picture for effective parenting of teens and provides empowering prescriptions for developing healthy Christian youth from home. The personal insights are moving and catalytic. Parents must read this book!"

—JAY AND LAURA MOONEY, director, Assemblies of God,
National Youth Ministries/Youth Alive

"*Parent Fuel* is just the ignition needed for every parent/child relationship today! Barry St. Clair deals with the tough issues of parenting that too often lay hidden! It is refreshing and applicable! This is an exciting approach to the journey of being the best you can be for the 'treasures' in your life! Gather around the campfire and watch as your parenting will begin to fan the flame of your child's heart!"

—JOE AND DEBBIE-JO WHITE, president, Kanakuk Kamps

"Parents want to find the one, single focus to guide them in raising their children. Barry provides that focus in *Parent Fuel* along with laser-like insights and applications on how to pursue the single focus of guiding our kids to love God with all of their hearts."

—BOB AND CHERYL RECCORD, chairman of Total Life Impact Ministries

"*Parent Fuel* is a powerful and practical resource both for parents and the kids they love. Barry St. Clair, one of the leading voices in student ministry for this generation, empowers moms and dads to shape the spiritual direction of their kids. This book shows them how."

—LOUIE AND SHELLIE GIGLIO, Passion Conferences and author of
the student resource *Wired for a Life of Worship*

"Absolutely outstanding! *Parent Fuel* is more than a book— it's a resource center for parenting. Having known Barry and Carol for many years, they have practiced what they've preached—and the rewards of their labors are evident in their kids. This truly is must reading for every parent."

—RANDY AND CAROL POPE, pastor, Perimeter Church

"Barry St. Clair is one of the world's top authorities on young people. His expertise and passion to help parents fuel the fire of faith with their children is life transforming. In this book we will learn what our heart already cries out for, and that is how to build a legacy of faith to the next generation."

—JIM BURNS, PH.D., president, HomeWord; author of
Creating an Intimate Marriage

"I started reading *Parent Fuel* this morning and have already been blessed by the stories of your children and your own testimony. I have been blessed every time I have heard you share, and your books through the years have ministered to me."

—JOHNNY HUNT, pastor, First Baptist Church, Woodstock, Georgia

"I've known Barry for over twenty-five years—I assure you, he lives his stuff. His hard-earned experience and godly maturity is a gift to all of us who love our kids and want to be better parents."

—PAUL FLEISCHMANN, president, National Network of Youth Ministries

PARENT
FUEL
BARRY ST. CLAIR

FOR THE
FIRE INSIDE
OUR KIDS

CROSSWAY BOOKS

A PUBLISHING MINISTRY OF
GOOD NEWS PUBLISHERS
WHEATON, ILLINOIS

Library of Congress Cataloging-in-Publication Data
St. Clair, Barry.
 Parent fuel : for the fire inside our kids / Barry St. Clair.
  p. cm.
 ISBN 13: 978-1-58134-830-9 (tpb)
 ISBN 10: 1-58134-830-4
 1. Christian education—Home training. 2. Christian education of children. 3. Parenting—Religious aspects—Christianity. 4. Child rearing—Religious aspects—Christianity. 5. Parent and child—Religious aspects—Christianity. I. Title.
BV1590.S695 2007
248.8'45—dc22   2006028593

VP		17	16	15	14	13	12	11	10	09	08	07
15	14	13	12	11	10	9	8	7	6	5	4	3	2	1

Reflecting on my life, I see both tragedy and triumph. God has been very good to me in both. He has graciously surrounded me with family who have loved me and whom I have loved. To them I dedicate this book.

To Carol. I express the deepest gratitude for the privilege of spending twenty-eight years with her. We loved each other deeply and invested that love in our children. One fall day we sat on the floor in a bookstore with scores of parenting books around us asking ourselves if we should write a book for parents. Surely everything had been said. In the end we believed that our relationship with God, each other, and our children would benefit parents. *Ignite the Fire*, the last project we worked on before her death, we wrote together. It expressed our parenting approach and the core values of this book. Almost everything I know about parenting I learned from Carol; so her influence on this book is enormous. I am so glad God gave us to each other, even though for a much briefer time than I had hoped.

To Lawanna. Where would I be without her? In a series of events that only God could orchestrate we experienced an almost immediate love connection. And then we joined our lives, our grief over the death of our spouses, and our hopes and dreams for the future. Now with kids scattered everywhere, we enjoy each other. Together we have a wholehearted desire to make the second half of our lives count for God's glory.

To our kids and grandkids. Plain and simple, I love my kids and grandkids. They light up my life. Scott and Cameron, Price, Blane, and Virginia; Bart and Katie, Caroline, Clair, and Mary Cameron; Charlie and Dava, Abby and Charles David ("Chucko"), Jonathan and Catherine and Ginny.

To my parents. My heritage in Christ is a gift that cannot be measured. Howard and Kitty St. Clair and their parents before them demonstrated the main theme of this book: love the Lord with all your heart, and guide your children to do the same. Carol's parents, Buddy and Bev Price, displayed the same with her, and they have loved me like a son. Truly our family is a product of God's promise that *he is the faithful God, keeping his covenant of love to a thousand generations of those who love him* (Deuteronomy 7:9).

PARENT FUEL KIT

FOR YOUR CHURCH OR SMALL GROUP

The **Parent Fuel Kit** by Barry St. Clair has more fuel for your parenting fire!

Parent Fuel Journal. This companion piece to the **Parent Fuel** book gives you the tools to reflect further on your parenting and your kids and then to implement the practical realities of the book.

Parent Fuel Audio CDs. Presented live before parents, these talks offer encouragement and guidance from Barry's parenting experience.

Parent Fuel DVD Series. This six-session highly interactive DVD series inspires and motivates. It features Barry St. Clair and a variety of parents expressing their struggles and successes in parenting their kids, along with plenty of small group discussion. These videos introduce the message of the **Parent Fuel** book to parents in your church, small group, school, or neighborhood.

Contents

Acknowledgments

The magnitude of this book project has proven quite a challenge, actually much more than I expected. Without the contribution of several special people you would not hold it in your hands now.

Greg Johnson, my agent and editor, who pressed me hard to make this book more excellent and then put his shoulder to the wheel for that to happen. I am grateful to have a literary guru like Greg come alongside me.

Ruthie Arnold, who helped in the editing process, causing the words and thoughts to flow smoothly. She improved the manuscript significantly.

Laura Thompson, who pored over the final manuscript, applying her considerable proofing skills.

Crossway Books, who took a risk on publishing this book. Thank you, Allan Fisher, Ted Griffin, and Josh Dennis, for patiently working with me to make it better.

The Reach Out Team, who released me from the office to write all summer and picked up considerable slack for me.

Cathey Goodroe, my one and only sister who loves her older brother in spite of himself. Thanks so much for taking your time to read the manuscript thoroughly and through your suggestions to soften my rough edges considerably.

To all of my kids, without whom this book would lose most of its good illustrations. I deeply appreciate all we have been through, both the fun and the pain. God has used it all to shape us and to draw us to Him and each other. His grace continues to take us deeper.

Lawanna St. Clair, my second-half life partner. Every day of my life without her is a treasure lost. Regarding the book, she not only read the manuscript thoroughly but also advised me, encouraged me, and stuck with me through the extraordinarily long days and late nights of the long, hot summer of writing.

Love the Lord your God with all your heart
and with all your soul and with all your mind.
This is the first and greatest commandment.

JESUS

Fuel!

Whoosh! When fuel touches the tiny spark, combustion occurs, and the fire flames with the *whoosh* sound.

Whoosh! happens when the fuel goes from its source, through the pump at the gas station, into a hand-held gas container. That fuel poured on a fire pit, like the one behind our house, then comes in contact with a lighted match—*whoosh!*

From the source, through the dispenser, to the spark—that's how the fire ignites. Similarly the Source pumps His fuel through parents who dispense His fuel to the spark He has ignited in our kids—*whoosh!*

the **Source**

from God

through Parents

to Kids

That image portrays our opportunity, mission, and charge as parents. Through our *relationship with the Source* and our *relationship with our kids*, we dispense the fuel of God onto the tiny spark ignited by God in our kids' hearts. Without the dispenser, the fuel cannot get to the fire! With parents as the dispenser, the fuel pumps a passion for Christ on the tiny spark, and it ignites into a flaming fire—*whoosh!*

It's all about the *relationship!* When parents connect with God and then connect with their kids, the fire of God can ignite and steadily increase the flame. This book *equips parents to go to the Source and then to dispense the fuel to their kids through relationships.*

It's like the relationship I have with my daughter, Ginny. We have experienced so much together. And I remember the crazy occurrence when we connected relationally and the fuel began to flow. On our first big trip together, we traveled to California after she turned ten. Five of our ten days together we spent in my world, speaking to a gathering of teenagers. The other five days we jumped into her world—Disneyland, Knotts Berry Farm, and Sea World. We had fun! To this day we cherish our picture together with Winnie the Pooh.

Yet beyond the fun our most memorable experience came on the day we drove to Balboa Island. A friend had loaned us a "nice" car. But when he handed us the keys he informed us that it had no air-conditioning and that the electric windows "might have some problems." Yes, they did! They did not roll down, and we had no AC. We tried to ditch the car and get a rental, only to discover that my driver's license had expired five months earlier. At that point I wondered if we might spend the day in the police station.

With the "nice" car as our only option, we drove that "wreck" onto sophisticated Balboa Island. When we parked it, the windows indeed did not work, nor did the doors—except one. To get out, Ginny had to climb out one partially open window and open the hatchback. Then I had to climb out of the driver's seat, through the backseat, and out the back of the car. At this point both of us had broken into a full sweat and had attracted a crowd of onlookers. We repeated that process every time we got out of that car—for a week. At the end we wanted to drive that car into the ocean!

As ridiculous as it may seem, that "hatchback bomb" experience symbolizes our bond. A bond that has grown through the sickness and death of my wife and Ginny's mother, through our "single" days together, through my remarriage, the family blending, and her delayed bout with grief. As her dad, my relationship with the Source fueled me, so in turn I could fuel Ginny. I could dispense the fuel, and she could receive it because of our ever-deepening heart-connection. Through our relationship, her tiny spark has ignited!

In our reading journey together we will discover how to make those relationship connections and pump the fuel from the Source to the spark. Then the fire will burn. And the more fuel we add, the hotter the fire burns.

Fire!

The bonfire burned hot as about a dozen of us youth leaders sat on the edge of the canyon watching the sunset. A wild three days together on a west Texas ranch had offered us some unique experiences. We had rappelled over a cliff and off a rock inscribed with the words, "Lean back and live!" We'd herded cattle on horseback, hiked through the canyon, and gathered for grub cooked over an open campfire. As darkness set in, I stared into the hot orange flames leaping from the mesquite logs. Mesmerized, I found myself lost in my thoughts—about fire and all the gifts this simple element brings to man.

Fire warms. On this increasingly cold fall night in Texas, I scooted as close to that fire as I could get.

Fire brightens. No lights anywhere! Away from the fire it looked darker than normal to this city boy. The fire offered our only source of illumination.

Fire consumes. The barbeque cooked over the hot, smoking wood tasted delicious. So did the baked potatoes, vegetables, apple pie, and coffee. The heat of the fire made the food taste better. But if we had left our meal on the fire too long, it would have burned into charcoaled nothingness. A bunch of grown-up little boys, we threw a few scraps of food into the fire just to watch them sizzle. Eventually the scraps disappeared completely, totally consumed.

Fire refines. Warren, our cowboy/guide, built the fire close to the corral. He had used that same fire pit many times to brand cattle and to shape horseshoes. He could fashion the horseshoes with his blacksmith's tools and the heat of the flames, which burned out all the alloys and left only the pure metal.

Fire can also describe God and our relationship to Him.

And in a most fascinating way it expresses how He wants us to parent our children.

When we begin a relationship with God, He builds a fire in us that warms us, brightens us, consumes us, and refines us. And as that fire burns in our hearts, God uses it to kindle a fire in our children's hearts.

Yet today that fire often gets doused in the hearts of teenagers. Maybe you find that true in your own home. Why so much widespread apathy—toward God, toward life, toward all things meaningful?

In many churches and families with teenagers, either the fire never started or only a spark remains. Josh McDowell summarizes the problem: "The reality is that the majority of our young people are adopting a 'Christianity' that is making little or no difference in their lives."

In other words, they have the words of faith but no fiery enthusiasm for their faith.

Why? Many reasons define the problem, and we'll take a shot at addressing those.

What can we as fallible, busy parents do not only to avoid spiritual apathy in our children, but more, to pour fuel on the fire of their hearts? I can hardly wait for us to go through this book so we can fuel this fire together!

Maybe you're worried that your past and/or your own spiritual life now don't exactly exhibit a shining example of sainthood. I have good news for you! I love the line from *My Big Fat Greek Wedding*, especially when applied to parenting: "Don't let your past dictate who you are, but let it be part of who you will become."

Don't let where your kids have been or where you have been in the past dampen your fiery enthusiasm for the future. To use another movie line, in this book we will look back but only to enhance the future. Back to the future, so to speak!

If you desire a fresh start when it comes to raising your kids, *Parent Fuel: For the Fire Inside Our Kids* offers you a new, fiery perspective on parenting filled with possibilities. In fact, as a result of reading and *applying* this book . . .

- You will move past your guilt over what you have not done.
- You will make your pursuit of Jesus a passionate priority.
- You will change from raising your kids by rules to raising them by God's amazing grace.

• You will take steps toward connecting or reconnecting in your relationship with your children.

• You will relate to your children from your heart toward your child's heart.

• You will invest in a discipling relationship with your kids and your kids' friends.

• You will exercise discipline that will move your children from dependence to independence.

• . . . and much more!

In a sentence, you will discover how to guide your children to passionately pursue Jesus, and in the process they will discover their hearts.

Once the fire starts, it spreads quickly. God ignites the spark; we pour the fuel on the spark in their hearts; the spark turns into a blaze; then their brightly burning fire spreads to others.

I hope that my experience as a dad and my own family's amazing journey will . . .

motivate
    encourage
        guide
            advise
                inspire you to *fuel the fire inside your child's heart!*

Fuel the Fire First in Us

To fuel a fire in our kids, first we fuel a fire in ourselves. An honest assessment of mistakes, priorities, and painful past experiences plus a desperate need for God's fuel gives us much greater potential to make a difference in our kids' lives. The fiery intensity of our own pursuit of God will determine the degree of passion with which we will pass on our faith to our kids.

1

*How do we break through our imperfections
to pursue God's purpose for our kids?*

Parents aren't perfect. They never have been, never will be.

Years ago a young couple came to visit my wife Carol and me to observe and ask questions about our close and loving family who had "successfully" traveled down the parenting road. They had recently started their own family and had feelings of inadequacy about raising their children. During dinner they peppered us with questions. All went well, until my son Jonathan, about ten at the time, spoke disrespectfully to his mother. Since disrespect meant discipline, I sent him to his room. He left with the chair screeching and his feet stomping.

Needless to say, the questions about our close and loving family lost a little zip. A few minutes later we moved downstairs to our den. On the way I dropped by Jonathan's room to check on him. I turned the door handle.

Locked.

"Jonathan, open the door," I whispered. No answer. I made the request again, turning up my volume a bit.

This time he yelled his refusal. "Dad, get away from my door!" His voice fell within easy earshot of our visitors. As I came back to the den, interrupting Carol's conversation with our guests, I could feel the tension rising in the discussion about how to raise a close and loving family. A few minutes later I walked back to Jonathan's bedroom door. When I knocked this time, there was no answer!

I knocked more loudly.

No answer.

I had no choice but to raise my voice to Yell Level, hoping our guests would not hear too much of the commotion. When it became clear that my son had no intention of answering, I walked through the den, past our parenting disciples, and out the door to get to the window outside his bedroom.

"Excuse me," I said, red-faced, managing a weak smile in the direction of our company as I passed by. "I have to go outside to look in my son's window." When I got to Jonathan's window, I found it open and his room empty.

Great. With perfect timing he had apparently decided to make The Great Escape and run away from home.

I loaded Carol in the car to search for our runaway son, along with our bewildered company who joined in the search. We drove in total silence until we spotted the escapee a few blocks away. He turned, saw our car, and took off running. Though impressively quick-footed, he wasn't quite as fast as a speeding car filled with frantic parents and confused passengers. It wasn't long before we had the little guy cornered and safely captured.

We pulled up into the driveway of our Home Sweet Home, and not surprisingly, the couple politely, but very quickly, excused themselves and left.

We never heard from them again.

When we spoke to Jonathan later, we resolved the problem. In fact, in later years it became a staple "tell it again" story when we'd gather as a family. We'd shake with laughter as Jonathan colorfully recounted the story about his "tyrannical oppressors."[1]

Imperfect Parents, Imperfect Kids

It bears repeating: Parents aren't perfect!

And surprise, surprise, kids aren't perfect either.

All this adds up to a firm common denominator: imperfect families.

Parents aren't perfect. Never have been. Never will be.

Have you ever considered this fact? Our grandparents and parents survived being raised in imperfection. Yet through the generations many of them took the job of fire-builders. This e-mail sent to me by a counselor friend might encourage you to see that we can survive parenthood in spite of our imperfections and still qualify to become fire-builders ourselves.

To the Kids Who Survived the 50s, 60s, and 70s:

First, we survived being born to mothers who smoked and/or drank while they carried us. They took aspirin, ate blue cheese dressing and didn't get tested for diabetes. Then after that trauma, our baby cribs were covered with bright-colored, lead-based paints.

We had no child-proof lids on medicine bottles, doors, or cabinets. When we rode our bikes, we had no helmets—not to mention the risks we took hitchhiking. As children we would ride in cars with no seat belts or air bags. Riding in the back of a pickup on a warm day was always a special treat. We drank water from the garden hose and *not* from a bottle. We shared one soft drink from one bottle with four friends, and *no one* actually died from this.

We ate cupcakes, bread and butter, and drank soda pop with sugar in it, but we weren't overweight because we were always outside playing! We would leave home in the morning and play all day, as long as we were back when the streetlights came on. No one was able to reach us all day. And we were okay. We would spend hours building our go-carts out of scraps and then ride down the hill, only to find out we forgot the brakes. After running into the bushes a few times, we learned to solve the problem.

We did not have Playstations, Nintendos, X-boxes, video games, 99-1000 channels of TV, no DVD movies, no surround sound, no cell phones, no personal computers, no Internet or Internet chat rooms. . . .

We fell out of trees, got cut, broke bones and teeth, and there were no lawsuits from these accidents. We made up games with sticks and tennis balls and ate worms and, although we were told it would happen, we did not put out very many eyes, nor did the worms live in us forever.

We rode bikes or walked to a friend's house and knocked on the door or rang the bell, or just walked in and talked to them!

Little League had tryouts and not everyone made the team. Those who didn't had to learn to deal with disappointment. Imagine that! We misbehaved at home or in school and our mother would say, "Wait till your father gets home." Then our father would say, "This will hurt me more than it will hurt you." But we did not believe him because the spanking *did* hurt. The idea of parents bailing us out if we broke the law was unheard of. They actually sided with the law!

Now we live in more uptight times. Voices speak to parents from many different directions telling us to feed, teach, and discipline our children in certain ways, and if we don't, we have set them up for certain failure.[2] It seems that at every turn others like to point out how we do it all wrong, and often we believe them.

Imperfections Magnified

Added to that, life and circumstances have a way of magnifying our imperfections. Carol, my first wife, and I were married for twenty-eight years before her untimely death (more on that later). We had what I call a "normal" family—two parents and four children doing their best to live life together. Yes, we had the typical disagreements, conflicts, hurts, and pains. And we tried to work through them by honestly facing our faults, admitting when we had treated each other wrongly, and finding ways to negotiate our disagreements.

It's within such a "normal" family structure that God gives us the best opportunity to raise children to become healthy adults. And we did that. Scott, Katie, and Jonathan, my three oldest children, fortunately lived nearly all of their childhood years "intact." And in spite of their parents they became healthy adults.

Then tragedy struck! On August 2, 1998, the wife of my youth, my Carol, died after a long illness. On that day my life changed in what seemed like ten thousand ways. Suddenly a reality I thought I'd never experience flashed in front of me like a neon sign: *YOU ARE A SINGLE DAD!*

At the time, Ginny, our youngest, was eleven. In the hearse on the way back from the funeral, she leaned her head on my shoulder and asked, "Dad, what can you cook?" Even as I waded through the mire of soul-numbing grief, I entered a sixth-grader in school and began a new phase of life, the hardest I've ever experienced. I survived as one person filling two roles. Constantly behind, constantly overwhelmed, I would stay up until 1 A.M. and get up at 5 A.M. just to meet the demands the new day would bring.

In the mornings the alarm would shake me to life, and I'd say, "Lord, please help me. I cannot move. Unless You get my foot over the side of this bed, I will never get out of here. I do not have the physical or emotional energy to get up and face the day." That went on for months until I found myself at the point of utter exhaustion. Being a single parent brought a challenge I could not meet. My imperfections glared at me. I felt as though I couldn't do anything, much less do anything right.

In an amazing turn of events, a friend sent me a book on grief—*A Grace Disguised* by Gerald Sittser. A year earlier, my friend too had lost her spouse. Her husband and I had actually enjoyed a long friendship. And she knew my wife Carol. As she and I exchanged e-mails about the book she sent and our common grief, we decided to get together and talk about it. When we met face-to-face a couple of months later, we connected on a deep level. That eventually led to an ever-increasing love. Some people never have the opportunity to love once. God gave us each the gift of loving twice. Lawanna Busby and I married several months later.

And so we lived happily ever after.

Not exactly! Yes, we love and enjoy each other. But blending families is not for the faint of heart. Life became . . . a bit complex, even complexly complex.

As a result of our union, our "trying to blend" family consists of five children (four of whom are married) and eight grandchildren. We pray hard and work hard at fitting all the pieces together. And guess what—it's not perfect.

Every parent, even every Christian leader I've known, struggles with the same imperfections you do. In fact, for me the more years of life I count, the more my imperfections become magnified. Yes, I stand with you as one of those imperfect parents.

Imperfection's Black Holes

In spite of those imperfections, I write this book to offer hope and help, especially for parents who struggle with their faults and who seriously question their parenting capabilities.

Have you ever been paralyzed over the guilt of your shortcomings? I sure have. Sometimes we become afraid to move in any direction for fear that we will do something wrong, perhaps even make things worse.

If we view our imperfections without the light of God's love, forgiveness, and grace, we can fall into emotional black holes that render us useless to anyone, especially our children! I've discovered that most parents tend to fall into one or more of four different black holes. Each one can engulf us in darkness and confusion about being the parents we want to be. By staying in one or more of these black holes, we never move beyond our own failures to fulfill our parenting purpose.

Black Hole #1—The "Done Its"

Some parents feel they have tried everything to parent well, yet it hasn't worked out for them . . . or their kids. Their precious little children have grown into angry, rebellious adults who bring more heartache than joy. Honestly, when we finish our primary parenting years, all parents question themselves. All of us ask the question, "Should I have done some things differently?" The woulda, shoulda, coulda voices can become a constant whisper as we see what we think is the finished product.

With sadness I listened to a longtime friend talk about his son. In more than one of our conversations this dad has been on the verge of desperation. At other times he had resigned heartbreak written all over his face. During adolescence this son began to put up a wall between himself and his parents. At first he erected it toward spiritual matters, then later toward moral issues. The wall grew quietly, insidiously, and before long it seemed insurmountable. At one point his parents had to do an intervention, forcibly removing him from their home and taking him to a facility for wayward young men. This gut-wrenching experience left the father and mother feeling like a pair of deflated balloons, fizzling and falling motionless to the floor. After much prayer and counsel, they have learned to cope with their unmarried son, who broke up with his girlfriend after the birth of a baby. These parents have endured their pain and embraced the baby who came out of this unwed relationship. Underneath, however, the heartbreak remains.

What should they have done differently? Having known this couple for years, the answer is . . . nothing. Certainly they made mistakes. Certainly they have their flaws. Certainly they were not perfect parents. But they loved, nurtured, and provided well for their son. They made a physical, emotional, and spiritual investment in him that for most kids actually works. In truth, they did all they could.

Until recently it didn't look like that investment was paying any dividends. But now, after years of patiently waiting while their son struggled, they have begun to see him come back to renew relationships—both with them as parents and with the Lord. The investment that they once questioned has begun to bear fruit again. What they saw in him as a teenager by no means will end up as the finished product!

Are you heading toward this same black hole of despair and resignation? Be aware, and be encouraged that "The Hound of Heaven" ever watches and woos your children back to Himself!

> **"The Hound of Heaven" ever watches and woos your children back to Himself!**

Black Hole #2—The "Haven't Done Its"

Parents often look back on their parenting experience and realize what they have *not* done. They wish they had done more. Living with that regret, they wonder if it is too late.

Because of the cultural lies that have been fed to this generation of parents, many of us get to a certain point in our parenting, glance back over our shoulders, and recognize that our children needed more of us. Due to dads who work too much and therefore physically and emotionally render themselves unavailable, often boys haven't had the fathers they need. With many working moms, other people have nurtured or not nurtured our children, as the case may be. Most of us wake up one day to the stark realization that the job we hold, the money we make, and the things we can buy simply do not measure up to the price we have paid in missing out on raising our children.

My friends Don and Cindi faced that dilemma and wisely decided to take a hard look at their parenting approach. Both worked for an airline company. Both lived with the long hours and the high stress of their jobs. After having children and realizing that they had fallen into the "Haven't Done Its" black hole, they creatively figured out how to get out of it. Cindi quit her job. Then she used her abilities to begin an outsourcing business with stay-at-home moms—from her home. She finds clients who need a specific labor skill and then connects them to stay-at-home moms who have those skills. The clients pay highly skilled individuals at a lower-than-market rate, but the moms get to stay at home with their children and yet bring in income. And the kids receive nurturing attention from their moms every day. Everybody wins! And Don, the dad, has figured out how to use his flying privileges to take the entire family to places around the world where they could never go otherwise. Don and Cindi saw themselves in a black hole but refused to stay there.

Whether we have fallen in the "Haven't Done Its" black hole only recently or long ago, we must understand that we *can* get out. When I speak to parents, inevitably they ask, "I have teenagers. Is it too late for me?" The answer is always the same: "Never!"

If you find yourself in this black hole, it's never too late to get out.

> **It's never too late!**

Black Hole #3—The "Undone Its"

These parents compare themselves to other parents and feel that they don't measure up.

One mom I know (let's call her Sandy) sent her children to the same school that our children attended. She had sharp kids. They received good grades in school. They had musical talent. They excelled in athletics. Yet she always compared her kids to other children. It didn't take long for her to start berating herself as a mom. "John just doesn't grasp spiritual things like Austin. Andrea isn't in the advanced class with Suzanne. Josh isn't scoring as many points as Michael. We must be doing something wrong." By comparing her kids in this way, she came up short in her view of her children, her husband, and herself.

Who suffered most? Everyone! Her low self-esteem that created these negative comparisons drove everyone up the wall.

These sorts of parents who feel like they don't measure up look around at what other moms and dads have, what they do, and what they say, then look at themselves with condemnation and think, *I fall woefully short of being a good parent.* Actually most of us who fall in this hole (and most of us have fallen in this hole!) have done and are doing many great things for our kids. But we feel like the negatives outweigh the positives. This sometimes leaves us feeling like a piece of dirt.

Notice that I have used the word *feel* or *feeling* three times in the above paragraph. Often, due to low self-esteem, we don't think consciously or act deliberately about the way we parent. Rather we respond emotionally, allowing our feelings to create our parenting reality. We see how our kids act and react in situations with other children. We observe that our children don't always measure up to others. And then we react to that by reaching negative conclusions not only about our children but also about ourselves.

Comparing ourselves with others, negatively or positively, leads only to a dead end. On the other hand, realizing that God created each of our children uniquely—and that each has a God-given destiny—will absolutely change the way we parent. And that change will usually move our children to fulfill that destiny, not to mention beginning to pull us out of the "my kids and I don't measure up" black hole.

If you find yourself in this black hole, don't pin the burden of your self-esteem on your child's shoulders. Instead face your insecurities and pursue your self-worth in Someone who can create real security.

> **Pursue your self-worth in Someone who can create real security.**

Black Hole #4—The "Half-Done Its"

Some parents, like me several years ago, function in the mode of single parent. Others operate with one parent pulling against the other, either in their personal relationship or in their parenting philosophy. These parents know that they do not and cannot operate at 100 percent capacity. Either 50 percent of the parenting team misses the action or 50 percent of the parenting team opposes what the other one wants. One produces a sense of inadequacy. The other creates high levels of tension.

Death, divorce, or spiritual opposition can leave a parent in this black hole. Every time I lead a parenting conference, tearful parents come to me begging for help. Desperately they search for an answer to their dilemma. At one such conference I listened empathetically as a mom of three teenage boys told me about the death of her husband and how it had devastated each of her sons. She felt completely inadequate. Her feelings of grief and abandonment overwhelmed her. She felt frustrated at her ineptness to do anything to guide her boys. She looked at the ground, shook her head, and cried. I cried with her.

Divorce leaves the family in an even bigger mess. Let's don't sugarcoat this: *children of divorce have deep wounds!* They become the victims of their parents' decision. That being said, a spouse sustains deep wounds and feels victimized as well. One of my friends (we will call her Julie) married her dream man and had her three dream kids, and her husband got the dream job with the financial pot at the end of the rainbow. Then he had an affair, and the dream turned into a nightmare. For years she has had to clean up the mess—not only her shattered dreams, but the shattered dreams of her children as well.

Spiritual opposition between Mom and Dad can create the biggest mess of all. A tug-of-war, with one parent pulling for God and the other parent pulling against Him, definitely confuses kids. Yet if we find ourselves in this tension, we can be encouraged. Our children are not stupid. They see the light in the midst of the darkness. With childlike clarity and simplicity, they know right from wrong. Perceptively, they know what emotional and spiritual death looks like as opposed to life, and they will opt for life almost every time. However, you face the battle of living with spousal tension 24/7 and in the midst of that tension the challenge of finding the wisdom to live life God's way in front of your family.

Helene had been looking for God for twenty years. After we talked, she realized that finding Jesus was the end of her search. But her husband would have nothing to do with that. He expressed (and still does) total opposition to God, Jesus, the Holy Spirit, or anything that remotely resembled spirituality. For years she lived with her husband's agnosticism and antagonism. Yet through her prayers and influence her daughter and later her daughter's husband, her son and his wife, and her grandchildren all became fervent followers of Jesus.

Even if you face such severe difficulties, you can dig out of this black hole over time with God's help.

You can dig out over time with God's help!

Beyond Imperfections to Purpose

If we find ourselves in one of these black holes, we need to admit that we feel defeated by our imperfections and guilt and ask God to lead us out. That's His specialty, you know. It's what Jesus came to do.

I saw a greeting card by Max Lucado the other day that made me smile. He suggested imagining God pulling a dump truck of His love up next to you and unloading its contents until you are absolutely covered with His love. The cure for our messed-up selves begins with letting God do just that. And consider this truth of equal value: the love of God offers the only answer for your children when they, too, come face-to-face with their own messy selves.

If we do not turn our eyes and hearts toward His love, we will continually feel guilty over what we have done, what we haven't done, what's undone, and what is half-done. Guilt only wastes our emotional energy if it doesn't lead us to reach for and be embraced by God's goodness and grace. But with the abundance of love we receive from God's embrace, we can move out of these black holes and move forward positively with our lives and purposefully toward our kids.

We need to remember the apostle Paul's perspective on our past imperfections:

Forgetting what is behind and straining toward what is ahead, I press on toward the goal to win the prize.
PHILIPPIANS 3:13-14

The apostle Paul said that he had learned to do two things when the thoughts of his past started to immobilize him: *Forgetting what is behind and straining toward what is ahead.* If an ex-murderer of Christians can get past guilt and go on, you can too. In fact, you owe it to your kids to do so, for two reasons: 1) They need a recovering, healthy parent who fully and joyfully shows up for them. 2) They need an example of how to handle life God's way when they hit the wall of their own failures. God and His love for you prevail over your imperfections.

God and His love for you prevail over your imperfections.

Whatever our personal life circumstances, whatever we have or have not done in the past, wherever our children are now, God wants to use us significantly in our children's lives.

In order for Him to do that, we must come out of the black hole and look upward, breathe fresh air, and move above our limitations and our past failings. Even in our imperfections, what does God have in mind for us? What's His purpose for us as moms and dads?

God has called us to be parents!

That seems readily apparent, but in our day the meaning of *parents* has gotten muddled. From God's viewpoint, what does He have in mind? He wants us parents to play the vital role with our kids in *fueling the fire for Him in them.*

For each child in each family, God wants *to ignite a fire in their hearts.*

And from before creation, God has had in mind for us parents *to kindle a passion for Christ in our kids!*

Do not put out the Spirit's fire.

When the apostle Paul wrote the book of 1 Thessalonians, he addressed believers as a caring mother speaks to her young and as a father deals with his children (see 2:7, 11). And in the closing verses of the book he says, *Do not put out the Spirit's fire* (5:19). God has placed the spark of His Spirit in each of our children. They want to know Him. However, we don't want to unwittingly throw water on the fire of His Spirit in our kids. Instead He desires to use us as the primary people who fuel the spark in their lives—*parent fuel.* Grasping this truth puts a match to our parenting purpose!

Taking Action

Think briefly about which black hole you tend to fall into. Ask God to show you why and how you have fallen into that hole. Ask Him to show you how to get out. Write down what you discover.

Penetrating Questions

1. On a scale of 1-10 how easy is it for you to admit that you are an imperfect parent?

2. What one example can you give of your imperfection with your children?

3. What one example can you offer of your children's imperfections? (Name only one.)

4. Which black hole do you tend to fall into most often? Why?

5. How do you think God wants to get you out, keep you out, and move you beyond that black hole?

6. In spite of your imperfections, what purpose does God have for you as a parent?

7. How do you see yourself fueling a passion for Christ in your kids?

Fresh Ideas

• Viewing ourselves positively, not negatively, provides one of the fastest ways to create fresh ideas about our parenting. That positive view of ourselves will begin to emerge after we admit our imperfections. Write down your parenting imperfections.

• After deciding which black hole you fall into most often, ask God to show you a specific plan to get out and stay out. Write out the plan.

• In a phrase that will fit on a T-shirt, write out your parenting purpose, then have it painted onto a T-shirt or some other surface. Display your purpose someplace where you will see it regularly.

• Share with your spouse what you have written above. Pray for each other about the parenting black holes you fall into and about your parenting purpose. Appropriately communicate the same to your children.

Further Reading

Brent Curtis and John Eldredge, *The Sacred Romance* (Nashville: Thomas Nelson, 1997). This book will allow you to see your imperfections against the story of God's love for you. It will help you see how you fit into God's story in spite of your flaws and failures.

Tim Kimmel, *Grace-based Parenting* (Nashville: W Publishing Group, 2004). This book offers grace and truth, love and purpose, as well as hope and freedom for our parenting adventure.

Stoke the Spark—
From God to Parents to Kids

*How do we connect with God's primary desire
for us and our kids?*

Barry, you have an invitation to meet the President tomorrow," my friend said calmly. My response, however, was not so calm. As a member of the National Prayer Committee, yes, indeed, I did have the opportunity to meet with the President of the United States (along with two hundred other people).

When I called home that night, my daughter Ginny said, "Dad, when you meet the President, tell him there is a fourteen-year-old girl in Atlanta who thinks he is really cool and is glad he is the President."

I responded, "Ginny, there is no way I am going to tell him that. Besides, two hundred people will be there."

"Please, Dad," she said.

I replied, "No way, Gin."

The next day I entered the East Wing of the White House, found my seat, and waited with anticipation for the entrance of the President. The voice in the back of the room announced, "Ladies and gentlemen, the

President of the United States." Everyone stood and applauded. After a brief speech highlighting the National Day of Prayer, the President concluded his remarks by saying, "Now let's have a little time of fellowship." I thought he would hang around for five minutes, then leave. I knew I would not get to shake his hand because I got stuck close to the end of the line. But he stayed and greeted each one of us . . . *personally.*

Somewhere along that line I began to think, *Okay, what do I say to the President of the United States?* Certainly he did not need my advice on energy policy or the Middle East. When he stuck out his hand, I blurted out, "Hello, Mr. President. My name is Barry St. Clair. There is a fourteen-year-old girl in Atlanta who thinks you are very cool, and she wants you to know that she is glad you are the President."

He smiled and asked, "What's her name?"

"Ginny," I said.

"You tell Ginny I said hello," he responded with a chuckle. We exchanged pleasantries, and then I moved on down the line.

The President's intern was supposed to take pictures of each of us with the President, but he stopped that routine about halfway through the line. When I exited the line, I saw Jim and Janice Weidemann, my friends who had set up this special opportunity. I commented, "What an awesome experience to meet the President. But I wish I'd had my picture taken with him. That's a once-in-a-lifetime opportunity." Janice agreed. So we looked back down the line to the President. Noting there were still four or five people in line, Janice and I took a back route and slipped in at the end of the line. When we got to the President, I said, "Mr. President, my name is Barry St. Clair. I came through the line a few minutes ago."

He said, "You're the one whose daughter thinks I'm cool."

"Yes, sir."

"What can I do for you?" he asked.

"Would it be possible to get an autograph?"

"Sure. Who do you want me to make it out to? Ginny, I'll bet."

"Yes, sir. And could we get a picture with you?"

"Absolutely. Logan [the intern who had said, "No more pictures"], take the picture." Both of us handed him our disposable cameras, and he took our picture with the President of the United States! Very cool!

Later that afternoon I went for a run through the National Mall. With each step I recounted with delight the details of my meeting with the President. As I ran by the Lincoln Memorial, the thought flooded my mind: *Barry, if you put your heart into loving Me as much as you loved meeting the President, we could have a fabulous relationship.*

The Lord stopped me in my tracks!

Exactly twenty-four hours later I attended a National Prayer Committee gathering. Everyone felt tired, sleepy, and ready to leave this late-afternoon meeting. Then one of the ladies made a profound comment about the Lord that changed the environment in the room. What happened next goes beyond my ability to describe. The Holy Spirit swept through that room. We fell on our faces before God and stayed there . . . *for three hours!*

We could hardly speak.

Tears flowed.

But mostly we remained silent.

All of us knew God had given us a special experience of His presence. Beyond anything I had experienced before or since, God spoke to me simply and clearly: "Barry, I love you, and nothing is more important to Me than your loving Me. More than ever, I want you to pursue Me with all of your heart!"

As great as it was to meet the President, having that encounter with the living Lord that day beat meeting the President hands down!

How does my experience with the President and with the holy presence of God Himself connect to our parenting? God's message came loud and clear to me: *I only want one thing: for you to passionately pursue Me with your whole heart.* God's message to parents contains equal clarity: *I only want one thing: for you to passionately pursue Me with your whole heart.*

When we as parents pursue God with all of our hearts, that provides the spark for our children to pursue God wholeheartedly as well. A heart wide-open to God—honest, available, tender, seeking—cannot be hidden from our children. They will see the spark in us and will desire it for themselves.

God's message to parents: *Passionately pursue Me with your whole heart!*

Lean the Ladder Against the Right Wall

"What can I do to make sure my children turn out right?" parents ask me all the time. My response? "Wrong question." That question leans the ladder against the wrong wall. Picture yourself climbing a ladder to get to something, but you cannot get it because you positioned the ladder in the wrong place. Most parents lean their ladders against the wall of per-formance—ours and our children's. Parents try to measure up to certain external expectations that we then internalize like "Set a good example for your kids." Or we expect our children to measure up to external standards that we deem important like "Get all A's." These external expec-tations lead both parents and children to climb the ladder of *extrinsic motivation*. At the top of that ladder we find superficial self-image and behavior based on other people's approval. Leaning the ladder against the wrong wall, asking the wrong question, gives the wrong result.

Let's lean the ladder against the right wall: "How can I help my chil-dren love Jesus more?"

Right question. Right wall. Now picture yourself climbing a ladder, knowing that as you climb, that ladder will take you to exactly the right place. When we lean our ladders against the wall of God's love, that love for us and for our children beckons us to love Him in return. This strong sense of God's love transforms "Set a good example" and "Get all A's" from an external expectation into an internal desire to please God, which leads both parents and children to climb the ladder of *intrinsic motivation*. At the top of this ladder we discover a *heart-to-heart* connection with God and our children. That in turn creates in our children a passion to pursue God with all their hearts. Then our example and our kids' grades find their proper place. Leaning the ladder against the right wall, asking the right question, gives the right result.

Love God with All Your Heart

When Moses gave his final message to the children of Israel, it must have been an electrifying moment. He found himself at the end of a long and arduous journey.

• Forty years of favor in Pharaoh's court.

• Forty more years of deepening discipline on the back side of the desert.

• Forty more years of frustration, trying to lead one million people to the Promised Land but instead wandering in the wilderness.

In each phase of his life Moses pursued his highest purpose (with a few detours along the way). After all, even the leader to whom God gave the Ten Commandments had his flaws. Although Moses died with unfulfilled hopes and dreams, he passed from this life to the next having finished the task God gave him. But not before offering an earth-shattering, final speech for the ages that began like this.

> *Hear, O Israel: The LORD our God, the LORD is one. Love the LORD your God with all your heart and with all your soul and with all your strength. These commandments that I give you today are to be upon your hearts. Impress them on your children. Talk about them when you sit at home and when you walk along the road, when you lie down and when you get up. Tie them as symbols on your hands and bind them on your foreheads. Write them on the doorframes of your houses and on your gates.*
>
> DEUTERONOMY 6:4-9

What message did Moses want to communicate to this audience of over one million people, mostly parents?

• God is God. There is only one God. He is Lord. He is our God.
• Love God with everything within you—heart, soul, and strength.
• Let this command impact you and consume you, and in it find your highest purpose.
• Once this command fills your heart, impress it on your children.
• Influence your children to love God with all of *their* heart, soul, and strength.
• Show them what it means to love God when you *talk, sit, walk, lie down,* and *get up.* (When else is there?)
• Post this as a constant reminder on your hand and forehead, on your front door and gate.

Only a fool could have missed the point, the one thing God desired of them. In a nutshell: *love God with all your heart!*

Parenting in a nutshell: love God with all your heart!

If someone argues that Moses' speech became an obscure Old Testament relic, no longer valid for us, then take a look at Jesus' main message in the Gospels. To keep us from losing sight of this highest priority, Jesus said in three of the four Gospels, *Love the Lord your God with all your heart and with all your soul and with all your mind* (Matthew 22:37-38; Mark 12:29-30; Luke 10:27).

If I am a parent who follows Jesus and who wants my children to follow Jesus, then when I reflect on Jesus' words, I must come to the conclusion that the purpose for my life and my children's lives reaches its peak in these words: *Love the Lord your God with all your heart and with all your soul and with all your mind.*

Once this is rooted inside our hearts, we will want to live the "Love God" message with such authenticity and will desire to communicate it to our children with such enthusiasm that they will find themselves surrounded by God's love at every place they touch our lives.

> **Our kids will passionately pursue what they see us passionately pursue!**

Passionately pursuing Jesus, to use a well-worn phrase, is more caught than taught. Our kids tend to passionately pursue what they see us passionately pursue! What we model for our children in relationships, attitudes, priorities, and actions shapes their lives. Rather than parent by mouthing the right words, performing the right actions, creating the right behaviors, and insisting that our kids do the same, genuine parenting transfers our passionate love for God to our kids. Then words, actions, and behaviors become teaching tools, opportunities to point them back to this one thing: *Love the Lord your God with all your heart and with all your soul and with all your mind.*

Rekindle the Flame Inside

So . . . what stokes the fire in you? Is Jesus the one who lights up your life, or is it something or someone else? Did the fire burn hot at one time, but now the embers have grown cold?

When Carol died, the rain of grief caused the fire in my heart to smolder. Grief, heartbreak, pain, and sadness poured over me in the loss of my wife and friend, the mother of my four children. God's love for me felt distant, and my love for Him felt numb. Death's long arms made every effort to pull me away from my loving Father. But at the funeral, sitting with my children and family, a friend offered a word of encouragement that I recalled several weeks later. It became a very personal word to me. That message began to rekindle the flame inside me.

Cliff Barrows, worship leader for Billy Graham, a survivor of his own wife's death and a mentor and friend to me, spoke and commented on these words:

> The LORD your God is with you,
> he is mighty to save.
> He will take great delight in you,
> he will quiet you with his love,
> he will rejoice over you with singing.
>
> ZEPHANIAH 3:17

God spoke through Cliff's few comments to stoke the fire in my heart. *I am with you. I am saving you. I delight in you. I am quieting you with My love. With joy I am singing songs to you.* While grief surrounded me, my Heavenly Father began rekindling the spark of hope in my broken heart.

Perhaps life's circumstances, pressures, and difficulties have caused your flame to fade. Problems in your relationship with your spouse or children have left you feeling like only a few dying embers remain in your intimacy with Jesus. Living in the real world douses our fire with these love-quenchers. But God stands over us ready to rekindle the flame, calling us back to a love relationship with Himself.

So how do we stoke the fire in our own hearts and in our homes?

Put Jesus in the Black Box

In his book *Halftime* Bob Buford told an insightful personal story that encourages us to look for the spark inside ourselves and our kids. One of his mentors gave Bob the assignment to bring a black box to their next meeting with only one thing in it—the most important thing in his life. The next week Bob came in with the black box and a list of four or five important items to go in the box. His mentor rebuked him and sent him away. "Come back next week with the one most important essential of your life to put in the black box. Just one." During the next few days Bob, a Christian, wrestled with this assignment. He had so many things he wanted in the box—his wife, his children, his career, his hopes and dreams. He struggled fiercely with this decision. The next week he showed up at his meeting with one slip of paper in the box. On it was written one word: *Jesus.*

Do you identify with Bob Buford's struggle?

I do . . . daily.

His story points out the difficulty of crafting our choices about loving God.

In one sense, making the decision to place Jesus in the black box of our lives occurs once in a lifetime; yet every day we must resolve to keep putting Jesus there in difficult daily life choices. An old quote says, "Love is like bread—it has to be made new every day." This is true in every relationship, but especially in our love relationship with God. When we don't make decisions on the basis of that relationship daily, we run into difficulties.

Running has been a passion for me since the seventh grade. Along with a few other weirdly-wired people, I love it. Even more, I can easily become obsessive-compulsive about it. Before my brother-in-law's out-of-town wedding, I decided to go on a run. Just one little hitch emerged—it was against my wife's wishes. But I didn't let that stop me. After we checked into the hotel, I had only a narrow time window to get in my quick jog. So I dressed quickly and took off. About twenty minutes out, I turned around to come back. Within a block or two I realized I had made a wrong turn and gotten lost. And the more I tried to find my way, the more lost I became. Ten minutes, twenty minutes, thirty minutes went by. Panic set in. The time passed for the entire family—about twenty people—to leave for the big event.

Needless to say, Carol panicked. Her dad panicked too. They drove around to find me, and when they did—um, let's just say *happy* did not describe Carol's feelings toward me.

Even though, surprisingly, I made it to the wedding on time, this story ranks right up there with "The Top Ten Barry Blunders." My selfish decision created havoc for the entire family. Everyone felt angry with me. That day I placed *myself* squarely in the black box. My decision to run that day not only went against my wife's desires, but also 180 degrees away from my lifetime black box decision for Jesus to be my life and His servant attitude to guide in my daily decisions. A tough lesson on black box decision-making!

Like you, I have so many important things to put in the black box every day. I get distracted, busy, stressed, and confused. I love my wife, children, job, friends, things, and playing—reading, exercise, movies. When do I have time for God?

Do you struggle like me to put Jesus in the center of your life every day in every decision?

For me, the black box represents my heart. Once I put loving God as my highest purpose and passion, I can make all of my other daily decisions based on that priority.

Right now, will you put Jesus in the black box? God will hear and respond to your simple prayer: *Jesus, I choose to put You in the black box of my life!* Then each day and in every situation, offer that simple prayer to God.

Jesus, I choose to put You in the black box of my life!

By making the black box decision and beginning to pray that prayer daily, you will stoke the spark in your heart as well as spark that same passionate pursuit in your kids. The fire in your heart will in time kindle that same fire in their hearts.

Place Jesus at the Head of the Table

For twenty-eight years Carol and I ate off the same kitchen table. We bought it early in our marriage at an antique flea market . . . cheap. The pine top was stained a natural color, while the legs were painted blue. The chairs around the table matched the blue color on the table legs, sort of. Although it wasn't much to look at, all four of our children slurped milk from their sippy cups and ate their food around that table. Our family told stories, laughed at jokes, shed tears, and experienced life around that table.

But there's more. That table became an altar. We brought every important decision to that table for discussion and prayer. These gatherings did not qualify as family devotions or religious observances as much as simple prayers offered in humble submission to God, asking Him to do His will. That table served as the place where our family drew together to bring our joys and challenges before God.

For example, one night Carol and I felt nervous as we ate our dinner with our three children, who at that time ranged in age from nine to fourteen. Our nervousness resulted from not knowing how they would react to the announcement we planned to make. We didn't know if they would laugh or cry when we told them the news about soon having a little sister. We felt great relief when they embraced the idea. That night, and many nights after that, we prayed around that table for their new little sister.

Carol and I had made the decision during our engagement that we wanted Jesus to be the focal point of our home. That table symbolized our desire for Jesus to take His rightful place as the Living Center of our home—the Head of our table.

Looking back on my twenty-eight years of marriage to Carol, my single-parent days with Ginny and me, my marriage to Lawanna, and our experience of trying to blend our families, one certainty stands out to me: When Jesus occupies the head of the table, when He takes His rightful place as the center of our homes, every meal tastes better, every discussion has deeper meaning, every conflict and hurt has the possibility of resolution and healing. Laughter and tears, words and actions become infused with the presence and power of God. Every decision takes on eternal significance.

God's love passes from our hearts to their hearts.

As the Lord of Love receives and accepts our standing invitation to the table, our children become surrounded by the love of God. Almost inevitably that will result in God's love passing from *our hearts to their hearts*. From the spark that grows into a fire in our hearts, God ignites a spark in their hearts. On both counts that beats meeting the President of the United States hands down!

Taking Action

Answer the question: Do I love God with all my heart?

If not, write down the reasons why and the consequences that has brought into your life and into your children's lives. Since there is no time like the present, write out your statement to God telling Him that you want to decide now to put Him in the black box of your life and place Him at the head of your family table.

If you do love God with all your heart, write in your journal the value and consequences of that decision in your life and in your children's lives.

Penetrating Questions

1. What primary desire does God have for parents and through parents to kids?

2. In what ways have you leaned your ladder against the wrong wall of "How do I make my children turn out right?"

3. In what ways have you leaned your ladder against the right wall of "How do I help my children love Jesus more?"

4. If "Love God" expresses the one clear message God has for you and your children, how do you see that working out with you and with your children?

5. How has the spark of love for God gotten doused? How do you think God wants to renew the spark?

6. Is Jesus in the black box of your life? What difference has that decision made for you and for your children?

7. Does Jesus sit at the head of the table in your home? What difference has that made for you and for your children?

Fresh Ideas

- Note your interactions with your kids this week, and give attention to which conversations focused on behavior and which ones focused on the heart.
- Memorize Matthew 22:37-38.
- Make a list of your passions. Decide which ones override your love for Jesus.
- To daily remind you to connect with God's primary desire for you and your kids, write "Love God" on one side of a piece of paper and "Jesus" on the other side. Put it in a black box or, if you prefer, in your wallet, on your dashboard, or on your computer screen.
- Realize that if you love Jesus, your kids benefit by hanging around you. Put on your calendar specifically when you will spend time with your kids this week.
- Around your kitchen table (or your special place to meet in your house) write personal and family concerns on a card. Pray about one of those concerns each night at dinner.

Further Reading

John Eldredge, *Wild at Heart* (Nashville: Thomas Nelson, 2001). Dads who want to passionately pursue God will love this book!

John Piper, *Don't Waste Your Life* (Wheaton, IL: Crossway Books, 2003). This book will challenge you to further explore your highest purpose.

3

Dry Out the Firewood:
Gain New Purpose for Old Pain

How do we find healing for our hurts without passing those hurts to our children?

The phone rang, interrupting my Sunday night reading time with six-year-old Ginny. Jonathan, then fourteen, talked to me on the phone while his sister, Katie, then seventeen, drove home from downtown Atlanta. At one point in the conversation I heard what sounded like static on the line. Then I identified the sound as breaking glass and crunching metal.

"Dad, we're in a wreck! We're in a wreck!" Jonathan yelled.

Panicked, I shouted, "Don't hang up!"

"Dad, we've been hit! Katie is bleeding. She's cut!"

I could hear Katie screaming.

I yelled, "Jonathan, get out of the car. Can you get Katie out?"

He cried out, "Glass is everywhere. Sparks are flying, and the car is rolled over on its top. I don't know if I can get us out or not!"

"Jonathan, get out now!" I screamed.

After a struggle he pulled his sister out of the car to safety.

With fear pulsing through my veins, I yelled, "I'm calling 911. Don't leave until I get there!"

I made the 911 call and sprinted to my car in the driveway. The twenty-minute trip took me all of eight minutes! When I turned the corner onto the street where the wreck had occurred, flashing lights lit up the entire block. In fact, the emergency vehicles threw off enough light to make it look like midday. Ambulances, fire trucks, and police cars covered the area. I ran to the scene.

The first thing my eye caught was our old Sunbird turned upside-down in a smashed heap—totaled. "Where are my kids?" I shouted to no one and to everyone. Then I spotted Jonathan wandering around in a daze. I ran toward him, pulling him into my arms. When I did, I spotted a blood-soaked green sweater on the sidewalk to my left. I didn't have to guess whose blood it was. "Where's Katie?" I inquired.

"In the ambulance, Dad," Jonathan responded, zombie-like with shock.

Again I sprinted, this time to the ambulance. Police and rescue workers crowded around the rear door. I pushed my way through, crawling on my hands and knees to get to my injured daughter. Blood covered her head and the upper part of her body. The moment we saw each other both of us began to cry.

Thankfully, neither of my kids sustained long-term, serious injuries from their wreck. In the aftermath of the trauma Katie's physical wounds healed rather quickly. But the emotional trauma lingered, as it does for all of us who have survived a similar crisis and lived to tell about it.

Like my kids' car crash, our lives often experience a crash emotionally, psychologically, and/or spiritually. In the aftermath we often can't see and don't realize the internal injuries resulting from trauma. Hidden from view, still they reside inside us. These wounds act like rain-soaked firewood. It's impossible to get the fire going without healing the hurts.

Often parents inflict such hurts. Frequently the emotional pain from these hurts can extend from parents to grandparents, going back for generations. Wrong choices, broken relationships, and selfish behavior created pain in that particular generation, and it then passed from generation to generation down to us and our children. In the preamble to the Ten Commandments God expressed clearly how this comes to pass:

> The LORD, the LORD, the compassionate and gracious God, slow to anger, abounding in love and faithfulness, maintaining love to thousands, and forgiving wickedness, rebellion and sin. Yet he does not leave the guilty unpunished; he punishes the children and their children for the sin of the fathers to the third and fourth generation.
>
> EXODUS 34:6-7

Sinful choices in previous generations create serious problems. God did not bury your great-great grandfather's pain-producing issues at his funeral. They were passed along. Many of us still live with the wrecks of our ancestors.

Because of these generational wrecks we can unwittingly hurt our children. We wound them because our parents inflicted pain on us, pain likely caused by their parents wounding them. Clearly children receive the residue of their parents' pain and often find themselves having to clean up the mess.

If the root issues that have caused the generational wreck do not get addressed and then dealt with properly, these wound-producing issues will carry on to future generations. The good news for us is that these deep-seated hurts can be healed; but we must remember two important thoughts.

1. Generational patterns of sin or dysfunction cannot be cured by ourselves. We need the Healer and support from each other.
2. The root, not just the fruit or symptoms, needs healing.

For example, I've known Christian parents who determined to break the curse of divorce in their family by sheer willpower. Often these marriages end up intact but void of intimacy and all that makes a God-blessed marriage a joy. Why? They've thrown the pink paint of "intact marriage" over the old dysfunctional ways of relating. The parents determined to avoid legal divorce, but they didn't deal with the roots that caused a divorce in their hearts years before. God desires a deeper healing. He always goes to the root if we allow Him to do so.

Find the Root of Parent-Inflicted Pain

The wounds that parents inflict on their children come in all shapes and sizes. Some come from physical abuse, others from verbal abuse; some come from neglect, and still others come from the normal bumps and bruises of living in a family. All can wound deeply.

Violent Wounds

After counseling with me, a very fragile-looking fourteen-year-old, Vanessa, wrote me this note:

> I really want Jesus Christ in my heart. But there is one thing that really hurt me a lot. My grandpa molested me. He's been doing this for two years. My parents found out, but they don't believe me. But I told my parents: Why should I lie? I told my mom: "You just have to face it, because it is true." I stay up all night crying because this is the thing that gives me great pain.

Only by confronting the reality of this issue can this young lady get past the pain. Good for her. She brought it into the light, her first step to healing and to a restored view of God and herself. Then an authority figure she trusts must hear, believe, understand her in her childlike vulnerability, and assist in completing the healing process.

Deep Hurts

I liked Randy (not his real name). He was the first boy who ever took my daughter out. Those teenage boys—you either like 'em or hate 'em! Randy struck me as sharp, friendly, and having a great sense of humor. For two years he participated in a high school discipleship group that I led. However, during his sixteenth year he discovered some things about his past that sent him into a tailspin. He learned that his father had left his mom when she became pregnant with him, saying he didn't want the responsibility of a child. Randy suddenly began dressing weirdly, acting strangely, and isolating himself from his friends. These nearly overnight changes outwardly reflected the deep wound he had experienced inwardly.

The pain of this father-rejection wrecked his life and created in him an overwhelming sense of grief that negatively impacted his life for years.

And for years the pain has kept him trapped in the wreckage. For Randy to live healthily, wholly, he must decide to dig deep into the wreckage, find healing, and move past the pain of that experience. But he cannot do it alone. He'll have to seek help—both from God and from God's people gifted in recovery from emotional wounds.

These violent wounds and deep hurts devastate. They can produce emotional and spiritual cripples, keeping people from reaching their full potential. The pain turns us in on ourselves, so that we lose sight of anyone else's needs. Unresolved wounds and hurts create dysfunctional families. And they shut off intimacy with a loving, healing Father.

I connected meaningfully with one of these walking wounded, named Richard. He came to our church and then made an appointment to see me. "I am dying of AIDS" was the first sentence out of his mouth.

I took a deep breath and listened with compassion as his story unfolded. He told me that as he grew up he was the All-American kid—athletic, popular, an Eagle Scout. Then one weekend his older brother invited him to Atlanta. What he didn't know was that his brother had planned a wild weekend. Before it came to an end, his brother's friend had raped him.

Devastated, all Richard knew to do was tell his parents, who, to Richard's shock and pain, became angry *with him!* This created a second wounding to his young and tender heart (all too common with those who have suffered sexual abuse). A few days later he asked his father for the keys to the car. His dad handed him the keys and said, "Going out with some of your homo friends again?" That hurt Richard so badly that he started a downward spiral of rebellion that, in his words, "left nothing undone. I did every perverted thing known to man." In the process he got AIDS. A few months after our first talk, he died.

Richard lived a tragically wrecked life, as did Vanessa and Randy. Hopefully their stories jolt us into the reality of our own wreckage, our own wounds and pain. No matter how healthy or dysfunctional a family is or how lovingly or unlovingly our parents care for us, hurts happen. All of us have wounds from our family, hopefully to a lesser degree than the examples above.

All of us have wounds from our family.

To address the pain in our lives, let's go back to the car wreck involving my children for a metaphor on surviving trauma. As indicated before, even though covered with blood, Katie's condition did not result in serious injury. She had stitches in her head and hand and missed several days of school due to pain in her neck and back. But the minimal damage done to her body, and Jonathan's body as well, did not lessen the impact of this experience on our entire family.

What happened that night created a symbolic visual image for our family. Through my kids' accident we saw more fully what to do with the pain of one of life's wrecks, addressed in the remainder of this chapter, and then how to clean up the messy aftermath, which we will address in the next chapter. Our family gained valuable insights from coping with this crisis, later giving us strength for handling other traumas, including the death of my cherished wife and my children's much-loved mother.

What most important discoveries about dealing with emotional trauma did we make from that physical wreck?

Call Out to the Wounded Healer

After I pushed my way through the crowd around the ambulance and got to Katie, she grabbed my hands. Through tears she told me, "Dad, I knew you would come. While the car spun around and crashed I kept yelling, 'Lord, please protect us.' And when I saw all of this blood and kept thinking I might be seriously injured and scarred for life, I kept calling out to God to help me and heal me."

Only Jesus can deliver us *through* our hurts and tears.

Looking at your life, where do you hurt? Behind the smile, where do you see bloodstains and tears? Do you realize that Jesus has already come to you and stays with you to bring healing to your hurts? Only Jesus can deliver us *through* our hurts and tears. He doesn't extract us from them or take us out of them—He leads us *through* them. God never guarantees us freedom from this world's pain, but He promises us His loving and healing Presence always. He can comfort us as no other because He lives in us as the Wounded Healer. Do you know that He has such great love for you that He would go through gunfire to rescue you? All who have turned to the Comforter for consolation in times of devastation will tell you they have grown better instead of bitter. Instead of their story ending in resentment, it concluded with inspiration.

Jesus experienced all of our pain ahead of us.

Much of that inspiration comes from knowing that whatever pain has been inflicted on us in life, Jesus has already experienced it.

He grew up before him like a tender shoot, and like a root out of dry ground. He had no beauty or majesty to attract us to him, nothing in his appearance that we should desire him. He was despised and rejected by men, a man of sorrows, and familiar with suffering. Like one from whom men hide their faces he was despised, and we esteemed him not. Surely he took up our infirmities and carried our sorrows, yet we considered him stricken by God, smitten by him, and afflicted. But he was pierced for our transgressions, he was crushed for our iniquities; the punishment that brought us peace was upon him, and by his wounds we are healed.

ISAIAH 53:2-5

Consider how Jesus experienced our wounds.

• For those who feel ugly, He had no beauty.

• For those who have been rejected, He was despised and rejected by men.

• For those who have experienced deep pain, He was a man of sorrows and acquainted with suffering.

• For those who blame God for what has happened, He was considered stricken by God, smitten by Him, and afflicted.

• For those who have been beaten and abused, He was pierced (wounded) for something He did not do.

• For those who have lost a child or other loved one to death, He was crushed by death.

Perhaps you've seen the movie *The Passion of the Christ* and got a glimpse of the price Christ paid to rescue us. In going to and hanging on the cross, Jesus experienced physical pain at its highest degree. The Roman soldiers scourged Him, which meant that they beat Him many times with a whip entwined with sharp objects. They spit on Him. They put a robe on Him and let the blood coagulate so that the robe stuck to

His body. Then they ripped it off. They placed a crown on His head made of one-inch thorns and pressed it into His skull, causing Him to bleed profusely. The soldiers made Him carry His own cross. Then they nailed His wrists and feet to the cross with long spikes. Once nailed, the soldiers lifted the cross into its socket, which ripped His flesh. All this caused intolerable pain and suffering. Cicero called crucifixion "the most cruel and horrible torture." What scholars have declared as the most terrible death ever invented by man, Jesus experienced to the fullest extent.

Many in Jesus' day faced death through crucifixion. For Jesus, however, beyond the physical pain of crucifixion He experienced the most severe emotional and spiritual pain ever known to man. He cried out with hurt beyond human comprehension, "My God, my God, why have you forsaken me?" (Matthew 27:46). For the first time since the beginning of eternity, Jesus suffered separation from His Father. At that moment His Father sent Him outside of His presence—to hell. Breaking this eternal relationship between the Father and the Son caused the worst possible pain for Jesus and His Father. They each experienced a wounded heart!

Meditating on the cross provides a fresh perspective on our hurts, pains, and suffering. And it offers hope for healing!

In Jesus' suffering, He identifies with our suffering. No matter how profoundly we have suffered, Jesus suffered beyond that. Whatever our parents, spouse, or children have done to us, Jesus empathizes with our pain—physical, emotional, or spiritual.

Through Jesus' suffering, He heals our hurts. On the cross Jesus not only identified with our suffering, but He could actually *do something* about it. Jeremiah, in the Old Testament, cried out:

> *Since my people are crushed, I am crushed; I mourn, and horror grips me. Is there no balm in Gilead? Is there no physician there? Why then is there no healing for the wound of my people?*
>
> JEREMIAH 8:21-22

The Father sent Jesus as the Balm of Gilead, the only One who can heal our wounds. The apostle Peter said it best: *He himself bore our sins in his body on the tree, so that we might die to sins and live for righteousness; by his wounds you have been healed* (1 Peter 2:24).

Where do we start the healing process? *Honestly identify your pain, and humbly ask Jesus to heal it.* Neil Anderson explains why taking this seemingly simple step makes so much sense.

> Refuse to believe that you are just the product of your past experiences. As a Christian, you are primarily the product of the work of Christ on the cross. You are literally a new creature in Christ. Old things, including the traumas of your past, are passed away. The old you is gone; the new you is here.[1]

Honestly identify your pain, and humbly ask Jesus to heal it.

Decide now that no matter how painful, you will let Jesus come into those wounded, hurt places in your life, diagnose your situation, and bring His healing touch. Your decision will break the cycle of sin, broken relationships, and wrong behavior, possibly passed down for generations. That same decision creates the wonderful possibility that from this point on you, your children, and their children can live healthier lives, lived to their maximum potential.

Like the Jaws of Life in the hands of the rescue workers at the scene of my kids' wreck, Jesus comes to cut you out of the wreckage that life has brought you. Like the ambulance that arrived to aid Katie, Jesus draws near, offering you help for your hurts. And like the EMTs equipped to handle their trauma, Jesus moves toward you to clean up the mess and bring healing. Because of what Jesus did on the cross, you can climb out of the wreck, get in the ambulance, and let the Wounded Healer heal you! When you do that, the firewood dries quickly, and then the fire is prepared to burn.

Taking Action

As you answer the seven Penetrating Questions, let the Wounded Healer rescue you, heal you, and remove your pain.

Penetrating Questions

Think about one of these questions each day for the next week.

1. What one major hurt have your parents inflicted on you?

2. What other wounds has your family painfully imposed on you?

3. What do you see as the results of those wounds in your life?

4. What impact have your wounds had on your children?

5. Why do you think Jesus, the Wounded Healer, can heal you? (Review Isaiah 53:2-6.)

6. What specific wounds do you want Him to heal?

7. How do you want to express your healing prayer to the Wounded Healer?

Fresh Ideas

Use any of these ideas to help you move from woundedness to wholeness.

• Identify any sin that has dominated your extended family. Trace it through your family tree as far back as you can.

• Create a picture of Jesus as portrayed in Isaiah 53:2-6. Then around that picture write the characteristics of the Wounded Healer.

• Then on the back of that paper draw a cross. Around the cross list all the wounds you have experienced, and then write next to each wound how Jesus experienced that same hurt, again referring to Isaiah 53:2-6. With each hurt express how Jesus, the Wounded Healer, wants to heal you.

• Record, in writing, your decision and prayer to let Jesus, the Wounded Healer, heal you.

Further Reading

Henri Nouwen, *The Wounded Healer* (New York: Image Books, Random House, 1979). Brief, yet profound, this treatise on Jesus as the Wounded Healer gives fuller explanation of Jesus' ability to heal our wounds.

Dry More Firewood:
Gain More New Purpose for Old Pain

*How do we follow through on our healing to avoid
imposing pain on our children?*

Katie and her younger brother Jonathan used to pick on each other mercilessly—until the accident—the one I described in the last chapter. Only three years apart in age, they duked it out constantly. The accident changed all that.

As we continue to delve into how Jesus rescues us from the wreckage in our lives, what can we discover from my children's physical wreck about dealing with emotional trauma? And how does that prepare more dry firewood in us that increases the amount of fuel we can use for our kids?

Value Precious Relationships

We did not discover until later that night—about 2 A.M., after spending several hours in the Emergency Room—that our son Jonathan had heroically rescued his sister from the wreck. Not only did he have the courage to get himself and his sister out of a car that could have exploded, but also he took care of Katie once he rescued her. Her blood-soaked sweater, which I had seen lying on the ground, got that way because Jonathan had used it as a pillow to cradle Katie's head as he held her in his arms until the ambulance arrived.

That night their relationship changed. Even though they still have their sibling spats, that night they gained a new love and respect for each other. Later on they attended the same university, and now they, along with their spouses, work together planting a church. The accident revealed to them how much they valued their relationship.

Often those closest to us can hurt us the most.

Often those closest to us can hurt us the most. Think about the real hurts in your life. The President of the United States didn't hurt you when he didn't pass a bill important to you. The mayor didn't wound you when he didn't pass a school bond. Those things may frustrate you, but more than likely they did not wound you emotionally. The deepest hurt and pain come mostly from family and friends—those closest to us.

Conflict is unavoidable!

Conflict is unavoidable! So in a highly valued relationship, how do we understand and deal with conflict? The most helpful tool I have found is what I call the Conflict Curve, which communicates the spirit of the apostle Paul's words in Acts 24:16: *So I strive always to keep my conscience clear before God and man.* Studying it will help us see how conflict escalates and likewise then how it has to de-escalate.

I have used this Conflict Curve in numerous ways over the years. Following its process became a powerful healing tool in one of my most important relationships.

I have one sister—Cathey. When I was sixteen and she was thirteen, I had a science project in process on our outdoor patio one spring afternoon. I asked her to get me a glass of water. Like a good little sister, she did. When she brought it, I told her, "I'm almost through. Hang on to the water for me just a few seconds." Seconds turned into minutes. After repeatedly asking me to take the water and my speaking to her rudely and still refusing to take it, Cathey in her frustration with me poured the drink on my project. I jumped up and slapped her. She ran into the house. I ran after her, and everything in me wanted to hit her again. Really she should have hit me!

Understanding Conflict[1]
Conflict Escalation and De-escalation as seen in a Reconciliation Curve

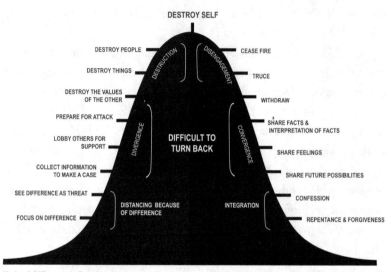

DESTROY SELF

DESTROY PEOPLE — DESTRUCTION / DISENGAGEMENT — CEASE FIRE

DESTROY THINGS — TRUCE

DESTROY THE VALUES OF THE OTHER — WITHDRAW

PREPARE FOR ATTACK — SHARE FACTS & INTERPRETATION OF FACTS

DIVERGENCE — DIFFICULT TO TURN BACK — CONVERGENCE

LOBBY OTHERS FOR SUPPORT — SHARE FEELINGS

COLLECT INFORMATION TO MAKE A CASE — SHARE FUTURE POSSIBILITIES

SEE DIFFERENCE AS THREAT — CONFESSION

DISTANCING BECAUSE OF DIFFERENCE — INTEGRATION

FOCUS ON DIFFERENCE — REPENTANCE & FORGIVENESS

Notice A Difference in Relationship ······ Place Value on Difference ······ Act On or Implement Difference

NOTES • Differences are often seen through the eyes of insecurity.
• Just as conflict escalated going up the curve, it must de-escalate by coming down the curve. Each parallel point must be addressed.

We smoothed over that incident, and life went on, but from that point on nothing I did for her turned out right. If I bought her something, I got the wrong size. If I set her up on a date, I picked a loser. Much later, talking to our mom about it, Cathey told her, "Barry has been a crummy big brother to me." It broke my heart when my mom told me about that. I didn't know what to do, but I realized that I had to do something. I knew my only sister had been hurt by me and that she still felt angry toward me. Also I began to realize that this incident fit into a pattern of my not valuing my relationship with her. I decided to talk with her about it. So I went to visit my sister. When I arrived we sat on the couch.

"Cathey, I haven't been the big brother I should have been to you," I began. Then I listed eight or ten ways I knew I'd failed her over the years, including the slapping incident. Then I asked her, "Will you forgive me?"

She sat there quietly for what seemed like an eternity. Then big tears welled up in her eyes. We slid across the couch to each other. When we hugged, the barriers between us came down. In the emotion of the moment she said, "I forgive you."

Conflict that had escalated over time began to de-escalate that night. Interestingly, within six weeks of that time I offered an option to her about a serious decision she was about to make. That decision altered the direction of her life. Often I have thought, *What if I had blown off the conflict as if it did not matter? What if I had said, "She's just my little sister and I only did what all big brothers do. So what? No big deal."* My lack of sensitivity and responsiveness to the relationship could have significantly turned my sister's life (and mine) in a negative direction. But because we both valued the relationship, we faced the pain of a relationship in conflict. We asked forgiveness and talked it through. We de-escalated the conflict. That began the process of reestablishing our closeness.

Pray for Protection

Earlier in the evening of Jonathan and Katie's accident, Carol and I had gone to a small group meeting with some couples in our church. Jonathan and Katie had gone downtown with their friends to a church service. In our small group we divided the men and the women. Each group went into a separate room to pray. In the men's group we began to pray for our children and for God's protection over them. We began praying quietly, but then with more intensity and volume we prayed for the Lord to watch over them. We prayed for them by name. Then I did something I had never done before and have not done since. I prayed Moses' instructions to the children of Israel in Exodus 12:21-23. I prayed the blood of the Lamb over the doorposts of our children's cars. That's when the prayer meeting got exciting!

Not an hour later I experienced the wreck through my telephone earpiece. At the accident site the policeman told me that if the Lincoln

Continental had hit six inches closer to the door on Katie's side, instead of the *doorpost* of the car, she would have been killed!

That still sends chills up my spine! God protected our children that night, no doubt about it. He has given us many promises about His desire to do that. This is one of my favorites: *The angel of the Lord encamps around those who fear him, and he delivers them* (Psalm 34:7).

But His promises for protection extend far beyond the physical into the emotional, relational, and spiritual realms as well. Satan desires to destroy our families. Watching him try to wreck our family, I have noticed that he attempts to destroy us at our weakest points. Often he attacks our relationships, especially inside the family. He likes to drive a wedge between us with hurt feelings, not being listened to, being treated insensitively, or rubbing another person the wrong way. The Bible calls that wedge a *foothold*. The apostle Paul challenges us: *In your anger do not sin: Do not let the sun go down while you are still angry, and do not give the devil a foothold* (Ephesians 4:26-27).

Potentially our most significant role as parents resides in praying for our children—consistently and specifically. In prayer we can pull out any wedge that exists in the family. We have God's full authority to resist Satan on behalf of our family and to cast him out of any situation, circumstance, or relationship in our family. The apostle John, the writer of Revelation, explained it this way:

For the accuser of our brothers,
who accuses them before our God day and night,
has been hurled down.
They overcame him by the blood of the Lamb
and by the word of their testimony;
they did not love their lives so much
as to shrink from death.

REVELATION 12:10-11

Pray for the blood of Jesus to protect and heal your family.

You don't want Satan to have the slightest foothold in your family. He does not have any business accusing you or your family about wounds over past or present conflicts. He has been defeated by the blood of Christ. All that remains to destroy any foothold is *the word of your testimony*—that is, for you to express openly that Satan has no place in your situation because Jesus is Lord over it.

Begin to pray now for your family, that wherever Satan has a foothold, Jesus will overcome him. Pray for the blood of Jesus to protect and heal your family. Jesus has the full authority and power to overcome any damage that Satan has caused by creating conflict, wounds, and pain in your family. Christ will bring healing through your prayers!

Offer Forgiveness Freely

The night of the wreck I struggled with my anger toward the driver of the Lincoln, especially before I knew the extent of my children's injuries. I had never met him, but I did not like him! I had to deal with forgiving him for what he did to my kids.

Over the years I've had many times like that night, when someone hurt me or I hurt someone else, either inside or outside our family. I have been stretched to the max with the challenge of giving and receiving forgiveness. Maybe you face a similar challenge.

Where do we begin to enter into forgiveness? We start by realizing that Jesus gave us no choice but to offer forgiveness. He stated our lack of options clearly.

> *For if you forgive men when they sin against you, your heavenly Father will also forgive you. But if you do not forgive men their sins, your Father will not forgive your sins.*
>
> MATTHEW 6:14-15

Without question God wants us to forgive those who have hurt us.

Without question God wants us to forgive those who have hurt us.

Yet forgiveness doesn't come easily! Do an experiment: make a mental list of people you know who do not follow Jesus but have forgiven others who have seriously wounded them. My guess is that you created a very short list. It's just human nature, apart from the Holy Spirit, to seek revenge, not forgiveness.

We followers of Jesus, of course, have a mandate and resources beyond ourselves to forgive others.

When we call on those resources and choose to forgive, it doesn't mean we choose to let the other person run over us. Rather, we choose to let God, the just Judge, work it out His way (Romans 12:19). We offer forgiveness, which in essence means we let go of the burden of being judge and jury—we trust God to bring justice.

As a single dad I discovered once again the value of offering forgiveness. During that time I worked eighteen-hour days, barely kept my head above water, and struggled to deal with my own grief. All three of my older children had moved away. My two oldest had married, and the youngest of the three was attending college. All of them had a serious concern for their younger sister after the death of their mother. When they called me and inquired about Ginny, they would say things like, "Dad, if you would just learn to cook, you and Ginny would not have to eat out all the time and you could eat more healthily." Or they would ask about the housekeeping and the finances, and then they would instruct me on how to keep the house cleaner and how to balance my checkbook. Although I knew this came from their concern for Ginny and me, their comments hurt me, and I became angry and resentful. I felt they not only thought they could parent Ginny better than I, but also that they felt obligated to parent me!

After this occurred a few times I realized what had taken place. They had the right motivation of concern for us, but instead of their well-intended words being helpful, they hurt me. When I saw that, I had a talk with the Lord about it, released my feelings of hurt and resentment to Him, and forgave my kids. When it occurred again, I brought it to the Lord again and forgave them again. As I let go of the hurt, the Lord released me from my angry feelings, and then without anger I had the freedom to call this dilemma to my kids' attention. Over time we worked through it.

We may say, "That person hurt me so badly, I cannot forgive him." But when we don't forgive, not only does our pain continue, it gets worse. We end up renting valuable space in our heads and hearts to bitterness and anger. And the relationship remains broken. God's blessing cannot flow. Forgiveness provides the only path to let go of the past, stop the pain, heal the relationship, and enjoy God's blessing.

Will you choose to forgive? If you can't seem to say yes for the sake of the other person, try saying yes to your own need for freedom and release.

If you did answer yes, then either one person or many people came to mind whom you need to forgive. Either way, decide whom you need to forgive the most and then follow this process.

1. Identify honestly what that person did to hurt you and why. Be specific.

2. Record your feelings about the pain that person caused you. Journal without restraint until you have released all of your feelings, unloading them all on paper.

3. Bring the incident and your feelings to the cross. Because Jesus died to forgive sins, the cross is the place of true forgiveness.

4. Offer forgiveness in prayer. Pray back to God what you recorded in your journal above. Then offer this prayer: "Lord Jesus, I choose to forgive (name) for (the offenses). I forgive him/her like You forgave me. In Jesus' name, Amen."

5. Give your emotions time to catch up. The act of forgiveness is immediate. The feelings of forgiveness may take time.

6. Don't expect the other person to change. Just because you forgive someone does not mean that he/she will respond differently toward you in either attitudes or actions. Knowing this, try to understand the actions, thoughts, and feelings of the person you have forgiven and the wounds that have caused his or her hurtful behavior.

7. Accept your part in the conflict. If you caused even minor pain to the other person by your actions, go and ask his/her forgiveness. With humility and with no expectation of that person asking your forgiveness in return, say, "I was wrong. (List the ways.) Will you forgive me?"

8. Continue to offer forgiveness to the other person when conflicting actions, thoughts, or feelings arise. Forgiveness often takes many times of giving the hurt back to God on an emotional level in order to relinquish it fully.[2]

Following this process of obedience, no matter how difficult, leads us to freedom from relational hurts and pains. As we obey we experience forgiveness, healing, and reconciliation. Of course, receiving this added benefit of emotional and spiritual freedom releases us to love our spouse and children with a greater capacity than ever before and then to parent out of the overflow of that love in our lives.

"Does this really work?" you may ask. "Can I get beyond the wrecked relationships to healing, health, and hope?" Ask Sally.

Sally came from a home with an alcoholic mother. Her father left the family during her junior high years. The sense of embarrassment over her mother's drinking and the disappearance of her father created deep wounds. One afternoon she poured out her story about her family to Carol and me. She had never told anyone before. We helped her follow the steps in this chapter. That began a healing process that continued over time. As a result of her working through the wreckage in her life, her brother had the courage to forgive as well. His journey to healing began when he became a follower of Jesus. Together they began to pray for their mother. Not too many months later, their mother decided to follow Jesus. And since that day she has never touched alcohol again. (God works in a variety of ways. Often He grants such dramatic, immediate deliverance from an addiction, and sometimes He works through a process over time. Either way, He heals!) Sally forgave her father too and went to him to reconcile the relationship.

As much progress as Sally had made, she recognized that she still had leftover anger from living in such a dysfunctional home. Often she directed that anger toward her children. Over several months of healing prayer, the Wounded Healer soothed her wounds, bathed her in love, and began to replace anger with a deep sense of God's love and acceptance of her.

Over time she created totally new ways of relating to her children. Now all of her children are grown. All of them love the Lord, love their parents, and have healthy relationships with their spouses or a "significant other." What once was a wreck has become a beautiful trophy displaying the power of Jesus to heal wounds, resolve conflicts, and forgive freely.

Jesus offers us forgiveness and healing, and we can offer it to others. We can receive it and give it as a gift now. And, as in Sally's case, forgiveness and healing can happen immediately; yet, as she experienced, emotionally the process of working through past pain takes time.

The outcome of offering forgiveness varies with every situation. As for the response of others, we cannot hang our healing on their response since we have no control of them or their responses and they may or may not change. But in spite of the time it takes or other people's responses, Jesus invites us to enter into receiving and giving forgiveness and healing.

Sally turned woundedness into wholeness. Like Sally, when we do our part to take every possible step of obedience in order to parent as a whole person, we have a *whole* lot more to offer our children! We have plenty of dry firewood to fuel our kids' fire.

Taking Action

As you answer the seven Penetrating Questions, take the steps of obedience needed to give and receive forgiveness in order to bring healing to you and to others.

Penetrating Questions

Think about one of these questions each day for the next week.

1. What did your parents do that lowered the value of relationships in your family and kept your relationships from being precious to each other?

2. What does your current family do that lowers the value of relationships and keeps your relationships from being precious to each other?

3. Do you see connections or patterns between questions 1 and 2? What are they?

4. Do you think Satan has gained a foothold in your family? If so, how?

5. How do you need to pray for spiritual protection for your family if in fact Satan does have a foothold?

6. With whom in your family do you have the most conflict? How can the Conflict Curve help you in that relationship?

7. Are you willing to forgive that person? If so, will you walk through the steps of obedience necessary for you to give and receive forgiveness? When will you begin?

Fresh Ideas

Use any of these ideas to assist you in resolving conflict, overcoming strongholds, and offering forgiveness freely.

- Write the names of each family member on a piece of paper, both the family in which you grew up and your present family. Identify where each person fits on the Conflict Curve.

- In light of what you discovered from the Conflict Curve about the relationships in your family, list the issues about which you will pray for each person. Divide the sheet in half so you can keep prayers on one side and answers on the other. Pray for these people daily.

- Consider how Satan might have gotten a foothold in your family. Write down what that looks like, and then write a prayer of protection for any or all of the people in your family.

- From your list of family members write the names of any people to whom you need to go and ask forgiveness (see Matthew 5:23-24). Write down what you will say to them. Then, one by one, go and ask forgiveness.

- From that same list write the names of any people who have hurt you, people whom you need to forgive. Write down what you will say when you ask God to help you forgive them.

Further Reading

Neil Anderson, *Victory Over the Darkness* (Ventura, CA: Regal, 2000). In this book you will find more depth and detail on how to give and receive forgiveness.

David Seamands, *Healing for Damaged Emotions* (Wheaton, IL: Victor Books, 1986). This powerful volume offers spiritual insight, excellent illustrations, and practical applications for healing and forgiveness.

5

How do we rely on God's resources to raise our kids?

Running very late for a 9:15 A.M. flight from Atlanta to Chicago, Bill and I made the mad dash down the long escalator toward the train that would take us to Concourse C and our gate. If we didn't catch that train, we had no chance of making our flight. As we got closer, the train door began to close. I lunged for it. The door closed on me with a thud. *No problem*, I thought. *Surely this will function like an elevator door and just pop open.* Wrong.

Now half of my body was wedged inside the train, half outside. The inside half consisted of one arm holding a backpack, one leg, and my head. The outside half included my other arm—holding my baggage—and my other leg extended in the air. The train door that held my body captive caused me no small amount of pain.

The nasal, robotic voice intoned over the loudspeaker, "The door will not close. Someone is blocking the door. The train cannot leave while someone is blocking the door." I wanted to yell, "Hey! That's me. You caught me. Way to go. Now get me out of this jam!"

I desperately looked for help from a train full of people in front of me. Each passenger stared at me with a blank gaze as if to say, "You idiot! You got yourself into this mess. Now get yourself out." No one made the slightest gesture to help. I was stuck and probably dead if the train took off, so Bill came up behind me and pried the door open. Both of us quickly hopped onto the train and eventually caught our plane.

That comedic picture of me in the door portrays most parents trying to raise their children. One side of us tries to raise children using our limited parenting skills, saying to ourselves, "I should be able to handle this." But after our puberty-induced son has hit his little sister for the tenth time today, another side of us says, "I can't handle this!" We realize that we need help beyond ourselves. Momentarily we wonder what Jesus would do but then revert to instinct and, um, raise our voices. Yes, we want to handle it differently, but we get caught in the door.

Outside the door (my skills, knowledge, and experience) versus inside the door (God's resources)—*we must understand the stark contrast of this choice.* Even with the finest parenting skills from the best experts we cannot . . .

- change a pouting, whining, screaming child into one at peace;
- root rebellion out of a teenager's heart;
- heal the physical or emotional hurts that wound a child;
- motivate a kid to think beyond himself;
- create a sense of purpose in life;
- open a child's heart to receive Christ;
- make Christ-pleasing choices for an adolescent.

Only the Lord God can bring about those internal changes.

Certainly it makes sense to apply the wisdom and insight we have learned through experience. But I'm convinced that our Heavenly Father wants us to submit our natural parenting abilities to Him so He can work through us to parent our children supernaturally.

What's the difference between parenting on our own and parenting in God's strength? *Relying on our own resources* leads to our children *relying on their own resources.* This results in both parents and children operating on the basis of *behavior, performance, and external motivation.* In contrast, *relying on Christ to work in us* leads to our children's similar response. This results in both parents and children *pursuing Christ, relating to each other on a heart level, and being motivated internally.* This latter approach certainly creates a draft that fans the flame in our kids' hearts. It results from opening the door and letting grace blow in.

How, then, do we define this contrast and then make parenting decisions on the basis of it? Let's go back to the door illustration.

Outside the Door—Relying on Our Own Resources

Often, even when we don't want to and when we know better, we find ourselves relying on our own resources to deal with our children. That puts us outside the door of God's resources. How does that happen?

Naturally we have concerns about how our children will turn out. We have this picture in our minds of their present and future success. Call it a photo album of our own expectations.

What are these pictures, and where did they come from?

From our parents. The most prevailing picture we have for raising our children comes from our parents. Since all of us have imperfect fathers and mothers, we see some negatives in our own parents' photo.

From our fears and insecurities. Not wanting our children to embarrass us, out of fear we enforce rules to ensure that their behavior will conform to the standard behavior of other children. We can get by with operating out of our insecurities with younger children because we make most of the decisions. But with the onset of adolescence when kids buck our rules, continuing to function from our fears and insecurities creates a badly smudged photo.

From our disciplinary methods. We want our children to turn out "right," so we have all sorts of methods of behavior modification—from rules and shaming to rewards and bribing. We believe such "discipline" will shape and mold the picture of their lives. And it does, but negatively instead of positively.

From our view of success. Parents try to shield their children from the "negative world" outside of our homes. Rightly so. Yet we tend to get blindsided by what we perceive as the "positive world." Overemphasizing our children's performance, position, success, grades, place on the team, social status, and material possessions can create "the picture of success." Yet success from "doing well" and "having the right things" proves as destructive to our kids as "doing and having the wrong things." We are easily duped into putting this picture in our album.

Parenting background, fears and insecurities, disciplinary methods, and views of success all contribute to the expectations picture album we create. All of these place us outside the door—relying on our own parenting abilities and producing in our children *performance-based external motivation.*[1]

The Parent Trap

When we find ourselves parenting outside the door of God's resources, pursuing our photo album of expectations, in time we stumble into the parent trap.

The apostle Paul explained to parents and other believers in Galatia how they had been caught in this trap. He showed why their expectations resulted in negative external motivation. The external motivation issue was raised by a group of people called Judaizers. They believed that the rules (expectations) of the Old Testament were binding on the New Testament church. They complained that Paul had removed the rules from the gospel in order to appeal to the Gentiles, and they insisted that Gentile converts had to abide by the Old Testament rules—over 600 of them! That's a rather large photo album full of expectations!

In no uncertain terms the apostle Paul responded by showing these rules and expectation gurus their place—outside the door. He told the Galatian believers:

> *I am astonished that you are so quickly deserting the one who called you by the grace of Christ and are turning to a different gospel—which is really no gospel at all. Evidently some people are throwing you into confusion and are trying to pervert the gospel of Christ.*
>
> GALATIANS 1:6-7

Paul argues that achievement by our own human effort (external motivation) has no connection whatsoever to the gospel of Jesus. Instead a world system coated with religious ideas, commonly known as legalism, motivates people to try to get something from God or to try to please God through human effort. From the beginning of the world's system of religion,[2] legalism has run rampant within us like a stinking sewer. And it still does today. We need to understand this as parents and take every step necessary to get it out of our family's system.

Legalism results in expectations that lead to external motivation, creating an extremely negative impact on the family. Paul says that when we live life and raise our families this way:

1. No one is acceptable to God because we can never reach His standard.
2. In turn, we are never acceptable to each other either because we can never measure up to each other's standards.
3. Carried out in practical living over time, we make ourselves and our children into *prisoners* . . . *locked up*, trapped in the expectations that lead to external motivation.[3]

Three Trap Doors

Often without even knowing it, we tumble into the parent trap of human effort through three trap doors.

Guilt. If we hear ourselves frequently saying, "You ought to . . . you should . . . you could," we know we are inducing a false guilt that causes us and our kids to feel like we and they will never quite do it right.

Fear. The fear we instill in our children results from our own fear. When fear drives us, our method is rules. And when children break the rules, we punish them. (Notice: I said *punish*, not *discipline*. More on this in Chapter 11). Fear reasons, "If we don't have strict rules, our kids will get into sex, drugs, and alcohol." Fear results in overreaction. Then our kids react to our overreaction. In this cycle not enough restrictions exist in the entire world to keep a kid from rebelling.

Performance. How easily we can walk into the performance trap. Through emphasis on performance we communicate, "You are not measuring up to my standards."

All five blue uniforms huddled around the basketball. Wherever it went, all five little girls followed it, including my daughter Katie. She had decided to try basketball for the first time. We watched her first game in agony. I had played basketball in college. So after the game I told her we would work on helping her play better. Later, on the court, I instructed her, "Katie, grab the ball and drive to the basket." Every day we worked on grabbing the ball and driving to the basket.

The next Saturday the same girls in the blue uniforms hovered around the ball with my Katie among them. I whispered to Carol, "She is not grabbing the ball and driving to the basket." Then I told Katie, "Grab the ball and drive to the basket." That fell on deaf ears. So I yelled to her, "Katie, grab the ball and drive to the basket." It still did not happen. So I stood up and yelled more loudly, "Katie, grab the ball and drive to the basket!"

She stopped mid-court, put her hands on her hips, and yelled back, "Dad, I'm trying to grab the ball and drive to the basket!" The gym fell dead silent. Everyone stared at me. Total embarrassment engulfed me. I felt like one of those dads they put in jail for abusing kids at ball games.

Old Dad had taken his years of basketball prowess, added guilt, fear, and performance, and tried to impose them on his unsuspecting ten-year-old daughter. She had no clue. The possibility of her measuring up to my standard was zero.

> **We naturally gravitate toward guilt, fear, and performance in handling our kids.**

I did that so naturally. And that's the point. We naturally gravitate toward guilt, fear, and performance in handling our kids. But God wants us to parent supernaturally! That places us in a completely different parenting paradigm.

Emotionally and spiritually, guilt, fear, and performance create negative responses (like Katie's) and leave parents and children feeling empty. In the long run parent traps create the opposite effect from what most parents desire.

Often we don't see the full impact of this until our kids graduate from high school. After graduation why do so many teenagers pack to move away from home but leave the religion/church bag behind? Why do so many church kids go berserk when they get away from home—drinking, using drugs, having sex? Of course, multiple issues contribute, but most kids maintain their religion at home and church because they are driven by external motivation—guilt, fear, performance—all in God's name. Then as soon as they move away from home they leave external religion behind because they see how superficial it is. They totally miss the connection with Jesus that is internally motivated, life-changing, and supernatural!

Yet most kids, if they see this internally motivated faith lived out by their parents, want to throw open the door and experience life on a level that only God can provide. If we parents open the door ahead of them, we can lead them away from the trapdoors and through the grace door!

Inside the Door—Relying on God's Resources

By discovering how to open the door and step into the supernatural resources of God, we move away from surface, legalistic religion into an authentic relationship with Jesus that leads to rich relationships within our families. It's our only viable alternative.

No one has expressed more clearly how we can live by God's resources than the apostle Paul. Picking up the other side of his argument against expectations that lead to external motivation, he offers us the positive alternative.

> *I have been crucified with Christ and I no longer live, but Christ lives in me. The life I live in the body, I live by faith in the Son of God, who loved me and gave himself for me. I do not set aside the grace of God, for if righteousness could be gained through the law, Christ died for nothing!*
>
> GALATIANS 2:20-21

To sort that out in simple terms:

• Jesus died, and God raised Him from the dead.

• When I enter into a relationship with Jesus, I die to my self-oriented desires, and I come alive to the resurrected life of Jesus, who then lives in me and enables me to live the way He desires.

• If I could have done this for myself, then Jesus had no reason to die—He died for nothing!

These three statements express the meaning of the word *grace*. Concisely defined grace means: God's supernatural resources in me through the cross and the resurrection.

Grace: God's supernatural resources in me through the cross and the resurrection.

Arguing against the legalistic, expectations-loving Judaizers in Galatia, Paul unlocks the prison door with the grace key, releasing us from the parent traps of guilt, fear, and performance. *God throws open the door and moves us into the freedom of His grace.* Applied to the family, we discover at least three dynamically positive effects on us and our children.

1. God accepts us, and we please Him simply because Christ's Spirit lives in us.

2. We can rely on the Spirit to supply us with all of His resources so that we are able to follow Christ faithfully and find fulfillment in Him.

3. Practically, we have the freedom to use His vast array of resources to internally motivate us and our children.[4]

As a result, instead of being trapped, we and our children experience freedom (Galatians 5:1, 13)! We wanted it from our parents, and our kids want it from us, and we have it in Christ.[5]

Consequently, we have what it takes to parent our kids! When we grasp the powerful reality of tapping into God's resources and living from those resources ourselves, we can internally motivate our children to do the same.

The Trust Factor

Practically working out how to gracefully motivate our children in a way that leads to freedom can prove somewhat tricky.

My son, Scott, had his learner's permit. Three afternoons a week I sat on the passenger's side as he drove to basketball practice across town in the Atlanta traffic. He had not quite mastered the use of the brakes. When the brake lights lit up on the car in front, instead of applying his brakes Scott would accelerate. (It's conceivable that he observed this accelerating habit in one of his parents—not his mom!) We had words about this several times, with me explaining, "Scott, one day you will not stop in time, and you will hit a car."

One afternoon as we were cruising along on the freeway, suddenly the brake lights of several cars came on in front of us. Scott just kept accelerating. But this time the cars ahead of us stopped more quickly than usual. Scott slammed on the brakes—hard. Tires squealed. I grabbed the dash, praying out loud, "Lord, help us." God answered that prayer. We missed the car in front of us by half an inch or less.

I looked over at Scott. Hands shaking and his face white as a sheet, he mumbled with a trembling voice, "Dad, I think you'd better drive." We switched places.

Later we stopped to get a burger—and to gather our wits. When we walked out of the restaurant, I headed toward the driver's side of the car. Then I stopped dead in my tracks. "Scott," I said, "you drive." I tossed him the keys.

That, ladies and gentlemen, demonstrated grace in action! With the sound of squealing tires still ringing in my ears, naturally I wanted to choke the boy! I would never have thought of tossing those keys on my own after that incident. Grace rarely surfaces as my first response. Usually I default to external motivation. "Scott, you could have killed us. You weren't paying attention. I'm taking away your driving privileges." Instead, led by the Spirit, I tossed him the keys. My *trust* response motivated him without saying a word. From then on when the brake lights came on, he never pressed the accelerator again!

No issue looms larger in applying grace than *trust*. Trust inspired the driving decision with Scott. And trust becomes a factor in almost every decision with our kids, especially teenagers. How do we build internally motivated trust with our kids?

With performance-based, external motivation we force our convictions on our kids, then we get upset if they reject them—it's "my way or the highway." That's because we don't trust our children with God or God with our children, particularly in their teen years. Without trust, establishing a rule for every situation remains our only option. How many rules will we need? We don't have enough paper to write them all.

But through grace we can trust God with our children and our children with God. For example, let's say your eighth-grade son keeps listening to music you don't approve of. Ask yourself:
- Does the Holy Spirit live in you? (Yes.)
- Does the Holy Spirit live in your eighth-grader? (We could debate if eighth-graders have souls! Just kidding. Yes, if he knows Christ.)
- Then why do you need to play the role of the Holy Spirit and tell

your eighth-grader what music to listen to? And who to have as friends? And what to believe? Etc.

Before you think I've weirded out on you, stick with me. If the Holy Spirit lives in you and in your child, can't the same Holy Spirit speak to him as well as to you? "He's not mature enough to hear," you protest. Tell that to Joseph, Samuel, David, and other young people in the Bible. Since *God is no respecter of persons* (Acts 10:34, KJV), why can't you trust God's Spirit to work in your child's life just as you expect Him to work in your life?

Catch this point because it looks into the heart of internal motivation. From early on we want our children to respond to God. But how can they do that if we always tell them what to do? Can we relate to our children in a way that helps them discover for themselves what God wants them to do? This doesn't mean we don't discipline our children.[6] But it does mean that the focus of our discipline, actions, conversation, and all the other ways we relate to our children teaches them how to hear the voice of God rather than just follow our directives. If we help them learn to listen to the Holy Spirit who lives in their immature human spirits, then with time and experience God will make them *strong in spirit* like John the Baptist (Luke 1:80)—the person Jesus described as the greatest human who ever lived (Matthew 11:11).

Our grace goal is *to help our children become strong in spirit as they learn to trust in the Holy Spirit inside of them.* Then as they get older and face more socially, morally, and spiritually demanding situations, they will possess the inner convictions to make Spirit-led decisions.

Four Graceful Actions

From the driving incident until Scott left for Duke University, we concentrated on keeping the grace door open, sometimes more successfully than others. God gave us and him many grace experiences similar to the driving incident. These trust-building encounters gave us confidence that we could rely on the Holy Spirit in him. When he went to college we never considered the possibility that he would not live for Christ. And during those four years at a school that is not known as a bastion of evangelical Christianity (but is great in basketball!) he lived true to Jesus Christ.

How did that happen? How can we open the grace door and keep it open—daily, practically, and specifically? How can we engender internal motivation in our kids? Taking these actions will make all the difference.

Decide Now to Open the Grace Door

We need to decide about the grace issue. All other parenting issues will flow from this one. This decision will determine how we operate as a family. Once we admit our inability to raise our children and desire to raise them by God's grace, all of God's resources become available to us.

And God is able to make all grace abound to you, so that in all things at all times, having all that you need, you will abound in every good work.

2 CORINTHIANS 9:8

For your own sake and for the sake of your children, make this significant decision now.

Pray the Grace Prayer Daily

We can pray this simple grace prayer daily for ourselves and our children.

Lord, I can't. You never said I could.
But You can. You always said You would.

Lord, I can't. You never said I could.
But You can. You always said You would.

Memorize this, and then pray it when things go well and when life falls apart. Make it your parenting prayer. Let it remind you on whose resources you can rely.

Share the Gospel with Your Children

One of the most meaningful ways to apply grace to your children is to explain the gospel to them. Don't worry about your ability or experience. It's God's job to draw them to Himself. At the right time they will want to know Him. Simply explain the message of the gospel.[7] Once they show interest and understand, ask them if they want to pray to accept Jesus. Lead them in a prayer to do so. It's a parent's greatest joy!

Once our children have begun a relationship with Christ, they can respond to God's grace because God's Holy Spirit living within them will enable them to do so. That gives them the internal motivation they need and makes our job much easier!

Appeal to the Holy Spirit in Your Children

When we face a trust issue, we can turn our normal "You ought to . . . you should" into a simple question: "What do you think God is saying to you about that?" The question may have many variations depending on the specific situation, but generally it turns the issue back to that child and to God, giving him or her room to work it out. For example, "You should not listen to that music. Turn it off" turns into "What do you think God is saying to you about your music? I would like to hear what you think God is telling you." Use caution, and phrase the question gracefully.

> ## Use the question,
> ## "What do you think God is saying to you about that?"

Using this question, we can appeal to the Holy Spirit in our children. Repeating this question-and-answer process over and over during their childhood and teen years, our children will develop their own convictions given by the Holy Spirit and based on God's Word. Over time they will become *strong in spirit* in three significant areas of their lives.

1. Self-image
2. Sexual purity
3. Self-discipline[8]

The gulf between expectations that lead to external motivation and grace that produces internal motivation is infinite. Once we experience grace we see the wide gap! No bridge can connect the two. When we go through the grace door, we enter a whole new world with our family. We can look out and see grace everywhere. We view our own lives and our relationship to our family completely differently. Our kids will change dramatically. Grace offers so many new expressions of life and freedom. We will know that our parenting ability did not cause the change. Rather, we will say, "God's grace changed my children." Both you and your children will know that grace blew in and ignited the fire inside them!

Taking Action

Open the door to God's grace by taking these actions quickly.

1. Decide to open the grace door.
2. Pray the grace prayer daily.
3. Share the gospel of grace with each of your children.
4. Appeal to the Holy Spirit in your children.

Penetrating Questions

1. In your own experience what example illustrates how you have relied on your own parenting skills? What example comes to mind that shows how you relied on God's grace with your children?

2. In your view, how has guilt, fear, or performance negatively affected your children?

3. From reading this chapter what has changed in your thinking about internally motivating your kids? About trusting them?

4. Will you make the decision to open the grace door for you and your family? What does that decision mean to you?

5. Will you memorize the grace prayer and pray it daily? What difference do you think this prayer will make?

6. When and how will you share the gospel with your children?

7. In what specific situations can you use the question "What do you think God is saying to you about that?" with your children?

Fresh Ideas

- Determine the trigger point when guilt, fear, or performance traps you personally. Ask the Lord to heal that by His grace.
- Evaluate the trigger point when guilt, fear, and performance trap your children. Ask the Healer to heal that also.
- Do a Bible study on grace. Look up all the grace verses in a concordance. Read one at each evening meal. Then ask each person to express thanks for ways they have seen God's grace expressed.
- Gather the material needed, and prepare yourself to share the gospel with your kids.
- Try using the "What do you think God is saying to you about that?" question in a variety of nonthreatening situations with your kids.

Further Reading

The Good News Glove, a Campus Crusade for Christ tract for leading your child to Christ; www.ccci.org/good-news/index.html. Or contact Reach Out Youth Solutions, www.reach-out.org, for material to lead your teenager to Christ.

Philip Yancey, *What's So Amazing About Grace?* (Grand Rapids, MI: Zondervan, 1997). This excellent book will expand your understanding of grace and broaden your view of how it works.

Kindle a Warm Relationship with Our Kids

God's fuel in us can kindle a fire that creates a warm relationship with our kids. When we connect with them at a heart level, offering them intimacy and positive communication, then we enjoy the kind of relationship that can dispense God's fuel by making disciples of our kids and their friends.

PART

2

Stir Up the Fire
by Relating to Our Kids

How do we connect with a disconnected generation?

Some years back our stepchildren, Charlie and Dava, needed a dog-sitter for several months. So Lawanna and I volunteered. Now I've always loved dogs. So when this seven-year-old golden retriever arrived, I got very excited. I made a long-distance call to my grandsons, aged four and two at the time, to tell them about Kelsey. Price and Blane pumped me with questions.

"Well," I tried to explain, "he's a hairy dog . . . and he's a handsome dog." They laughed, and Price yelled into the phone, "He *can't* be a *handsome* dog! There's no such thing as a *handsome* dog!"

"Oh, yes," I replied, getting somewhat carried away, "Kelsey *is* a handsome dog. In fact, he's such a handsome dog that he belongs to a club for handsome dogs. It's called The Handsome Dog Club." Now I was *really* getting into my story. "He is the president. And I am the only member that is not a dog. However, I will talk to him and see if you guys can become members." Clearly my excitement had rubbed off on them.

"Please, Papa Bear, go talk to him *now* and ask him if we can join the club!"

Smiling to myself, I said, "OK, boys, I'll call you after I talk to him." I "chatted" with Kelsey and then called back.

"I talked to Kelsey. He said he would be very glad to have you guys in The Handsome Dog Club." They squealed with excitement.

"Can Daddy be a member too?" I could see this thing had begun to escalate. Every time I called they would say, "Hey, you Handsome Dog!" Every conversation became dog-related. Their food became dog food. Their cookies became dog bones. Their haircuts became dog cuts. When the boys began introducing themselves as "Price, the Handsome Dog" and "Blane, the Handsome Dog," their mom tried to put a stop to it.

Too late. Lawanna and I had already started having a tree house built for our grandkids, and when they found out about it they wrote me a letter suggesting we call it "The HSM Dog Clubhouse." (Price writes in shorthand, so HSM is short for handsome.) I told them when they came for a visit we would have an official meeting of The HSM Dog Club in the tree house. They couldn't wait.

By the time we had our first official meeting, we had completed the tree house, and Lawanna had created plaques for each of us inscribed with "The HSM Dog Club," our names, and a real picture of Kelsey. We also had official name tags—"dog tags"—to match. We called our first meeting to order and immediately decided on our official "paw shake." Then we ate our dog food (dinner), later had a dog bone (snack), got into dog beds (sleeping bags), and spent the night in The HSM Dog Clubhouse.

Yep, this thing spiraled out of control! And it continues to do so to this very day. My grandsons will remember it when they become grand-dads. And I have loved every minute of it.

In this fun adventure I discovered what a big influence I have on those boys. I have reflected on how quickly I ignited the HSM Dog Club idea in them. I have seen how rapidly I can influence them and how extensive that influence is. Really, when I think about it, I realize I have that kind of significant influence with them because of my relationship with them. The family connection makes all the difference! I wish I had seen this more clearly when my own kids were growing up. I would have wielded that influence more wisely.

To wisely wield our influence with our children, we need a strong relationship with them. Following our fire analogy, our influential relationship can stir up the fire in our kids. Using a parallel analogy, parents can positively and powerfully influence their children by becoming the relational bridge that connects God to their kids and their kids to God.

Design the Bridge

A bridge—that's our major role as parents, and more so as our kids grow older. We have prepared ourselves to be a relational connector if we have taken action on the important issues discussed in Chapters 1–5. By applying what we have learned, we become the kind of bridge that David described in a little verse tucked into the end of Psalm 78.

> *And David shepherded them with integrity of heart;*
> *With skillful hands he led them.*
>
> PSALM 78:72

Our children live in a generation in which all kids experience some disconnectedness and most kids experience severe disconnectedness. Because the bridge is out, our children need our influence to help bridge the gap between them and God. *To connect God with our kids and our kids with God creates the ultimate bridge of influence.* For us to use that influence with them, they need us to *shepherd them with integrity of heart* and to lead them *with skillful hands.*

> **To connect God with our kids and our kids with God creates the ultimate bridge of influence.**

Like David, we must have *integrity of heart.* Recall that David was not perfect. He made several huge mistakes both personally and with his family. In spite of his mistakes, David was still known as *a man after [God's] own heart* (1 Samuel 13:14). He carried that reputation throughout his life.

As David possessed the *skillful hands* of leadership, so can we. He did not shrink back from his role as leader, either of his nation or of his children, though he experienced some very difficult circumstances with both of them. Some of David's difficulties came because of the rebellion of his people and his children. Other problems, quite frankly, David brought upon himself. Still other thorny issues arose because of the outside influences on his nation, his family, and himself. Yet in spite of these difficulties David continued to lead his nation and his family with *skillful hands*.

When David drove his own personal chariot into the ditch, affecting his nation and family, what got him back on the road again? The central focus of *loving God with all his heart* renewed and revitalized him to shepherd and lead. In the midst of personal, family, and national disconnectedness, loving God above everything else placed him in a position to significantly influence a disconnected generation. And amazingly, he continues to do so over three thousand years later! May no less be true for us!

Living in a disconnected generation, our kids unquestionably need our *integrity of heart* and *skillful hands* as a bridge of influence into their lives. These qualities result from applying what we have already learned in this book. Once applied, through Christ, we can be confident that we can build a relationship of influence with our kids. God designed us to be the bridge. But before we find out what that means first we must understand the great chasm of disconnectedness.

See the Chasm

To act as a bridge of influence that connects with our kids, we must comprehend the wide chasm that the disconnectedness of their generation creates. Count on this: the teenage world looms as a mountain of difficulty today compared to the molehill of problems we faced as teenagers yesterday.

It's much different today. Families have split apart. The church has lost much of its influence. Many families don't even know their neighbors. If schools and teachers discipline, they get slapped with a lawsuit. And kids have disconnected themselves from their friends and even from themselves with electronics, headphones, and video games. These disconnections have led to massive dysfunction, resulting in unimaginable problems and pain.

We live with a disconnected generation.

Too many parents have their heads in the sand regarding their children's hazardous world. To connect with our kids we need to understand what they face. Only when we get it can we help them through it. As we examine a small slice of their world, we must do our best to place ourselves in the raging river that engulfs our kids daily. Try to get a feel for what it's like to struggle to survive in that river.

Culture Is Destroying Them

Our children swim 24/7 in the sewage of our culture. Teenagers get bombarded with the Big Lie from the media—namely, that they can have it all—the body, the hair, the makeup, the looks, the car, the toys, the guy, the girl, *ad nauseam.* Then they're left, drenched in the sewage, to flail their arms and cry for help as they try to decide on their own identity, beliefs, and behavior, often without much positive adult guidance.

We can easily make the case that the adult world intends to destroy our kids! Trash floods over them—filthy lyrics in their music, ultraviolence in their video games, TV and movies laced with blatant sex, pervasive Internet pornography, beer ads that cost millions to entice them to drink. And that's the short list. Who creates this stuff? Adults, of course. I am not a naysayer with a doomsday message. But we must grasp the fact that the world wants to take over our parental influence and then severely damage our kids.

For example, according to Juliet Schor, a sociology professor at Boston College, in her book *Born to Buy,*[1] advertisers slip past parents' defenses and specifically target our kids for financial gain. Marketing to our children has become a multibillion-dollar effort that is uniformly bad for our kids. She writes, "Kids and teens are now the epicenter of American consumer culture. We have become a nation that places a lower priority on teaching its children how to thrive socially, intellectually, even spiritually, than it does on training them to consume. The long-term consequences of this development are ominous."

In her research Ms. Schor surveyed hundreds of ten- to thirteen-year-olds about their "stuff." "What I found was very strong evidence . . . that kids who are more keyed into consumer culture are more depressed, they're more anxious, they have lower self-esteem, and they have worse relationships with their parents. Conversely, the kids who are less involved with consumer culture are much healthier."[2]

We can expand on this culture theme in any direction and see that, left alone, present culture desires to destroy our kids.

Parents Have Abandoned Them

Wanting love, security, and support from parents, this generation more than any other is isolated from caring adults. Almost half of today's young people have lived through their parents' divorce. Sixty-three percent live in households in which both parents work outside the home. Only 25 percent of teenagers say their mothers are always home when they return from school. Teenagers spend an average of three and a half hours every day—20 percent of their waking hours—alone.[3]

Josh McDowell explains:

> Twenty-first-century teenagers experience an alarmingly high degree of loneliness and alienation. Many of them lead lives of quiet desperation and isolation. They may not even know what they are feeling, but they lack a sense of connectedness . . . they are isolated to an extent that has never been possible before.[4]

Look around at the kids you know. Undoubtedly you can confirm quickly that lonely and alienated kids result from absent parents.

Sadly, our kids inherit this mess and hate it. They desire a close relationship with their parents. They see family as a big deal, regardless of how they act or what they say. According to George Barna, "It is the rare teenager who believes he or she can lead a fulfilling life without receiving complete acceptance and support from his or her family."[5] Seventy-eight percent acknowledge the major impact their parents have on them.[6]

Parents who have checked out *must* check back in!

Parents who have checked out *must* check back in! We must step into the vacuum in our kids' lives, reconnect relationally, and exert our influence spiritually. It may seem unlikely, but if we move toward them, they may just take off their earphones and say, "Cool."

The Church Struggles to Be Relevant to Them

Somehow busy, churchgoing parents have gotten the impression that they can drop their kids off at church in the seventh grade and pick them up in the twelfth grade, believing that the church youth group will take care of their teenagers' spiritual needs. Nothing could be further from the truth.

Inside the church, students cheat, lie, get drunk, and have sex at the same statistical rate as non-church-attending students.

Outside the church 90 percent of teenagers never darken the door of a church. And when they do, most churches don't want them there unless they are the "right kind" of kids. Very few teenagers today fit the bill.

Generally speaking, we have created a church culture that remains shallow and frenetic, lacks challenge, and appeals to teenagers for all the wrong reasons.

Youth leaders offer a couple of hours a week of "spiritual entertainment," all of which has left our teenagers unequipped to handle their world and their relationship with God. We can conclude that most church youth ministries find themselves a mile wide and an inch deep.

As a result the church has lost much of its influence on the younger generation. Right now many churches must stop doing inane, non-life-influencing stuff and make a radical, revolutionary return to Jesus and His way of doing ministry![7]

Teenagers Are Searching for God

Most people who enter into a relationship with Christ do so before their eighteenth birthday. Today spiritual issues have captured teenagers' interest. Yet George Barna's research shows that confusion abounds on teens having a clear view of the Christian faith.

Nearly 9 out of 10 teenagers believe that Jesus Christ was a real person who lived on earth. Almost 8 out of 10 believe that He was born to a virgin. But more than half of all teenagers, with no perceptible difference between born-again and non-born-again teens, also believe that Jesus committed sins. About the same number believe that Jesus was crucified and died, but they do not believe that He returned to life physically. In other words, they do not believe in the Resurrection—the bedrock of the Christian faith![8]

Deeply interested in God, but totally confused about who He really is, teenagers need adult bridges who can lead them to know what they believe and how to express it.

Right now the river rages, and the culture sucks our children into the undertow. Many parental boats, designed to keep our kids safe and to get them to their destination, have tossed them into the raging water. And the church vessel passes by the drowning passengers, ignoring them because the church either isn't paying attention or doesn't know what to do. As we see the fury of the water and the width of the chasm, we must step into our God-given role of rescuing the younger generation in general and our own kids in particular by bridging the gap of influence to them. That begins with finding out what's on God's heart about the kids who live in our house.

Bridge the Gap

What's on God's heart? By that I mean, what connecting role does He desire for parents to play as bridges to our kids? Simply put, *each parent bears the responsibility and enjoys the privilege of bridging the gap from God to our kids and from our kids to God.* Possibly this idea and the actions that follow suggest a totally different way for you to think about how you relate to your kids. Please consider this line of thinking and relating because in God's plan Mom and Dad function as the most reliable bridge to span the gap into their kids' lives. In this way we connect God to our kids and our kids to God.

The Bridge

From Genesis to Revelation God has made it clear that He has set His heart on bridging the gap to the next generation with these two essential spans of the bridge: 1. Connect God to our kids. 2. Connect our kids to God.[9] In Psalm 78 the God of the next generation reveals His "secrets" in doing that. Look for the *hidden things* He wants to show you so you'll know exactly what to see and do to connect with your kids. You might be surprised!

> *O my people, hear my teaching;*
> *listen to the words of my mouth.*
> *I will open my mouth in parables,*
> *I will utter hidden things, things from of old—*
> *what we have heard and known,*
> *what our fathers have told us.*
> *We will not hide them from their children;*
> *we will tell the next generation*
> *the praiseworthy deeds of the LORD,*
> *his power, and the wonders he has done.*
> *He decreed statutes for Jacob*
> *and established the law in Israel,*
> *which he commanded our forefathers to teach their children,*
> *so the next generation would know them,*
> *even the children yet to be born,*
> *and they in turn would tell their children.*
> *Then they would put their trust in God*
> *and would not forget his deeds*
> *but would keep his commands.*
>
> PSALM 78:1-7, EMPHASIS ADDED

Often what is hidden we find right in front of our eyes! "It was there all the time," we say. We just did not see it. What secrets to spanning the bridge must we bring out of hiding?

Secret #1: Experiencing the Dynamic, Supernatural Power of God

Experiences drive kids' lives. They prowl around all day looking for or creating the next adventure. The adrenaline pumps, anticipating the next, the newest, and the most satisfying experience. To gain influence with teenagers, we must engage them in experiences that move them out of the mundane routines of life.

In their fast-paced world of video games, the intrigue of the Internet, and the energized action of sports, drama, bands, etc., the church, which represents God, often seems boring!

But God is *not* boring! Just the opposite! Dynamic, supernatural power more closely describes God. The psalmist encourages us to find the secret of God's power and to tell it to the next generation so they can experience *the praiseworthy deeds of the LORD, his power, and the wonders he has done* (v. 4).

So where do kids discover that secret?

My son Jonathan and I took a road trip to the Brownsville Revival in Pensacola, Florida during his senior year in high school. Imagine that—going to church for a high-schoolers road trip! What would cause any high school kid to enjoy that? Well, for starters people waited in line from 9 A.M. until 7 P.M. to get a seat in the church. Anticipation abounded. Then when the action started, no one sat in their seats. Several times each night they had to tell those in the balcony not to jump up and down out of concern that it could collapse. We exercised so vigorously during the worship that everyone broke out in a full sweat. People told how God had radically changed their lives and then got baptized. Sick people had someone pray for them, and many were healed. The service ended with prayer. Not boring prayer, but teams of people praying over people who had a need, often with a dramatic, on-the-spot demonstration of God's power. Jonathan and I couldn't wait to go to those four-hour church services.

"Weird," you may say, "we don't do church that way." Weird or not, my son loved it and certainly did not get bored! It reminded me of what the church must have looked like in New Testament times.

After they prayed, the place where they were meeting was shaken. And they were all filled with the Holy Spirit and spoke the word of God boldly. . . . The apostles performed many miraculous signs and wonders among the people.

ACTS 4:31; 5:12

Put this New Testament norm next to our kids' normal church experience, all the while remembering their penchant for exciting experiences. With that in mind let's refer back to Psalm 78 and ask ourselves a few penetrating questions.

• When did your kids last experience *the praiseworthy deeds of the LORD* in powerful worship?

• When have your children seen the *power* of someone being physically healed?

• When did your family experience *the wonders he has done* in a person's being converted to Christ?

Exposing our children to the dynamic, supernatural power of God reveals one secret of spanning the bridge that connects them to God. Where can you take your kids to experience that secret now?

Secret #2: Teaching the Commands of God

All teenagers try to kick down the fence that any authority puts around them. They don't like the closed-in feeling of boundaries. Instead they desperately desire that their parents and everyone else let them do their own thing. Yet wise parents know that authority gives structure, protection, and guidance and actually paves the path to the freedom our kids crave.

When we can offer our kids the opportunity to live under authority that leads to freedom, we have uncovered a secret worth millions, but for which most people won't pay two cents. God's secret? The authority of His Word. *He decreed statutes for Jacob and established the law in Israel, which he commanded our forefathers to teach their children* (v. 5).

Interestingly, the Book that is filled with the Word of God and with the words of God gives structure, protection, and guidance, yet day after day is rarely opened by most Christians. What most of us pick up from God's Word tastes like ABC gum—Already Been Chewed. A pastor or teacher has done the chewing, then offers it to us. Gross. Tasteless. Left over. No wonder kids think of the Word of God as boring. Since it has little appeal to them, they don't read, study, or memorize it, much less apply it. When I ask church kids to quote a Bible verse, 90 percent of them can't get one verse past John 3:16. Our kids' brains contain the words to hundreds of songs that they can quote verbatim. But their brains come up empty when trying to quote God's Word. If they don't know it or apply it, then God's Word has no authority in their lives.

Somewhere along the way the Word of God, as accessible as it is to us, has become one of those *hidden things*. To connect God to our kids and our kids to God, we must bring it out of hiding. For our children's sake we need to divulge the secret.

> *The word of God is living and active. Sharper than any doubled-edged sword, it penetrates even to dividing soul and spirit, joints and marrow; it judges the thoughts and attitudes of the heart.*
>
> HEBREWS 4:12

Our kids like to experience things alive, active, and sharp. We wield enormous influence with them when we pull the *double-edged sword* of the Word of God from the sheath and make God's Word alive, active, and sharp for them. When we show our kids how to use the sword, they will learn to *correctly handle the word of truth* (2 Timothy 2:15). At that point the internal influence of God's Word transforms their lives. It *penetrates* their innermost being and points out to them God's thoughts and attitudes as opposed to their own *thoughts and attitudes*. Through His Word He shows them His heart so they can know Him intimately, and He reveals their own *hearts* so they can know themselves. Now that's a powerful weapon with authority!

How powerful? How much authority? Psalm 119:9-11 confirms that once God's Word begins to work in our kids' hearts, it produces three very positive results.

1. It keeps our kids pure.
2. It motivates them to pursue God with all of their hearts.
3. It protects them from sin (and all of its ugly results).

When we commit ourselves to teach our kids God's Word, we will begin to see the authoritative Word work inside them. The internal Word sets the external boundaries. Instead of parents trying to get inside our kids' heads by making a bunch of rules they hate and then trying to enforce them over everybody's dead bodies, *the sword of the Spirit, which is the word of God* (Ephesians 6:17) does the work. Eventually they will set their own boundaries.

Our kids then begin to see that Jesus, who is the Word, is better than they ever imagined. Their personal knowledge of God expands their thoughts about Him, deepens their experiences of enjoying Him, and leads them to actions of honoring Him. They find their confidence in God and His Word soaring. They discover the guidance they need for following Jesus and the courage for making the hard daily decisions that come with following Him. Through this process He changes our kids from the inside out and empowers them with spiritual influence to lead others to change.

Now we know that teaching our kids the Word of God explains one secret to spanning the bridge. So what will you do to explore that secret for yourself and for them?

Secret #3: Passing on a Passionate Faith through Disciple-making

Parents get scared when their kids turn into teenagers! It's like they turn into werewolves! When our kids start acting weird and make it clear they want us to drop off the face of the earth, we panic. One day they hug us, and the next day they hate us. One moment they want to be around us, and the next they treat us like we have leprosy. True, but we make a huge mistake when we get caught on this roller-coaster ride and as a result pull back from our kids relationally and spiritually.

So how do we resolve this dilemma? We explore the secret of passing on a passionate faith to our kids through disciple-making. That means we search prayerfully and creatively to find new ways not only to relate to our kids but also to intensify our spiritual investment in them.[10] When we unlock the secret of a disciple-making relationship with our children, over time they will learn to . . .

- *put their trust in God,*
- *not forget his deeds,*
- *keep his commands* (Psalm 78:7).

Every God-fearing family and church in the world wishes for these results—kids who genuinely *trust God* with issues such as rejection by a friend; who positively *remember His deeds*, such as seeing a friend come into a relationship with Christ and then thinking God will do it again with the next friend; who fervently *keep his commands* to remain sexually pure when most of their peers have sex every weekend. Those characteristics don't just appear automatically in kids' lives. Over the years I have observed that no approach other than investing in a disciple-making relationship with our kids produces these characteristics in them.

> **We cannot depend on the church or other people to disciple our children.**

Most parents hand the spiritual development of their teenagers to the youth pastor or other volunteer youth leaders. When we do that, we make a tactical error of gigantic proportions. That's a big mistake because God has called parents to be bridges, the primary loving relaters and spiritual leaders, to our kids! They desperately need us to play that role. My friend and veteran youth leader Benny Proffitt confirms this important responsibility.

> When I became a dad, I had been involved in ministry long enough to know I couldn't depend on church programs, a special book or other people to disciple my children. . . .
> As a youth pastor in a church with more than a thousand teenagers, I told parents I wasn't there to disciple their kids. . . . They had the God-given privilege and responsibility of being the hands-on, day-to-day disciplers.[11]

> **Bridge the gap: bring together the power of God and the Word of God through relational disciple-making.**

We partner with God in discipling our kids. More in tune than anyone else to our kids' needs, He entrusts their spiritual care to us. Our everyday adventure of following Jesus ourselves leads us down the path of taking our kids on that same adventure with us. We have already confirmed that kids love adventure, relish relationships, and desire the input of their parents, even when they cannot bring themselves to say so. Knowing that, we can boldly step out with confidence and pursue a discipling relationship with our kids.

Realizing that an important secret to spanning the bridge is passing on a passionate faith to our kids through disciple-making, will you decide now to pursue that secret?

A bridge solves the problem of disconnectedness. Once the bridge opens, people can relate in ways not possible before. We, too, can solve the problem of disconnectedness with our kids. As the bridge opens and we relate to our kids, we will have an influence on them beyond our wildest dreams. That influence stirs up the fire that burns in their hearts.

Taking Action

Gather the thoughts you discovered in this chapter about connecting with your kids. Then pray about and decide what God wants you to do to become the bridge that connects God to your kids and your kids to God. Consider how you will bring together the power of God and the Word of God through relational disciple-making.

Penetrating Questions

1. What do you think influence is?

2. What factors in the culture, your family, and your church contribute to the disconnection with your kids?

3. What can you do specifically to minimize those negative influences that disconnect?

4. In what ways do you see your children searching for God?

5. Do you see yourself as the primary influence in your children's lives? Why? Why not?

6. Will you take on the influential role of a bridge by connecting God to your kids and your kids to God? How do you see yourself doing that?

7. What did you discover from Psalm 78 that has been hidden, but now you see? From those discoveries will you make the decision to show your kids the power of God and the authority of the Word of God by meeting with them to pass on a passionate faith? If so, how do you think that might look?

Fresh Ideas

• Pick up a teen magazine at a newsstand, read it, and make notes on what you observe.

• Go to the web site of the Center for Parent/Youth Understanding (www.cpyu. org), and read their reviews and updates on today's youth culture.

• Create a brainstorming discussion with your spouse and/or family on how the culture destroys young people, how parents abandon them, how the church struggles to relate to them, and yet how kids are searching for God.

- Take your kids to a bridge and explain to them your role in their lives as a bridge—connecting God to them and them to God. Then ask them to talk to you about how you can help them in that role. Ask what they need and want from you.

- Create a Bridge the Gap Profile. In it you can put items such as:

    - A description of the ways your kids buy into this disconnected generation.

    - A list of the ways you are disconnected from your kids.

    - A report on a conversation with your child on how he/she sees this generation as disconnected.

    - An account of a conversation with your child on how he/she sees himself/herself searching for God.

- When you see opportunities to connect with your kids, write them down, then follow through on some of them later.

- Jot down your thoughts about how to show your kids the power of God and the Word of God through meeting with them to pass on a passionate faith. Brainstorm ideas on how you can do that.

Further Reading

Walt Mueller, The Center for Parent/Youth Understanding, www.cpyu.org. This dynamic web site will offer you frequent updates on various elements of our culture that influence our kids.

7

Burn Away the Junk to Find the Heart of Gold

How do we help our children discover their hearts?

Ginny, my youngest and the only child at home, had recently turned eleven when her mom died. In the months after the funeral Ginny would cry regularly, but when I asked her how she felt, I only got "Fine" in response. Several times I pressed the issue, but to no avail. She decided to put an end to my questioning.

"Dad," she said firmly, "I have my feelings locked in a box. I have the key, and you cannot get in."

My heart felt heavy because I knew that although her grief ran deep, she could not let go of it. From time to time I continued to probe the subject, but she was not ready to talk. I knew that one day the top of that box would fly open, and her grief would come pouring out.

And it did. In her sixteenth year, Ginny's junior year, her attitudes, words, and actions changed from the sweet little Ginny I knew. Attitudes turned sour. The dreaded first boyfriend entered the picture. Words and actions did not always match. Anger emerged. As all of this unfolded before me, I could sense the top of the box bulging.

My heart broke for Ginny. When I asked God what to do, two impressions came clearly to mind. First, the Lord encouraged me to delight in Ginny even more. That wasn't hard. She was (and is) the delight of my life. "Find more ways to enjoy Ginny, her friends, her world," the Lord seemed to say.

The second impression was, "Meet with Ginny every week to find out what's in her heart, and more importantly, so *she* can discover her own heart."

After reflecting on that quiet message from God for several days, I approached Ginny and invited her to meet with me just to talk. I let her know, "I want to know you better, to know your thoughts and feelings. But more importantly, I want you to know yourself."

I could feel her reluctant response. She seemed nervous about what she might discover about herself. But when I suggested meeting at Starbucks and I would pay, she agreed to meet—once.

Before I met with her that first time, the Lord made this clear to me: "Zip it! Ask questions, and listen—really listen!"

Over coffee I focused on Ginny and *her* agenda, not me and my agenda. (Like most dads, that's a hard concept for me to grasp!) So I asked questions. She talked. Friends. Boyfriend. School. Homecoming. Clothes. Money (always needing more!). Car. School. Grades. I listened. We had the constant interruption of her cell phone. I sat patiently as she talked to her friends. After she hung up, I asked more questions. No easy task for an impatient person!

About six weeks into our meetings, the lid finally blew. Something came up about Ginny's mom, and she reacted. I asked her about her reaction, which brought more reaction—frustration, anger, and tears.

"Gin," I asked, "are you angry?"

"Yes."

"At whom are you angry? Are you angry at me?"

"Yes."

"Are you angry at Lawanna [my wife and her stepmother]?"

"Yes."

"Are you angry at God?"

"Yes."

"Are you angry at your mom for dying?"

"Yes."

Her anger came streaming out. Inside of her, a rushing river of grief overflowed its banks, beginning that day and continuing over the next few weeks.

As I listened, processed our conversations, and listened some more, I watched what happened with a sense of amazement. As the grief and anger came out, Ginny experienced an increasing release in her spirit, in her heart. A burden lifted. A weight came off. Her attitude changed. Positive music replaced negative music. The dreaded boyfriend went away. (*Thank You, Lord!*) I sensed I could trust her word again. Ginny's interest in her friends' relationships with God increased, as did her positive influence on them.

We made progress. Did Ginny get all of her grief, pain, and anger issues resolved then? No. Is there more inside work to do? Yes. (Yes for all of us!) But Ginny and I got a good first look at her heart. From that point we continued our weekly meetings at Starbucks during her senior year and beyond. Her cell phone still interrupted, and she still allowed me to pay the bill. During our times together many other heart issues emerged—for her *and* for me. Through our heart discovery process we experienced and continue to experience the ultimate value of burning away the junk in our hearts to find our hearts of gold.

From Heart to Heart

In my interactions with Ginny, what I did as her dad illustrates the core concept of this book. Ginny's issues were not about her behavior but about her heart. We miss the point when we respond to our children on the basis of their emotional outbursts or out-of-bounds behavior. Those responses only indicate what's going on deeper inside, at a heart level. God wants us to respond to our children the way He responds to us—focused on the heart. He desires for us to take keen interest in our children and to learn to respond to them—*from our hearts toward their hearts!*

Parents to kids: from our hearts to their hearts!

We employ many expressions about the heart. We say, "Have a heart." We call people "heartless," "halfhearted," "wholehearted," "lighthearted," and "brave-hearted." When we get hurt, we say we experience "heartaches" and feel "brokenhearted." If we don't want to do something, we lament, "My heart's not in it."

To pursue our kids' hearts, we must first figure out what the Bible has in mind with its 750 uses of the term *heart*.[1] Without overdosing on detail, the Bible characterizes the heart in a variety of ways:

• the chief and most important organ of physical life (Leviticus 17:11);

• a person's entire internal self—mental, emotional, and moral (1 Samuel 16:7);

• the real inner person (Proverbs 27:19);

• the place from which human depravity springs, where sin resides and defiles (Jeremiah 17:9; Matthew 15:18-20);

• the sphere of God's influence to change us (Ezekiel 36:26; Acts 15:9); and

• the place where God dwells to fill us up with Himself (Romans 5:1-5; Ephesians 3:16-19).

Just a quick glance at the Bible shows us how far our hearts penetrate and influence every aspect of our beings. From our hearts come our moral and spiritual life (2 Corinthians 3:3), grief (John 14:1), joy (Psalm 4:7), evil desire (Matthew 5:28), affections (Acts 21:13), perceptions (John 12:40), thoughts (Matthew 9:4), understanding (Matthew 13:15), reasoning (1 Peter 3:15), imagination (Ephesians 3:14-20), conscience (Acts 2:37), intentions (Hebrews 4:12), purpose (Matthew 22:37), will-power (Colossians 3:23), and faith (Romans 10:8-10).

John Eldredge brings all of these profound and multifaceted attributes of the heart together in one focused idea: "It is in our heart that we first hear the voice of God and it is in the heart that we come to know him and learn to live in his love."[2]

The bottom line is: our kids have tender hearts!

God designed the home as the place where our children have their sensitive yet complex hearts formed, either negatively or positively. Outside the family, kids get wounded, broken, and hard. Inside the family they can find love, nurture, and strength. That's the way God intended it.

Yet, from my counseling experience with parents and kids, more often than not children's hearts become wounded, broken, and hard *inside the family.* And most likely the parents, knowingly or unknowingly, cause the wound. Why? Because we want to hurt our children? No. Yet we do, primarily because we do not know our *own* hearts. Honestly, most of us parents seem to know more about our favorite sports team than we know about our hearts!

In *The Sacred Romance* John Eldredge challenges us on the issue of our lack of heart knowledge.

> For what shall we do when we wake one day to find we have lost touch with our heart and with it the very refuge where God's presence resides? Starting very early, life has taught all of us to ignore and distrust the deepest yearnings of our heart. Life, for the most part, teaches us to suppress our longing and live only in the external world where efficiency and performance are everything. . . . Very seldom are we ever invited to live out of our heart. . . . We divorce ourselves from our heart and begin to live a double life. . . . On the outside there is the external story of our lives. This is the life everyone sees. . . . Our external story is where we can carve out the identity most others know. . . . Here, busyness substitutes for meaning, efficiency substitutes for creativity, and functional relationships substitute for love. . . . The inner life, the story of our heart, is the life of the deep places within us, our passions and dreams, our fears and our deepest wounds. . . . The heart does not respond to principles and programs; it seeks not efficiency, but passion. . . . Most Christians have lost the life of their hearts, and with it, their romance with God.[3]

So how do we burn away the junk that covers up our hearts and find our own hearts of gold? Once we find our own hearts we can help our children do the same.

> **Above all else, guard your heart, for it is the wellspring of life.**

Comprehending Proverbs 4:23 will aid us in our heart search. The world's wisest man of his time wrote these words: *Above all else, guard your heart, for it is the wellspring of life* (Proverbs 4:23).

Or as another Bible translation puts it: *Keep your heart with all vigilance; for from it flow the springs of life* (RSV).

Above All Else

One night a thief came through our yard, broke into Ginny's car, and stole her CD player and her lifetime collection of CDs. Stunned. Mad. Violated. That's how we reacted. Do you think we just went back to business as usual—unlocked cars, unlocked house? No way! Right now our house seems like Fort Knox. We now have a dog, lights that come on when someone comes close to our house, and an alarm system so good that when we forget it's on, it calls the police on us. I've almost gotten arrested in my own house!

The alarm company put in the alarm system, but I am responsible to set the alarm every time I go out of the house. Similarly, we must know that Jesus keeps our hearts and our children's hearts, but we have the responsibility to protect our hearts and theirs by setting the alarm—*above all else*.

Solomon makes the urgent appeal, *above all else, guard your heart*. John Flavel, who lived from 1630–1691 and wrote *Keeping the Heart*, a masterpiece on Proverbs 4:23, describes the high value of taking care of our heart as if someone had broken into our house!

> Alas, how easy a conquest is a neglected heart! It is no more difficult to surprise it than for an enemy to enter that city whose gates are open and unguarded.[4]

A house, a city, or a heart—they're similar entities. The enemy tries to attack from without and/or within. That's why the word *guard* in Proverbs 4:23 has a fuller meaning in Hebrew—*guard with all guarding* or *guard, guard*. The idea is: set double guards to protect yourself against the enemy from without and from within.

With the extremely challenging external temptations that can lure us and the internal lies about ourselves that can deceive us, *above all else* our hearts need double guards. We only win the battle for our hearts when, *above all else*, we stand double-guard over our hearts and help our children do the same.

According to Flavel, where we focus our attention determines our success in the battle for our hearts.

It is not the cleansing of the hand that makes the Christian (for many a hypocrite can show as fair a hand as he), but the purifying, watching, and right ordering of the heart.[5]

We miss hitting the enemy when we aim at external behavior, either ours or our children's. But we do hit the bull's-eye when we focus on the internal "purifying, watching, and right ordering of the heart." When, aware and attentive, we *above all else, guard* our hearts, outward behavior changes over time.

> **When we *above all else, guard* our hearts, outward behavior changes over time.**

Guard Your Heart

In our Starbucks conversations Ginny and I read and reread Proverbs 4:23. We wondered, "What does it mean to us personally to *guard your heart*?" From our chats we each decided to ask ourselves these questions:

- What is in my heart now?
- What do I need to remove from my heart?
- What do I need to put into my heart?

These questions deeply affected Ginny and me as we interacted with them, as they will all of us, because, in a nutshell, we all need to guard our hearts by having a change of heart. We need a double guard because of the double lies of the enemy. Attacking us from without and from within, he wants to infect our hearts. When we understand his twisted lies, we realize how far we can stray from God's view of our hearts. Many of us have believed these lies; so we might find it rather hard to acknowledge them and then lay them aside. Yet by exposing these lies, we guard our hearts with the double guard that protects us and our children.

The Big Lie: "I Am a Good Person"

That sounds like an innocent statement. But actually this Big Lie rises up like a monster inside us and roars loudly, saying things like:

- "I am no worse than the next guy."
- "I've never killed anybody or robbed a bank."

- "I do lots of good things for people, and besides I go to church."

With those statements people justify their motives, no matter how twisted, and make excuses for their behavior, no matter how wicked. We make those statements to justify ourselves before God and other people. But they just don't fly!

God expresses just the opposite. When we look at what He says about our hearts, we're stopped in our tracks.

The heart is deceitful above all things, and desperately wicked: who can know it?

JEREMIAH 17:9, KJV

What a hard pill to swallow! Nobody likes to think of themselves as *desperately wicked*! But God says we are. The apostle Paul states clearly in Romans 1:21 that our *foolish hearts were darkened*. He later adds, *There is no one who does good, not even one* (Romans 3:12). Jesus said, *There is only One who is good* (Matthew 19:17), referring of course to God. That's pretty clear! Even though few people are willing to admit this reality, we need look no further than the evening news to verify its truth. Or we can take a look inside ourselves.

As a teenager I told myself, "I am a basketball player and a leader at my school. I have good parents. I go to church." I tried to create the image of a good person. Yet when I took a hard look inside myself, I had to admit the obvious. "God, I agree with You: my heart is deceitful and desperately wicked." I knew it was true! I treated my sister terribly. I had out-of-control lustful thoughts and actions. I lied to my parents. Whenever I messed up, I wanted to blame someone else. When confronted I had to admit that the motives of my heart were wicked and depraved. I was *not* a good person.

Most parents hold the view that we are "good" people, and so are our children; that we have always had a good heart, not an evil one. We find it very difficult to admit, "I have an evil heart." But God says it's true. We begin to guard our hearts when we humbly and honestly admit the truth about ourselves and lead our children to do the same. Then we have taken the first big step to move from an evil heart to a good heart.

The Bigger Lie: "My Heart Is Not Good"

It looks like I did a 180 degree turn here! Actually God did it. He planned for a stunning turnaround. Once a person with a wicked heart realizes and admits his condition and turns to Christ for forgiveness, God promises to change that person's heart from wicked to good. He gives that person a new heart, a changed heart, a good heart.

I will give you a new heart and put a new spirit in you; I will remove from you your heart of stone and give you a heart of flesh.

EZEKIEL 36:26

But almost always, the enemy of our hearts comes along and entices us to believe the bigger lie: "My heart is *not* good." This Bigger Lie is bigger because we human beings find it harder to believe something good about ourselves—"you have a good heart"—than something bad—"you have a bad heart." Go ahead, say it and see how strange it sounds: "I have a good heart." We tend to doubt that God has done what He promised to do.

But Jesus confirms His promise.

The good man brings good things out of the good stored up in his heart.

LUKE 6:45

How could a person be a *good man* who brings *good things* out of *the good stored up in his heart* if that person's heart is still evil? Jesus transforms our wicked hearts into good hearts!

In the Parable of the Sower Jesus verifies this reality. He explains that some seed falls on good soil, and *good soil stands for those with a noble and good heart* (Luke 8:15). Jesus Himself tells us that we can have good hearts. So what happened to the *desperately wicked* heart? Jesus places His seed into the soil of our hearts and changes them from *desperately wicked* to *noble and good*! When Christ comes to live in our hearts, the *desperately wicked* heart simply disappears. *Poof—gone!*

Only Jesus has the ability to change a person's heart and make it good!

> **Only Jesus has the ability to change a person's heart and make it good!**

When we, as parents, look at our own hearts and our children's hearts, we must focus on and desire a changed heart for each one. We all need our hearts changed—from stone to flesh, from wicked to good, from corrupt to noble. Do we really believe that Jesus can (or has already) make that exchange so that we have a good heart?

One reason we struggle with the Big and Bigger Lies is, we believe the Biggest Lie of all!

The Biggest Lie: "God Does Not Have a Good Heart"

The Biggest Lie is also the oldest. It began with a corrupted heart, Lucifer's, the angel turned devil. Isaiah said this about him:

You said in your heart,
"I will ascend to heaven; I will raise up my throne
above the stars of God. . . .
I will make myself like the Most High."

ISAIAH 14:13-14

His corrupted heart caused Satan to fall from his glorious state as a mighty warrior of God and to take on the form of a crafty serpent. His first recorded words asked the question, *Did God really say . . . ?* (Genesis 3:1). Right out of the blocks his bad heart questioned God and God's good heart. Satan created the "God is not good" lie when he sowed the seeds of doubt in the minds of Adam and Eve. He got Eve to question God with the argument, "If God were really good, He would not hold out on you and keep you from eating from the tree of the knowledge of good and evil. God does *not* have your best interests at heart." The serpent deceived Eve, then Adam, and the rest is history.

Like smoke after a forest fire the *Did God really say . . . ?* question has lingered. Sure, God is powerful, big, forceful. He causes tsunamis, hurricanes, earthquakes, and fires. But why does God make bad things happen to good people? We, like Satan, call God's good heart into question, especially when some difficulty arises. God may be God, but He is not good, we think. As Herman Melville said, "The reason the mass of men fear God, and at bottom dislike him, is because they rather distrust his heart, and fancy him all brain, like a watch."[6]

Notice that Satan got Adam and Eve to side with him by sowing the seed of doubt in the first parents' minds. "God's heart really isn't good. He is holding out on you. You have to take things into your own hands." And since then that's what we have done. We suffer, have cancer, lose a loved one, or go through a divorce—or a boyfriend/girlfriend breaks up with our child or one of our children faces a big disappointment—and we question God. "Why did You do this to me? What do You think You are doing? Why would You do a bad thing like this to a good person like me?"[7]

As I grieved my way through the death of my first wife, Carol, I questioned God. I had begged Him not to take her. When He did, I said to Him, "It's bad enough to leave me without the love of my life, but look what You've done—You have left an eleven-year-old girl just going into adolescence without a mother." My words betrayed my heart attitude: not only was God not good, He had no idea what He was doing. Yet, as the Lord lovingly took me in His arms and helped me grieve, I rediscovered over time two overwhelming realities that anchored in my heart: 1) God is great; 2) God is good.

Many people—even church people, Christians, parents, and children—believe the "God is not good" lie. We believe it because it was in our original heart of stone to believe it. Intuitively we assume it without even thinking about it. Possibly our parents believed it. Of course, rarely do we say it. Nevertheless, most of us believe it. However, we begin to lose the lie when we have a change of heart. God changes our perspective. We look at the cross, and we begin to see the true heart of God—loving, caring, *good!* And then, in one of the most wonderful adventures of all, we begin leading our children to see God's goodness.

Like a tortilla around meat and beans, Jesus wraps Himself around us. He is the one who guards our hearts. Ruthlessly He routs the enemy. Gently He shows us the lies we have believed about ourselves and about Him. And then He burns them away to reveal a heart of gold!

Jesus is the one who guards our hearts and our children's hearts.

Using powerful imagery John Flavel confirms who has the responsibility for guarding/keeping our hearts.

> Whereas the expression "keep the heart" seems to put it upon us as our work, yet it does not imply a sufficiency or ability in us to do it. We are as able to stop the sun in its course or make the rivers run backwards as by our own skill and power to rule and order our hearts.[8]

Jesus, not us, guards our hearts and our children's hearts. Once we, *above all else*, place our hearts inside His fortress-like protection, *the springs of life* will flow inside our hearts.

The Spring Flows

In the early days after Communism crumbled, I took my kids and a group of their friends to a youth camp in Romania. The only water at the camp came from a spring high up on a hill above the camp. Without a spring we had no water. Without water we had no camp. So every morning a team of people would go up to the spring, clean out all of the debris that had gathered since the day before, and let the pure water flow into our buckets.

The spring had existed there for centuries. But that didn't matter unless we first found the spring and then cleaned out the debris. Without both actions, either we would have had no water or we would have had impure water. The result would have led either to dehydration or dysentery. Finding the spring and cleaning it proved vital to our camp!

Even more vital in ancient times, the water supply in a city determined whether or not that city would survive. When Solomon wrote Proverbs, people built cities around a water source. And around the cities they built walls, generally to protect the citizens of the city, but also to guard the water supply from capture or pollution. The city leaders knew that if their enemies cut off their water or polluted it, they would die. But as long as the spring of water flowed, they could live.

The free-flowing spring creates a picture for us of the outcome of guarding/keeping our hearts. The Guard of our Hearts values our hearts so much that He has built His double guard of protection around us to protect the spring of life that flows inside of us. He knows that life for us comes from the spring in our hearts. The Source creates *a spring of water welling up to eternal life* (John 4:14) that continually fills us with Himself.

110

The health of our hearts depends on it. When we come to the Spring of Life to drink, we first clean the debris from our hearts so the Spring of Life can create purity in us. Then we drink from the free flow of the Water of Life that cleanses our desires, attitudes, thoughts, actions, and words and fills us with God Himself. As long as we *above all else, guard our hearts* we have a free-flowing Spring of Life within us!

My Heart

2: What do I take out of my heart?

3: What do I put in my heart?

1: What is inside my heart now?

How do we continually experience the flow of the Spring of Life in our hearts? Do the suggested heart exercise in the "My Heart" chart. Just as

Ginny and I looked at our hearts in Starbucks, examine yours. Write your response to these questions:

- What is in my heart now?
- What do I need to remove from my heart?
- What do I need to put in my heart?

From your heart flows the Spring of Life!

When we decide to *above all else, guard* our hearts, we can have confidence that the Spring of Life is flowing into our hearts and into our children's hearts. Then the Spring inside of us and our kids, who also blazes as the Fire inside of us and our kids, will burn away the junk, and we will find our hearts of gold!

Taking Action

Focus on the "My Heart" page. Answer the following:

1) What is in my heart?
2) What do I need to remove from my heart?
3) What do I need to put in my heart?

(Decide what you need from God so He can fill you from His source. These verses will get you started: Psalm 51:10-13; Psalm 119:11; Matthew 5:8; Romans 5:5; Galatians 5:22-23; Ephesians 5:18.)

From what you write, pick one heart issue and pursue it with God. (See Appendix 1 on page 247 for a more in-depth approach.)

Penetrating Questions

1. In the story I told about Ginny, to what aspect of the story did you relate in particular?

2. On a scale of 1–10 how well do you know your own heart? Your child's heart? Why did you give yourself that rating?

3. How would you describe one specific situation where you did not guard your heart and/or your child's heart?

4. Have you believed any or all of the lies discussed in this chapter? How do you need to *guard your heart* against these lies?

5. What do you need to do now to place a double-guard around your heart against the enemy without and the enemy within?

6. When you filled in the "My Heart" page, what did you deem most important about what you took out of your heart and about what you put in?

7. What specific change(s) do you need to make to stop responding to your kids' outward behavior and to start responding from your heart toward their needs?

Fresh Ideas

• Meet one-to-one with one of your children—just to let him or her talk and for you to listen.

• At a meal or family time read, discuss, and memorize Proverbs 4:23.

• During a meal with your family present the Big, Bigger, and Biggest Lies to your family. Talk about them. Look up the verses and discuss them. See if you can reach a conclusion about each lie.

• Watch this week to see where the enemy tries to invade you and your family.

• Create your own "Examine My Heart" retreat. Use the *Parent Fuel Journal* to guide you. During the retreat you can read this chapter again, then meditate on the John Eldredge quote on page 103. Spend time expanding on the "My Heart" page. Concentrate on Proverbs 4:23, and consider how it applies to you and to your family.

Further Reading

Dave Busby, *The Heart of the Matter* (Minneapolis: Full Court Press, 1993). This dynamic video series will help your teenagers connect with their hearts. (Order from www.reach-out.org.)

John Flavel, *Keeping the Heart* (Morgan, PA: Soli Deo Gloria Publications, 1998). This classic book from the 1600s offers amazing insight into Proverbs 4:23 and the heart.

Gary Smalley, *The Key to Your Child's Heart* (Dallas: Word, 1992). This valuable resource from this renowned expert on love and relationships provides more insights on how parents connect to their kids' hearts.

Build a Fire That Blazes with Intimacy

How do we love our kids unconditionally?

When my first wife, Carol, took a turn for the worse and the doctors gave us the devastating news that her disease was terminal, I called all of our children. Scattered around the Southeast, they came home for the weekend. We told them the distressing news and put our arms around each other as a family. Katie spent the night with her mom in the hospital. Early the next morning Katie called me and said, "Mom wants to talk to you."

"The Lord has answered my prayer," Carol said weakly. I knew what she meant. For the last month she had asked the Lord every day to either heal her or show her what He wanted for her. Every two or three days she would tell me, "The Lord hasn't answered my prayer yet." This day, August 2, He did. "I had a dream," she continued. "I was standing on the porch of our dream house. I saw Jesus down below. He beckoned me to jump, and I did. I fell a long way, floating through the air, and landed in His arms. Then He carried me up into the bright light." After a pause she asked, "Honey, do you think I am going to die today?" I sat in stunned silence.

At 6 o'clock that evening her dream was fulfilled, her prayer answered.

Carol's death created more emotional pain for our family than can be described. Twenty-eight years earlier, Carol and I had made a vow to God and to each other "for better or worse, 'til death do us part." We had fulfilled our vow.

For me, once she was gone, grief set in and continued to intensify. Over the next several months I reflected on our life together, looking back through a series of intimate experiences that we had shared during her sickness, suffering, and death. And I considered our years of marriage, most of them spent raising our children. During those years we were simply "doing life together." From our early days together until Carol's death, the tiny spark of our love grew into a fire of intimacy, lending warmth to our entire family. Looking back from death's door, I could see how our growing understanding of God's unconditional love had caused that fire of intimacy to blaze!

Carol and I never got to live in that dream house pictured in her final dream. But we did live in a dream home. No, it was not perfect—not our relationship, our children, our home. Far from it. In fact, we had some serious nightmares! But in spite of our flaws, fits, and flounderings over the years, God's great love made it our dream home, where He built an environment of genuine intimacy.

Whether husband and wife, parent and child, or any other family relationship, the flame of intimacy finds its spark in God's unconditional love that originates from Him and no one else. Ephesians 2:4 speaks of God's *great love for us*. How do we build the blazing fire of intimate relationships based on God's unconditional love? How do we build our dream home established on that love? And in that home by the blazing fire, how do we love our kids unconditionally?

Pour the Foundation of Spirit Love

Madly in love when Carol and I married, to our great surprise the honeymoon soon ended. The realities of life together overtook us. We realized that we needed more than romantic feelings for our relationship to work. No matter how hard we tried, we did not meet each other's needs. We had to move beyond, "If you meet my needs and I meet your needs, we will live happily ever after."

This marriage thing didn't seem quite as wonderful as we had imagined. Frustration and disappointment set in. Stuck, knowing that the answers to our issues did not reside within either of us, we began to look beyond ourselves. Thankfully, we did not say, "We just don't love each other anymore." We did love each other, but we felt the distress of having lost our grip on that love. Then we discovered something that radically changed our relationship.

In a general sense we knew that God loved us. But, specifically, we began to grasp that God had placed His love inside of us through love insights like this:

> *. . . God has poured out his love into our hearts by the Holy Spirit, whom he has given us..*
>
> ROMANS 5:5

We possessed His love. And in four simple words we found out how we could give it away to each other: *. . . love in the Spirit* (Colossians 1:8).

We began to rebuild our relationship on similar love expressions: God is love; God loves us; He expressed His love in Jesus on the cross; His love lives in us through the Holy Spirit. These insights helped us see how God's love works. We discovered that to *love in the Spirit* we needed to *be filled with the Spirit* (Ephesians 5:18). Our spirits, filled with God's Spirit, released His love to flow freely into, through, and out of us to each other. As we prayed Colossians 1:8 back to God, He began to infuse the love of His Spirit into our human spirits. Over time our meager capacity to love God, each other, and our children enlarged.

The foundation for intimacy had been laid.

. . . love in the Spirit.

"Sure," you may say, "that sounds good, but practically, how does it work?" In our families all of us see the flaws in each other. Those flaws can frustrate and irritate us to distraction. Before we discovered *love in the Spirit*, Carol and I focused on each other's flaws, each trying to change the other. When we became aware that we could build the foundation of our relationship on *love in the Spirit*, that gave us the option to look beyond each other's flaws. We could quit trying to change each other (that's God's job) and could express the love of the Spirit to each other in practical ways, like my cleaning dirty dishes and changing diapers and fixing broken things.

Love in the Spirit changes a marriage because the Holy Spirit creates a desire in us to move beyond self-centeredness to meet the needs of the other person. Then that *love in the Spirit* attitude in the marriage spills over to change our children.

> **The greatest gift we can give our children is to love our spouse!**

The greatest gift we can give our children is to love our spouse! Spirit love gives parents the capacity to give that gift of love to their children. It creates such a solid foundation at the ground level of a marriage that it leads to three cause-and-effect benefits for our children.

Physical affection. If your kids have ever caught you smooching, you probably heard something like, "Gross me out!" Interpreted that means, "Cool. They love each other." Children whose parents touch, kiss, and hug see affection demonstrated. And when we touch, kiss, and hug them, they physically experience our love. Then when hormones rage in adolescence, they will intuitively find their security in Spirit love rather than in lust that looks for love in all the wrong places.

Conflict resolution. Husbands, have you ever walked into the house after work and blurted, "This place looks like a disaster"? Tears flow, tension fills the air, and the house still looks like a disaster. You have created a conflict. Now what do you do? We all say and do things we wish we could take back. All couples find themselves in conflict. But too rarely do these small and large conflicts get resolved. They build until a major explosion occurs. But with the capacity to *love in the Spirit*, we possess the necessary resources to resolve conflict. We can give and receive forgiveness (see Chapter 4). Humbly we can say, "I was wrong for that negative outburst. Will you forgive me? Now let me pick up the kids' toys." Parents who resolve conflict by asking forgiveness teach their children the skills to resolve their own conflicts.

Lifetime commitment. Unknown to us, ten-year-old Katie overheard conversations Carol and I had about a divorcing couple. We noticed that Katie seemed worried. When we probed, she burst into tears. "I'm afraid you'll get a divorce like those other people!" she said.

Realizing what had happened and the depth of Katie's feelings, we sat down with all of our children, looked each one in the eyes, and said confidently, "We promise you we will never get a divorce, because of our love for God and for each other." After a silence, then a few tense giggles, they gave a big sigh of relief and an even bigger hug. The subject never came up again. Children fear abandonment! But because of *love in the Spirit* parents can make a solemn promise never to divorce, and can stick to it. The effect on our children is that faithful love overrides their fear of abandonment, giving them security and freedom to love others.

Love in the Spirit, given to us as a gift by God, can grow in us. As it does, we become more aware of how to apply it properly. Through some very real tension in our own family and the honest conversation that resulted, we pinpointed some questions that have helped us grow in and use properly our *love in the Spirit*.

• Do I accept the other people in my family without reservations or expectations?

• Do I adapt to other family members' needs and desires?

• Do I admire people in my family openly?

• Do I appreciate others in my family by listening to them?

• Do I act with kindness toward others in my family?

These questions, remembered and acted upon, will cause couples and kids to mature in their *love in the Spirit*.

When we *love in the Spirit* we have poured the firm foundation we need for intimacy with our spouse and kids.

Put Up the Frame of a Healthy Marriage

On the day long ago when Carol and I returned from our honeymoon, we boarded a plane to Squaw Valley, California to start a church. By planting a church the week after we married, we held in our hands the prescription for disaster! Getting adjusted to married life and to each other would have proven hard enough in normal circumstances, but starting a church brought increased frustration, irritation, and tears. We discovered streaks of selfishness and rebellion in us that we never dreamed existed.

On a midsummer day, while still in the throes of discovering these things, the phone rang. Calling from the bus station, a desperate family had found the name and number of our church and wanted help. They had traveled across the country and had arrived in beautiful Lake Tahoe. Uprooting their entire family, they had paid for five cross-country bus tickets and brought "all their earthly possessions," meager as they were, to find the place where *Bonanza*, the sixties western TV show, was filmed. I wanted to say, "You've got to be kidding!" They asked if we would provide them with food and a place to stay since they were broke.

Quite a heated discussion ensued between the newly married St. Clairs! We both wanted to help them, but our disagreement came over how to do it. Finally we reached a compromise. Carol would prepare dinner, and I would find them a place to stay, not letting them invade our small honeymoon suite. Carol decided to cook venison that someone had given us, and having never cooked venison before, she prepared it like any other steak. As we tried to eat it, we appeared to be chewing rubber hoses. After exhausting their jaws, I loaded the *Bonanza* family in our car, took them to the local fleabag hotel, and paid for their room. Nicely I told them that eating and staying with us put more of a strain on our new marriage than it could bear; they would have to meet Little Joe and Hoss by themselves. Really, I think they felt relieved that they wouldn't have to face the venison again at breakfast! When I returned home, Carol and I went out for a talk over some ice cream. We soothed over one of many incidents in our discovery of how to put up the frame of a healthy marriage.

That summer we began realizing that the strength of the structure of our home would come through knowing each other more intimately— our personalities, gifts, and abilities—and finding and fulfilling our God-given roles in our marriage. Since that summer I have taken many couples through premarital counseling. Because all couples today live in a culture of divorce and family breakdown, I recognized early on the value of helping couples entering marriage to understand how God has structured the home. Many homes fall apart because they do not have a frame, a structure built on God and His Word. As the first assignment in premarital counseling I ask couples to study thoroughly Ephesians 5:18-33 on marriage, writing down the roles of the husband and the wife.

Immediately in this passage the apostle Paul unloads the marriage frame. When two people, filled with God's love, pour out that love to each other, then indeed that couple can *submit to one another out of reverence for Christ* (v. 21). That's a God-sized task in any relationship! Yet the attitude of submitting to each other's needs builds a powerful structure that connects the relational roles between a husband, a wife, and later the children. Answering two questions about the roles of the husband and wife will nail together the frame.

> **Submit to one another out of reverence for Christ.**

How Does a Husband Love His Wife?

Most husbands do not understand their primary role in marriage. That has led to a countless number of unhappy wives, many of whom have become fed up and have walked out. A different outcome results when husbands construct their part of the marriage frame. Paul lays out the lumber to build the masculine/husband frame in Ephesians 5:21, 25-33.

Submit to our wives' needs (v. 21). You may have thought about this the other way around! Yet because we follow Jesus, the Servant-Leader (Matthew 20:26-28), husbands must take Paul's command seriously: *Submit to one another out of reverence for Christ.* No one can force submission; rather the one who submits initiates it. God put us in our marriages to meet our wives' needs. Initiating submission in attitude and action leads to meeting needs such as building her self-esteem, relieving her from daily stress, giving her mature companionship, and enjoying a romantic relationship. Only by submitting ourselves to serve her can we meet those needs.

Protect our wives from danger (v. 23). In what has become a very controversial statement, Paul said, *the husband is the head of the wife.* Often people do not complete the sentence: *as Christ is the head of the church.* The "head" is not a dictator or controller but takes responsibility for his wife with awareness of her needs, with sensitivity to her thoughts and feelings, and with a burden for her well-being. A husband covers his wife—like putting up an umbrella in the rain—to protect her.

Sacrifice for our wives' well-being (vv. 25-27). As one husband said, "Our home is not our castle; it's our Calvary." Paul must have had that idea in mind when he wrote, *Husbands, love your wives, just as Christ loved the church and gave himself up for her* (v. 25). When we choose the lofty goal of sacrificing for our wives, it is like sunshine on a flower. Our sacrifice allows her to blossom as a woman. She experiences fulfillment. In these verses Paul reveals how our sacrifice brings deep and meaningful satisfaction to our wives.

Our sacrifice *sets her apart for sacred service.* The word *holy* (v. 26) literally means "to set apart" or "fulfills her proper use." Our sacrificial approach releases our wives to pursue God—the first expression of her *sacred service.* Then her intimate relationship with God leads her to discover His unique design for her—the second expression of her *sacred service.* Her ultimate fulfillment comes from living out of these two expressions of sacred service. By doing so, she becomes *holy—set apart.*

What's more, our sacrifice causes her to *shine with splendor.* The word *cleansing* (v. 26) literally denotes *washing.* In ancient times when a woman was clean, that brought out her beauty. We offset the smudges of the negative messages our wives receive daily by *cleansing her . . . through the word* (v. 26). By often expressing to her God's affirmation of who she is, we bring her inner beauty to the surface so it can shine with splendor.

Furthermore, our sacrifice *shields our wives from scars.* Just as Jesus will present the church to His Father *without stain or wrinkle or any other blemish* (v. 27), we can do the same for our wives every day. By putting her needs before ours, we offer protection and healing from worry, fear, anger, irritation, and bitterness. Like the Bride of Christ, our bride becomes *radiant . . . holy and blameless* when we shield her from these scars.

Nurture our wives' total health (vv. 28-30). Tenderness does not come naturally to most men. Surprise! But it does come *supernaturally!* According to Paul, we husbands enjoy the privilege of nourishing and cherishing our wives. Spiritual or sexual resistance often indicates that our harsh treatment has missed the mark of nourishing and cherishing. However, when we give positive attention to our wives' relationship with God (spiritual nourishing), handle her feelings tenderly (emotional nourishing), care about what she thinks (mental nourishing), and show interest in her daily activities (physical nourishing), we usually find our-selves with a healthy and happy wife who will openly share the deepest parts of her life with us.

How Does a Wife Respond to Her Husband?

Every woman wishes to have a husband like the one described above. Yet most husbands, like me, still struggle. Women, perhaps the follow-ing describes your dilemma. You want your husband to be filled with the Spirit, but he seems a thousand miles away from any spiritual interest. You wish he would think about your needs, even once a week, but amaz-ingly he doesn't even know what your needs are. You want him to protect you from the onslaughts of life, but he can't even manage to get the lawn mowed. You would like for him to sacrifice for you in a way that shows he knows you are special, but sports occupy his free time. You hope for tenderness, but he comes across as tough. According to Ephesians 5:22-24, 33 how can you respond to him—whether he's tuned in or tuned out—to create a feminine/wife frame for your home?

Play your role in God's authority structure. Yes, your husband's less than perfect responses impact you negatively. Yet his responses do not have to keep you from playing your vital role. What do you need to do to build a positive relationship with him? The apostle Paul offers two uniquely feminine responses to your husband—*submit* and *respect*. More often than not, these words produce a negative, knee-jerk reaction.

• "I refuse to be a doormat!"
• "Who says women are inferior to men!"
• "I am not going to wear a ball and chain."

Please don't blame God or the apostle Paul for these action verbs! The problem does not lie with *submit* and *respect*, but with husbands and wives who do not step into their roles. Really, *submit* and *respect* play out nicely against the backdrop of *Submit to one another out of reverence for Christ*. Obviously wives can implement these words more easily when both parties play their proper role. But having no control over another person's actions, how do you apply these words sensibly, regardless of your husband's response?

Husbands and wives are equal but different![1] Confusion comes when the husband's or wife's equality gets mixed up with the authority structure. God has given an authority structure to the home in the same way He provided structure for the entire universe. In the same way that He brought the universe into order out of chaos, He structured our homes to protect us from chaos. Here is the structure: *Now I want you to realize that the head of every man is Christ, and the head of the woman is man, and the head of Christ is God* (1 Corinthians 11:3). Visualize an umbrella. The top of the umbrella represents God, the Ultimate Authority. The shaft of the umbrella represents Jesus, submitted to His Father. The husband holds onto the shaft and to his wife, providing protection for her. Then the woman holds onto Jesus under her husband's protection. After that the children grab hold of Jesus under their parents' protection. As all *submit* to God's authority and as each plays his or her God-given role, the family lives under the Ultimate Protection.

Help your husband reach his full potential. Wives have a profound influence on their husbands, either positively or negatively. That influence expands when she chooses a healthy *submit* and *respect* approach toward her husband (Ephesians 5:22, 33). Resistance to these two qualities creates severe damage, causing feelings toward your husband of resentment, bitterness, indifference, and loss of confidence. Replacing resistance by embracing a *submit* and *respect* approach leads to wives' positively coming alongside their husbands as a *helper suitable for him* (Genesis 2:18), helping him reach his full potential.

Create dynamic oneness in your relationship. The Father, Son, and Holy Spirit functioned in perfect dynamic oneness (Genesis 1:26-28). They operated equally in their roles but differently within the authority structure (John 5:26-27). The Father loved the Son (John 5:20). Jesus honored His Father, always doing what pleased Him (John 5:19; 6:38-40; 8:29). The Holy Spirit came to glorify the Son (John 16:13-15). Each entity of the Trinity submitted to and respected the other. In their respective roles, love and honor were given to and received from each other!

In the same manner that the Father, Son, and Holy Spirit related to each other, husbands and wives can choose to relate to each other. For wives that means embracing your equality and then living out your God-given role. With the Trinity as your model and inspiration you have all you need to dynamically relate to and influence your husband.

Husbands and wives who build into their marriage a God-given structure and roles based on God's unconditional love create a frame for intimacy in their relationship. And who benefits? Everyone, including the children!

Raise the Roof of Authority Over Our Children

Our family lived in the same house for twenty-seven years. We remodeled twice. After our first bout with remodeling chaos, we decided never to remodel again. But necessity stepped in. Katie (ten) and Jonathan (eight) shared a room, creating a high level of tension. As they grew older, the room got fuller. We tried to solve the space problem by taking their bunk beds apart, but that only increased the tension about which part of the room belonged to whom. One day the situation reached a boiling point.

Katie stomped ardently into the kitchen. "I am old enough to have my own privacy," she announced with great gusto. "Since you all won't do anything about it, I have divided the room with masking tape!"

"So where's Jonathan?" we asked.

"He can't get out of the room," Katie explained gleefully. "The door is on my side of the room!"

The next day we placed a long overdue call to the builder. And we creatively designed guidelines for dual occupancy of the bedroom in dispute until we completed the remodeling.

Those guidelines fit under the roof of authority. Early on we discovered that without the roof of authority, chaos rains into the house. People tend to yell and scream at each other. Sarcasm and criticism fill the air. With each added family member, the confusion intensifies. As children grow older, they express themselves more freely (a good thing), and they do their own thing (not always a bad thing), but often to the detriment of the other family members (a bad thing). A roof of authority protects family intimacy from the threat of a downpour of chaos and confusion.

Authority, properly understood, provides kids with clear and reasonable guidelines. Please don't confuse this with legalism (see chapter 5); rather consider it in the realm of discipline (see Chapter 11). Exercising authority does not mean we need a National Football League-sized rule book. Actually, by maximizing the positive role of authority and minimizing rule-keeping, we simplify life, both for ourselves and for our kids. Simple, clear guidelines show our children where they fit into the family authority structure and how that leads to their well-being. In Ephesians 6:1-3 Paul raises the roof of authority with two simple guidelines for our children.

> *Children, obey your parents in the Lord, for this is right. "Honor your father and mother"—which is the first commandment with a promise—"that it may go well with you and that you may enjoy long life on the earth."*

Often I ask teenagers, "Why do you think God gave you parents?" I get fascinating responses like "to feed me," "to buy me a car," "to mess up my life," "to keep me from having a good time." (Notice the *me* emphasis!) Then I ask them, "What do your parents have in common with teachers, employers, government, police, and God?" They always nail that one. "Authority." I try to explain that *an authority is any person or agency God has placed in our lives to accomplish His purpose for us.* Then I speak for all parents of teenagers everywhere: "You want your parents to give you all of the authority but none of the responsibility. Authority comes when you take the responsibility to obey and honor your parents." As you might imagine, the sparks fly!

> **Authority: any person or agency God has placed in our lives to accomplish His purpose for us.**

As parents we have to apply the authority/responsibility balance with our children delicately. For example, at six years old Ginny had almost no responsibility and no authority. I would never say, "Ginny, drive to the store and buy some milk." She had no authority to take that responsibility. But when she turned sixteen, she had some authority and some responsibility. She made her own decisions about clothes and friends, and she could drive to the store to buy milk. Now that she is living on her own, she has almost all authority and all responsibility. She decides when she eats, attends class, and studies. And we work hard at getting her to pay her bills! Parents and kids have no small task in finding this delicate authority/responsibility balance!

> **We lose our balance when *disobedience* and *disrespect* rule our homes.**

We lose our balance when *disobedience* and *disrespect* rule our homes. But we strike the balance when we employ the two guidelines from Ephesians 6:1-3.

Obedience. How about this for simple and clear? *Children, obey your parents in the Lord, for this is right* (v. 1). Practically applied, when Mom says, "Take out the trash," it's God saying, "Take out the trash." Simply put, when parents speak, it is as if God is speaking!

When we teach our children to obey like this, then in turn we will listen more intensely to God ourselves before telling our kids what to do. That leads to children gaining confidence in our ability to hear from God and thus obeying more readily. Children who learn to obey like this become confident about hearing God's voice themselves. Amazingly, it sounds like their parents' voice!

By the way, when the apostle Paul uses the phrase, *Children, obey your parents . . . for this is right*, he nails the truth! Even if parents don't always get it right in their directives, a child still learns to obey. That in itself makes it right!

When our children grow up responding in positive obedience to a parent, that child does not need to take a long leap to obey God, to respond positively to other authorities, to develop a positive outlook on life, or to engender a strong work ethic. Through obeying their parents they already possess these highly valuable qualities!

Respect. Paul quotes Moses in Ephesians 6:3, saying, *Honor your father and mother.* That command applies to any person of any age at any time in history. God the Father desires His children to honor their parents. If parents have learned to honor their parents, then the children who follow will have a much easier time following suit.

The word *honor* translates into respect. Because kids get disrespected every day by their peers, shaping attitudes and actions that show respect presents no easy task. However, they do learn respect from us as they watch the way we express respect at home. These Top 10 Ways to Build Respect may ring a bell.

Top 10 Ways to Build Respect

1. Instead of yelling, speak softly.
2. Instead of speaking negatively, positively express appreciation.
3. Instead of giving the silent treatment, talk openly, especially about feelings.
4. Instead of responding to a request with, "No, because I said so," give reasons why.
5. Instead of insisting they come to your world, enter their world.
6. Instead of throwing out quick answers, pray about how to respond.
7. Instead of just telling kids what to do, get their input first.
8. Instead of telling lies, tell the truth.
9. Instead of always having to be right, confess when you are wrong.
10. Instead of withholding the words "I love you," say them often.

Honor grows in an honest environment. Honesty makes honor possible. But respect and honor get undermined when someone says one thing and does another; then nobody knows who or what to believe. Lying quickly erodes family trust and the communications structure.

Kids want to trust their parents, and parents want to trust their kids. But when lying creeps in, trust gets broken. Consequently we must learn to *speak the truth in love* (Ephesians 4:15). Our kids need to hear, "No matter how hard it is for you, tell the truth. We will not think negatively about you or hold it against you." In saying that they need to know that we tell the truth.

Honesty leads to honor. That makes sense since both words come from the same root. If we want our children to honor us, then we must create an environment of complete honesty with them.

The result of *disobedience* and *disrespect* needs to be severe disciplinary action. Yet *obedience* and *respect* call for positive affirmation. By instilling obedience and respect, our kids become happy and healthy! That's God's promise when the apostle Paul says in Ephesians 6:3, *that it may go well with you* [happiness] *and that you may enjoy long life on the earth* [health]. When we raise the roof of authority, we lead our children to live intimately with God the Father and to enjoy His promises—happy and healthy!

It takes time, energy, and effort to construct a house and even more of the same to build an intimate home. When we build it on unconditional love, a healthy marriage, and obedient and respectful kids, then no matter how bad the weather of circumstances outside, we can sit by the warm, blazing fire and enjoy the intimacy of our well-constructed home.

Taking Action

With your spouse, draw a picture of a house with a foundation, frame, and roof. Determine how each one enhances and/or diminishes the intimacy in your family. Decide on one step of action to build intimacy in your home.

Penetrating Questions

1. How has intimacy burned more brightly or diminished toward your spouse over the last few years?

2. What positive effect can *love in the Spirit* (Colossians 1:8) have on your spouse and children?

3. Knowing that the greatest thing you can do for your children is to love your spouse, what practical action will show your spouse that you love him/her unconditionally?

4. How do you see yourself growing in your marriage in the following areas (1 = the fire is out; 2 = the fire is still burning; 3 = the fire is hot)?

   • I accept my spouse without reservations or expectations.

   • I adapt to my spouse's desires.

   • I admire my spouse openly.

   • I appreciate my spouse by listening to him/her.

   • I act kindly toward my spouse.

5. How do you see yourself growing in your relationship to your children in these areas (1 = the fire is out; 2 = the fire is still burning; 3 = the fire is hot)?

   • I accept my children without reservations or expectations.

   • I adapt to my children's needs.

   • I admire my children openly.

   • I appreciate my children by listening to them.

   • I act kindly toward my children.

6. From looking at Ephesians 5:18—6:3 how has your view of your role in your family changed? Your spouse's role? Your children's?

7. What actions do you need to take to create an environment of obedience and respect with your kids?

Fresh Ideas

   • If you struggle to love someone in your family, write out a prayer based on Romans 5:5 and Colossians 1:8. Daily pray that prayer for that person.

   • With your spouse, read Ephesians 5:18-33. Write down how you view your role (not the role of the other person) and how you can carry out that role more effectively. Without trying to change the other person's viewpoint, communicate what you wrote with each other.

   • Look at Ephesians 6:1-3 with your spouse. Write down your children's role in the family. Talk together about what you need to do to help your kids pursue that role.

   • Attend a marriage retreat with your spouse to rekindle your intimacy.

Further Reading

David and Teresa Ferguson, *Discovering Intimacy Workbook.* Both this workbook and the one following will give you more tools for developing intimacy in your family; http://greatcommandment.com/store.php?c=19.

David and Teresa Ferguson, *Parenting with Intimacy*, http://greatcommandment.net/content.php?id=64.

9

Feed the Fire with Communication

How do we communicate positively with our kids?

"You are so precious to me." These words were the last words my mother ever spoke to me!

When I hung up the phone that day, tears filled my eyes, and I said aloud, "That's the message I've heard from Mom and Dad all my life." Then I packed my bags and went to be with Mom during what I knew would be her last days.

Kitty St. Clair came to the end of her life on this earth ten days shy of her ninetieth birthday. I spent the final six days with her until she breathed her last breath. Mom couldn't talk, but I talked to her. I told her how much I loved her and how beautiful she was. I thanked her for being such a great mom. The words came from deep inside me after a lifetime of words and actions from my mom that expressed, "You are so precious to me."

In a day when parents tend to douse the fire inside their kids with shame and negative communication, it seems wise to ask what my parents—both mom and dad—did to communicate positively a sense of preciousness to my sister and me. What can we do to feed the fire in our kids by positively communicating love to them?

Opening the Bank Account

Kids need a big bank account with their own checkbook! Now that I have your attention . . . let's think about positive communication as a bank account with a checkbook.

When we go to the bank with our kids to open an account, we make a required initial deposit. Likewise, in the Unconditional Love Account[1] we make the required initial deposit of unconditional love—intimacy that leads to our kids knowing they are precious to us. That opening deposit creates a healthy amount of "communication cash" that allows withdrawals later. Without it our kids operate from a deficit.

Parents who have not opened this account for their kids either have not experienced God's unconditional love for themselves or don't know how to express it to their kids. Either way, without adequate love funds we cannot raise emotionally and spiritually healthy kids.

Without unconditional love our attempts to love our kids turn out shallow and superficial, which comes across to our kids in two ways. We parents communicate "if" love to our children, meaning we offer love only "if" our children perform properly. For example, a parent may say, "I love you *if* you get good grades." This performance-based expression of love causes children to feel loved not for who they are but for what they do. Or parents convey "because of" love. We may say, "I love you *because* you are beautiful (or handsome)." Our children get the message that they have value based on some external quality instead of being valued for their true selves. These two common love expressions undermine our children's sense of security and significance and leave them with a love deficit.

However with "in spite of" (= unconditional) love, we can make not only the required initial deposit but numerous and generous other deposits along the way that keep a surplus in our love account. So how do we communicate "in spite of" love to our kids?

Making Liberal Deposits

Parents can ensure that their kids' love accounts get replenished with deposits regularly and liberally. Our love will flow through us to them by the communication channels of *time* and *focused attention*. Moses gives us some pretty good advice on how to do that. We discovered earlier God's main message to us parents and our children: *Love the LORD your God with all your heart* (Deuteronomy 6:5). Following that, Moses offers us clear direction on *when* we are to communicate God's message.

> *Talk about [God's message] when you sit at home and when you walk along the road, when you lie down and when you get up.*
>
> DEUTERONOMY 6:7

When else is there?

How do we develop this strategy? To find out let's follow Moses' line of thinking.

When You Sit at Home

Moses hits a nerve here! Sitting at home is a lost art in family life. It's an antique, but maybe we need to bring it out and dust it off. Possibly we think we can't. "I'm too busy!" That's the standard line I hear everywhere I go. I hear myself say it. Honestly, creating the time to sit with our families takes hard work. With kids going several directions, seemingly all at once, with dads on cell phones and PDAs and with soccer moms chained by seat belts like slaves inside their minivans, we need to *stop* and answer this question:

> Do our priorities and time commitments reflect a child-focused home or a Christ-focused home?

Once answered, we may need to make a Not to Do list, re-prioritizing our children's activities and ours as well.

If we want a Christ-focused home with a close-knit family, we need to make a plan to sit down together. A well-planned family time might look like this.

- All hands on deck. No excuses.

135

- A delicious meal (cooked or brought in).
- No TV, iPods, video games, cell phones, PDAs. No interruptions—period.
- A prayer before the meal, expressing thanks to God for food and family.
- A good time eating and laughing—no stress-producing topics discussed.
- Asking each person what happened during the day.
- Listening carefully to each family member.

An energized conversation follows as everyone joins in—talking, listening, laughing, relating, communicating. The following questions, and others you can create, will help stimulate the expression of thoughts and feelings.

- If you could change your age, what age would you rather be? Why?
- If you were President of the United States, what two actions would you take first? Why?
- Tell about a time when you felt proud of yourself.
- How do you think you look when you are happy? Sad? What causes you to look that way?

Planned often and regularly, these "sit at home" experiences of positive interaction make a deposit in our kids' accounts.

When You Walk Along the Road

Moses said this because he walked everywhere. We don't, but we *can* walk *somewhere*. Close to the house where our family lived, Lake Avondale waited every day for someone to walk around it. Over twenty-seven years we walked or ran around that lake thousands of times.

Most likely the place where you live offers walking, jogging, or biking options that, when used with your children, will stimulate conversation and closeness. So go take a hike!

The many miles we drive offer an *along the road* alternative. Driving can accomplish the same objective as walking—time for communication and closeness. Yet this only works when we become aware of the opportunity and use the time. During his ninth-grade year, Scott and I left at 7 A.M. every weekday to drive the twenty-five minutes to his school.

We had each other's undivided attention—radio and earphones were banned! Basketball and biology, girls and geometry—it all got discussed. We worked on memorizing Bible verses. We prayed together as we rounded the corner to the school. To be honest, early on I found myself tempted to complain about the traffic, talk on my cell phone, or try to get him other rides. But then I got it! This time became *our* time—*along the road!*

For people who travel, taking our kids on trips with us scores big with them. At age five my dad took me on a four-day road trip to Baltimore. He included me on the adventure—the long ride with snacks and drinks, a stay in a hotel, big offices, his friends, and a baseball game. Wow! I've never forgotten it. And that's the point—*time given* and *attention focused* leads to communication and closeness . . . and memories.

> **Time given and attention focused leads to communication and closeness.**

It's fun to plan special trips for just one kid. In Scott's eleventh year I took him camping. The first night we built a fire and cooked "silver turtles"—a dining delicacy! The next day we hiked up Blood Mountain on the Appalachian Trail. At the top, exhausted, we leaned back on a big rock, ate our snacks, and talked as we gazed out over the breathtaking view. Back at the campsite, we listened to some recorded messages on sexuality and other topics prepared for Scott's age. After a CD on self-esteem, I asked Scott what he liked and did not like about himself.

"There's nothing I don't like about myself," he declared. "I like everything about me." That ended that conversation! We picked up the sex topic the next day with a little more lengthy exchange. Those brief camping conversations opened the door for many other love, sex, and dating conversations over the years. And we had a fun trip!

Whatever the venue or age, each "walk and talk" makes a deposit in the bank.

When You Lie Down

Moses, a father, must have known the significance of putting children to bed. Taking a cue from him, why not make putting our kids to bed a big deal? Talk about an opportunity to connect!

Early on we learned about and used "The Garden" technique. We would begin a back rub by "digging" out the rocks from the soil. As we playfully dug into a child's back to yelps and squeals, we'd talk about the "rocks" of the day—a fight with a sibling, taking another person's toy, another person taking his or her toy. Then we "planted" rows of seeds, poking with our fingers straight down a child's back. With each poke we discussed what we needed to plant to replace the rocks—sharing, listening, helping. Finally the warmth of the imaginary sun represented by a very soft back rub led us to quietness and prayer together. Designed to send kids right off to sleep, it worked well—after they went to the bathroom four times!

Of course, children outgrow things like "The Garden." One night, when Scott was about twelve years old, we realized that he had outgrown "The Garden" ritual.

"I can tuck myself in," he announced. "And I can say my own prayers. I can also kiss myself good night!" So he tucked himself in, and then I took a flying leap onto his bed. Of course, a wrestling match ensued. Wrestling and prayer—with boys it's a great combo.

As our kids moved into high school, they stayed out later. Carol never went to sleep, and I tried to wake up when they came in. We would ask a simple question—"How was it?" Conversations ensued about friends, relationships with the opposite sex, feelings, and frustrations.

Money cannot buy those opportunities! Nor can it replace them. That's why every day calls us to deposit those "lie down" occasions in the account.

When We Get Up

It's a stretch, but I think Moses hated getting up early in the morning. That's why he placed getting up last on his list even though it occurs first in the day. Like Moses' distaste for getting up, most of us hate alarm clocks and look like death warmed over until we take a shower and inject coffee into our veins.

Admittedly, our family struggled to find continuity and meaning in our morning routine. We often asked, *How can we get our family started on the right foot with God and with each other considering our varying body clocks and different time schedules?* We tried many answers to that question over

138

the years. Most of them didn't work or worked only briefly. Then we'd adjust. Quickly we got over the looming guilt about "meaningful family devotions." We never quite arrived. Burps, bathroom runs, or unbridled laughter derailed many a well-prepared devotional thought. In the beginning we felt the frustration. But we learned to be flexible.

To create family togetherness in the morning, we must keep our objective in mind: *to carve out a brief time to get our hearts in tune with God.* The methods to do that can have a thousand variations. These perspectives and approaches helped us focus our family on Jesus at the beginning of the day.

• Block out this time and value it, no matter how you use it.

• Understand that a little communication works better than none.

• Eat breakfast together at a preannounced time.

• Expect and insist that everyone show up on time.

• Prepare the night before. Once the process begins, this requires only a few minutes.

• Dads need to take the leadership. That may mean eating and leading at the same time.

• Be brief, hit the target, stop.

• Focus on one verse or short passage of Scripture. Ask who, what, where, when, and why questions. Call on one person to get the conversation going. Let the kids talk.

• Pray together. Ask one person to pray that day's verse back to God. Find out what each person faces that day; then pray one-sentence prayers for the person on the left or right about those concerns.

• Relax and flex!

In spite of the wildness, craziness, and laughing that kids bring to the table, a morning time together will create a family focus on Jesus that launches your day. This effort will be rewarded over time.

By using Moses' strategy of giving time and focused attention to our children, we build added reserves into our kids' accounts. Over the long haul these seemingly small daily deposits become a huge investment.

Avoiding Unnecessary Withdrawals

Living in a fallen world of imperfect parents and kids, we don't always create an environment that positively communicates unconditional love. Not that we don't love our kids. We do. But communication break-downs can stifle the flow of that love. Just as too many withdrawals from a bank account leave it overdrawn, overdrawing our love account with our kids enough times leaves a relationship depleted, and then it shuts down.

Over years of talking to teenagers, many of them have told me how much they want to communicate with their parents, but their parents just don't get it. What don't we get? We parents tend to miss our kids' struggle with three core adolescent needs.

A search for identity and self-esteem. Even when kids flounder in trying to discover their identity, they want and need significant adults to respect them as individuals. Their request is: "Give me the opportunity to find my true self."

A reaction against authority and discipline. Negative reactions to parental authority arise from kids' need for time and space to discover themselves. They beg their parents, "Treat me like an adult, not like a little kid."

A frustrating failure to communicate. Teenagers desperately need open communication lines with their parents, even when they seem to do everything in their power to shut them down. Their heartfelt desire is: "Please listen to me, and don't just talk at me."

How do we positively communicate about these mostly unspoken needs? To do so, we need to understand what happens when children grow into adolescents. It's like they go from an open field into a dark cave. Somewhere in adolescence we can count on our kids "going into the cave." They withdraw inside themselves and pull their thoughts and feelings in after them. That happened to Rick. His easygoing, talkative personality with his friends disappeared at home. He was there, but he was not there. In the cave most of the time at home, he didn't talk to his parents except in one-syllable words: "Ugh." "Yep." "Hmmm." "Wha?" He refused to allow his parents into the cave to find him.

Adolescents go into the cave for many reasons. Often it's just because they have entered adolescence. This becomes very difficult for parents. When we reach into the cave, we don't know if they will kiss our hands or bite off our arms! Yet because of the critical importance of not los-ing touch with our kids, we must try to "get it" by looking beyond their behavior and into their hearts. We must keep the lines of positive communication open. For that to happen, we need to understand and respond constructively to the messages coming out of the cave.

> **Respond constructively to the messages coming out of the cave.**

You don't understand me. Teenage kids don't think their parents know them anymore. And they think that if their parents did know them, either "they wouldn't like me" or "my parents are so out of touch." Kids think, "My dad's best friend is Fred Flintstone." So they say things like, "If my parents knew, they'd kill me. I could never tell them about this."

You embarrass me. They assume that we will say or do something stupid around their friends. The fact that we even exist embarrasses them. And sometimes we do embarrass them. One mom of a middle-schooler dropped her son off at school in front of his friends. Remembering what she had forgotten to tell him, she blurted out, "When you get home you'd better pick up your dirty underwear." Now *that's* embarrassing!

You don't pay attention to me. Often our children feel like we shut them out, whether we do or not. If we get preoccupied with the computer, phone, TV, newspaper, a project, or whatever, their heightened sensitivity to our behavior causes them to think that our pursuit holds a higher priority than giving them our attention. When they think that, they won't communicate because they don't think we care about what they have to say.

You put me down. Our children, especially teenagers, tend to internalize negative messages they receive from us. Even when we gently try to correct them or when we mean nothing by a negative comment, they interpret it as, "Don't act like such a jerk!" or "You never do anything right." When we serve up a menu of negative comments, condemning statements, teasing, and sarcasm, that definitely hurts our kids. They clam up. Deep inside they not only feel the sting, but they think we hate them.

You won't let me grow up. Teenagers want their freedom, and they usually feel that we don't trust them. Adolescents do need space to grow. Often parents see their own loss of control and in fear try to rein in their kids. Then kids tell parents to "Buzz off." Often we respond by either restricting them or withdrawing from them. This scene is a wreck waiting to happen!

Count on this: our kids will go into the cave, and in time they will come out of the cave. During this time we will make withdrawals from our account with them. In the face of rarely knowing when to give space and when to tighten the reins, when to let go and when to grab hold, when to give attention and when to ignore, when to speak and when to shut up, we keep on making loving deposits of positive communication. No parent on earth can do that without living in the unconditional love of Jesus and then speaking to our children in each situation with His love. That is no small task for any of us!

Knowing How to Use the Checkbook

To take on this huge task we must remember that "in spite of" (unconditional) love supplies all the assets we need to resupply our teenager's bank account. That love gives us the courage to stay focused on the main objective of our communication: . . . *speaking the truth in love* (Ephesians 4:15).

In our Unconditional Love Account we have seven *speak the truth in love* checks as seen in Ephesians 4:22-32. With checkbook in hand we make both necessary deposits and withdrawals. Developing our skills in using these checks affords us the opportunity for increased positive communication with our kids.

Positive communication: speaking the truth in love.

Communication Skill #1: Change Our Attitude

The apostle Paul offers us the skill of *being made new in the attitude of your minds* (v. 23). When our kids consistently exhibit in-the-cave behavior, a frequent attitude check becomes necessary for us. We can remind ourselves that no matter how difficult or distant our kids become, amazingly, in both ideal and less than ideal situations we can have *the mind of Christ* (1 Corinthians 2:16) by simply asking for it.

This communication tool supplies us with our overall mind-set for handling our responses to our children and their responses to us.

Communication Skill #2: Speak the Truth

Another powerful communication tool offered by the apostle Paul is: *put off falsehood and speak truthfully* (v. 25). In the Garden of Eden Satan lied, and he has been lying ever since. He tries to influence us to lie in order to draw us and our children away from God and from each other.

Our family's ability to function healthily rests on whether or not we learn to discern truth from lies and then tell the truth—to God, ourselves, and our children. Homes produce either truth-tellers or liars.

How do we apply this truth-telling skill with our kids? In their early years somewhere along the way every one of our kids lied to us. Each untruthful event and the guilt they experienced following it led them to see the depravity of their own hearts, to understand their need for Jesus, to give their hearts to Him, and to let Him change them. That unfolding sequence of actions has always fascinated me. It seems to me that in spite of the wrongness of lying, God can use the lie to draw us and our kids to the truth. Therefore, parents must be on the lookout for lying. When we spot it in ourselves and our children, we must confront it, ask forgiveness, and walk toward the truth.

Parents must go first! Remember, we were kids once. We lied and maybe even made a habit of it. And we still have the capacity to lie. I wish I had a dollar for all the times I have had to go to my family to confess a lie (whether a half-truth, exaggeration, misstatement, or whatever). I hated it every time. But confronting it sets the pace for the rest of my family on facing down a lie and turning toward the truth. Our children intuitively know whether or not we tell the truth, even if they cannot express what they know. So *putting off falsehood and speaking truthfully* (v. 25) becomes critical to our own credibility with our kids.

We may find speaking the truth rather painful, creating tension, awkwardness, and/or negative feelings for a time. It may disrupt family closeness. But the truth ultimately wins. In fact, *speaking the truth in love* (Ephesians 4:15) always brings health and healing to our relationships.

Communication Skill #3: Stop Negative Communication

Negative words come easily. We litter our daily conversations with them. The apostle Paul knew that, so he advised us, *Do not let any unwholesome talk come out of your mouths* (v. 29).

About the time our kids launched into middle school, our family fell into the habit of negative comments. Middle school . . . negative comments . . . hmmmm! It became so bad that Carol and I decided to call a family meeting to address it. We came up with the acrostic NUB. That stood for "Not Up-Building." If someone said something negative, the person who heard it would reply, "NUB." Five NUBs brought negative consequences. Yeah, it was kind of goofy, but remember our target audience. It took a while, but the flow of negativism slowed considerably. And it brought to everyone's attention, including mine, how negatively we spoke to each other without realizing it. Even as adults my kids still say "NUB" if someone speaks negatively.

During our junior high "NUB" phase we discovered three actions, stated negatively, that when stopped helped curb negativism.

Don't cut. Teasing begins with funny comments but spirals down into sarcasm and cynicism.

Don't judge. No one likes to be judged. We can remind ourselves and our kids, "God only created one Judge to rule the universe. And you are not Him!"

Don't threaten. A threat sets up an "us versus them" situation. One teenager told his parents, "I am sick of living with your rules. I'm joining the Marines." Time for a reality check for that kid! Since we all belong to the same team, we don't need to resort to threats.

And along with these negatives throw out curse words, slang expressions about body parts, dirty jokes, and sexually oriented remarks.

By picking up the trash of negative communication we set up the opportunity for positive communication.

Communication Skill #4: Start Positive Communication

Positive communication leads the family to *build others up according to their needs* (v. 29). Going back to our NUB example, whoever made the NUB remark had to replace it with a positive one—an UB, if you will. Finding something positive to say sometimes felt forced, but after some practice we got the hang of it.

During the junior high NUB–UB phase, we found three positive actions that, when put into practice, encouraged positive conversation that built each other up.

Consider words carefully. When someone would blurt out unkind words, Carol or I would say, "Let's go back and try that again." In a moment of frustration, instead of just saying whatever comes to mind, pause to hold back or retract the unhelpful words and identify the right words to say. With practice our kids went from exclaiming, "Dad, you bug me!" to "Dad, what you just said frustrates me because it embarrasses me in front of my friends. Would you not do that?" We can help each other stifle the wrong words and find the right words to express our thoughts.

Control the tone of voice. A person's voice can communicate a wide range of emotions. If someone says, "Great," what does that mean? With that one word a person's tone can express enthusiasm, discouragement, sarcasm, or nonchalance. Families increase their emotional health by helping each other identify feelings and express them with the appropriate tone of voice.

Choose the appropriate time. Our children want to talk *now or never*. But effective communication means speaking the right words at the right time. They can grow from pulling on our leg yelling, "Mommy" fifty times to saying, "Mom, I know you're busy now. When can I tell you something important?" And we can say, "We can talk in five minutes"—and not forget! By honoring other people's time, we show that we value them.

Using these ideas, with our own unique twist, we move communication in a positive direction.

Communication Skill #5: Listen Actively

Nothing frustrates children more than parents who don't listen. A predictable grunt, a pat answer, or an inattentive response causes our kids to want to yell at us, "You're not listening!" Our kids wish the apostle Paul could shout into our ears, *Listen* (Ephesians 4:29). Parents who don't listen cause their kids to bottle up feelings and disregard underlying heart issues.

To improve our ability to listen, we can practice the "Stop! Look! Listen!" approach.

STOP your mind from focusing on the distraction.
LOOK with your eyes into the eyes of your child.
LISTEN with your ears to the words spoken.

Once we tune in, we can develop the conversation by asking clarifying questions. "That's interesting. Tell me more." "I am interested in your viewpoint. Will you explain it further?" "That seems important to you. Can you tell me why?"

To stop, look, and listen involves more than hearing words. We want to listen and then help our children identify and verbalize perspectives, thoughts, and feelings. Not only does this help them understand and express themselves, but as an added bonus we strengthen the cords of our relationship.

Communication Skill #6: Avoid Conversation Stoppers

Negative emotions expressed negatively take the legs out from under a conversation and leave it without any way to walk forward. Using conversation-crippling emotions to communicate *grieves the Holy Spirit* (v. 30) because people get wounded with words. That's why the apostle Paul says, *Get rid of all bitterness, rage and anger . . . slander . . . malice* (v. 31).

When negative human emotions are unleashed in a conversation, we will hear conversation stoppers like nagging, threatening, ridiculing, breaking a confidence, silence, sarcasm, name-calling, demands, defensiveness, attacks, and bringing up the past. These destroy positive conversation and hurt people badly.

At times all of us fall into the trap of negative emotional responses. But we must recognize that these hurt us and our children. If any of these conversation stoppers afflict us, we need to find the cause (review chapters 3–4), and ask for God's healing. Ridding ourselves of these puts legs under our conversations again and frees us to take long strides toward positive communication.

Communication Skill #7: Pursue Conversation Enhancers

Conversations, like yarn, can get tangled very quickly. When emotions run high, especially in a tension-filled conversation, we can get confused about how to respond when another person says something hurtful, and also we can make inappropriate remarks that hurt. However, we can get the kinks out of the conversation by being *kind and compassionate to one another, forgiving each other, just as in Christ God forgave you* (v. 32).

Consequently, we will find ourselves responding to our children and others by:

- not arguing with our children's feelings,
- not being threatened by our children's attitudes,
- accepting our children without condoning their behavior,
- treating our children respectfully,
- replying sensitively to sensitive issues,
- overlooking irritating behavior,
- making a decision and sticking by it,
- not retreating into silence.

With kindness, compassion, and forgiveness knitting a conversation together, we can ask questions, listen, sympathize, and express our viewpoint, knowing that the Spirit of Jesus will graciously untangle the yarn of knotted emotions, straighten out the confusion of inappropriate responses, and untwist misspoken words, thus creating clear communication.

Precious. That's me. I know that because my parents positively communicated it to me. Into my bank account they deposited unconditional love; they made withdrawals when necessary; and they wrote checks that spoke the truth in love to me. All the children in the world want that kind of love communicated to them, but far too few actually experience it. For a brief time in your home with your children the "precious" bank account remains open. Make the deposits while you can. And as you do you will feed the warm and blazing fire of unconditional love in your kids!

Taking Action

Ask your spouse and your children to give you honest feedback on how you communicate with your children. From that feedback consider three ways you can improve that communication. This week act on one improvement by building it into one activity that will give time and focused attention to your child.

Penetrating Questions

1. How did your parents communicate unconditional love to you, and how did that affect you? If they did not communicate unconditional love to you, how did that affect you?

2. Reflecting on Deuteronomy 6:7, what are you doing with your children to make

liberal deposits of time and focused attention? What needs to change in your priorities and time schedule to make more deposits in them?

3. Specifically how do you withdraw love from your children's account? Give an example.

4. If your child/teenager has gone into the cave or will at some future time, what specific action do you need to take to work through or prepare for that experience?

5. What do you think the apostle Paul means when he uses the phrase *speaking the truth in love* (Ephesians 4:15)?

6. Of the seven communication skills, which one do you use best, and which one do you need the most? Why?

7. From your answer to #6, what specific action will you take to improve one communication skill with your children?

Fresh Ideas

• Following the outline of Deuteronomy 6:7, design your plan for making positive, daily deposits of unconditional love in your children.

• Analyze your Unconditional Love Account by reviewing your deposits and withdrawals for each of your children. Create two columns labeled Deposits and Withdrawals, listing positive and negative communications with examples. Reconcile your account by deciding how to improve communication with your children and then acting on what you decide.

• Using the seven communication skills, write down one check you want to write to each of your children. Give each one his or her check!

• Make a large deposit by planning a special one-on-one time with one of your children this week. Think creatively about an activity that he or she would enjoy, and then do it. Each week do the same until you have had one-on-one time with each child. Consider continuing this on a weekly basis.

Further Reading

Ross Campbell, *How to Really Love Your Child* and *How to Really Love Your Teenager* (Colorado Springs: Cook Communications, revised editions 2004). These books have been around a long time. That's because they express the timeless truth that loving our kids with God's love is the basis of everything else that parents do.

10

Pour Fuel on the Fire by Making Disciples

How do we invest in Jesus-focused relationships with our kids and their friends?

Chick-fil-A on Lawrenceville Highway in Lilburn, Georgia at 6:45 A.M. on Tuesday mornings. For four years that's where I met with my son Jonathan and his friends Tim, Trent, Rodney, and Christian—a motley crew of ninth- and tenth-graders when we began.

All of them had mega-energy. Like Trent. He had the hyperness of a kid with a six-pack of Mountain Dew coursing through his veins. One summer I took my guys on a trip to Romania. The day we arrived at the camp, about ten of us jammed into one small room with bunk beds. Standing outside, I heard a commotion in the room. I walked in to find Trent bouncing on his top bunk bed, hitting his head on the ceiling with each bounce and laughing every time he hit his head!

Fairly typical teenagers, these guys played basketball and soccer; they obsessed about girls and struggled with lust. They didn't always get along with their parents. And some of their parents struggled. Neither preparation for the group nor their attention span while in the group would have won any awards.

Yet huddled in a booth at a fast-food restaurant we went places that very few parents get to go with their kids and their kids' friends. I invested my life in a Jesus-focused relationship with my son and his friends. I poured fuel on the small fire in their hearts, and slowly but surely it began to burn.

The Return on Our Investment

When we open an account to invest our money, what do we expect? We hope for a return on our investment. We expect to receive a dividend later that is greater than the initial investment. That return on investment idea must have been what the apostle Paul had in mind when he wrote his first letter to the Thessalonians.

> *For what is our hope, our joy, or the crown in which we will glory in the presence of our Lord Jesus when he comes? Is it not you? Indeed, you are our glory and joy.*
>
> 1 THESSALONIANS 2:19-20

When we invest our money and our time—our lives, we desire to invest sensibly. So we must ask ourselves, what is our hope, our joy, our crown of boasting when Jesus returns? When we stand before Jesus, and the important issues of life become clearer than we have ever seen them before, what will truly be important? Those of us who know Jesus will surely hold out to Him our relationship with Him above all. After that we will offer Him our investment in other people, particularly our family and our children. If we choose to invest wisely—that is, in relationships— then, regarding our children, we must answer this question: How do we invest in Jesus-focused relationships with our kids and their friends?

> **How do we invest in Jesus-focused relationships with our kids and their friends?**

Investing in a Jesus-focused, disciple-making relationship with our kids and their friends seems abnormal and sounds weird because it has become so foreign to church life and to family life. Jesus had twelve disciples, and He spent three years investing in them. Every Christian knows that, but today who invests in discipling relationships? Since Jesus made this the highest priority of His earthly ministry, maybe we need to change our investment strategy!

But how do we invest in discipling relationships like Jesus did—especially with our kids and our kids' friends? To answer that question, we can read the four Gospels to see what Jesus did with His disciples.[1] However, for this brief chapter we will condense our approach by looking at how the apostle Paul invested in Jesus-focused relationships with the believers in the church in Thessalonica.

Writing to the Thessalonian church, Paul uses a family-related theme. In 1 Thessalonians 2:6-7, 11-12 he tells them, *As apostles of Christ we could have been a burden to you, but we were gentle among you, like a mother caring for her little children. . . . For you know that we dealt with each of you as a father deals with his own children, encouraging, comforting and urging you to live lives worthy of God, who calls you into his kingdom and glory* (emphasis added).

Applying this to investing wisely in our children, we fathers and mothers can deal with our children as the apostle Paul dealt with the Thessalonians. We do that by investing in three accounts.

Account #1—We *encourage* our kids by praying for them.
Account #2—We *comfort* our kids by relating to them.
Account #3—We *urge* our kids by discipling them.

Our investment in these accounts will lead our children and their friends to grow up to *live lives worthy of God* (v. 12). How do we make an investment in these accounts that will ensure a fantastic return?

The "Encourage by Praying" Account

Long ago a troubled Abraham Lincoln said, "I have been driven to my knees many times with the overwhelming conviction that I had nowhere else to go." For most of my parenting days I have felt that same desperation—the kind that has driven me to my knees. If we find ourselves there and with a desire to invest in Jesus-focused relationships with our kids, then with confidence we can say that "To My Knees" must become our investment motto.

With that same idea in mind the apostle Paul opens his first letter to the Thessalonians with these words of encouragement: *We always thank God for all of you, mentioning you in our prayers* (1:2).

Fortunately my parents and Carol's parents gave us that same kind of prayer encouragement. For example, Carol's parents started their day at 5:30 A.M., praying, in part, for their family. When I joined the family, I became a recipient of their prayers also. Then when the grandchildren and great-grandchildren came along, they became the beneficiaries of their prayers. Every morning they took Communion and then prayed for each of us by name. Eating the bread, they asked that the life of Jesus nourish each of us. Drinking the juice, they prayed the protecting power of the blood of Jesus over us. For over thirty years we have received that incredible gift daily.

So our parents inspired Carol and me to pray for our children. I created a notebook with a prayer page for each of our kids, writing down their needs and leaving a space for an answer.[2] Those pages filled up with God's amazing answers to prayer.

For instance, praying for my son Jonathan and his friends became part of my investment in them. In our Tuesday morning group we began each meeting praying in groups of three (prayer triplets). They prayed for each other and for three friends at school. At first they could not get through a brief prayer time without laughing, burping, or making other gross bodily noises. Like most kids, they had rarely prayed out loud. As they learned to pray, we began to ask God to use them at their school.

Some time later as I prayed for them, the Lord led me to mobilize them to pray for their entire school. With my encouragement they started praying during lunch with other friends, seventeen guys, in prayer triplets. Not much happened at first. But they continued to pray faithfully through the school year.

The next fall, sitting around a bonfire on the first night of a school retreat, the students began to confess their sins to each other and make relationships right. That gathering lasted over three hours. That evening sparked a fire of spiritual enthusiasm, often hard to come by in a Christian school. Following the retreat the juniors and seniors began speaking and leading worship at chapel. In Jonathan's senior year his class led the first chapel, with the seniors washing the eighth-graders' feet! Astonishing since seniors don't usually acknowledge that eighth-graders even exist, much less serve them! God changed the environment of the entire school, much of it because of the prayers of those young men.

To pray meaningfully for and with our kids involves carving out space for the presence of God to reside with us and time for the power of God to work in us. Mother Teresa issued this profound but practical prayer challenge to us:

> Love to pray. Feel often during the day the need for prayer, and take trouble to pray. Prayer enlarges the heart until it is capable of containing God's gift of himself. Ask and seek, and your heart will grow big enough to receive him and keep him as your own.

We can respond to that prayer challenge in a variety of ways, but let me offer two specific approaches.

Carve Out Your Own Daily Time with God

If you have not developed this habit of spending time alone with God every day, begin now. It creates a time and place to meet God daily. Start with at least fifteen minutes a day, then after a month add five minutes a day each succeeding week. Soon you'll spend one hour a day in God's presence. To guide you, use the Prayer Action and Bible Response templates provided in Appendix 2 on pages 250-251. Either create your own notebook or order the *Time Alone with God Notebook*.[3]

Use a Prayer Notebook to Pray for Your Children Daily

Follow the Praying for My Kids template on page 249 to begin. Also create one page for each of your children, then journal your prayers for them every day. After one week of doing this, go back and read the answers. You'll be amazed at how often, how quickly, and how specifically God acts on behalf of your kids!

God answers the prayers of parents!

God answers the prayers of parents! John Bunyan, author of *Pilgrim's Progress*, once stated, "You can do more than pray after you have prayed, but you cannot do more than pray until you have prayed." If we don't make the prayer investment, everything else will feel like plowing concrete. Prayer activates God's Spirit in us and in our children. When we engage Him on our children's behalf, He begins to work inside their minds and hearts to create a fresh hunger to know, love, and follow Jesus. At that point discipling our kids becomes a real possibility for us.

The "Comfort by Relating" Account

Children have always needed the comfort of a close relationship with their parents. But because we live in a culture where kids are "isolated to an extent that has never been possible before," that need has become accentuated.[4] Our kids' disconnectedness, addressed in Chapter 6, has cut them off from caring adults. Yet they want love, security, and support from their parents. By investing in Jesus-focused relationships with our kids, we can give them a closer relationship than either they or we ever dreamed possible. We reverse the disconnectedness when we adopt the "In Their Lives" investment motto.

That motto must have motivated Paul when he wrote his highly relational letter to the Thessalonians.

> *We loved you so much that we delighted to share with you not only the gospel of God but our lives as well, because you had become so dear to us.*
> 1 THESSALONIANS 2:8

In this verse we find the motivation needed to relationally invest in our kids. Like four mighty converging rivers, the apostle Paul shows what makes a strong discipling relationship. Our love for our kids (*we loved you*), combined with our desire to communicate with them (*we delighted to share with you*), then choosing the gospel as our topic (*the gospel of God*), in the context of life-sharing relationships (*share with you . . . our lives*)—all of those come together to give depth and meaning to our relationships with our kids and their friends. Then we will say with Paul about our kids and their friends, *you had become so dear to us.*

From this highly motivating verse we can conclude that *when our kids connect with us, they find it easier to connect with God.*

> **When our kids connect with us, they find it easier to connect with God.**

If we agree with that conclusion, then we need to decide exactly what

"In Their Lives" investments we will make. We have many options, but all of them lead to *informal discipleship.*

We engage in *informal discipleship* when we involve ourselves in the daily routine of our kids' lives. In that routine we look for teachable moments—a TV show, a bad grade, a friend. When we spend time together with our kids, we'll have hundreds of these teachable moments. We don't need to give a lecture or point out a spiritual insight in every situation, but we can look for ways to casually talk through any large or small situation—responses, choices, and actions—offering words of wisdom that the Holy Spirit will give to us in the moment.

For example, during Jonathan's junior year in high school he surprised his soccer team by playing better than anyone imagined he could play. Although a big fish in a small pond, suddenly our son became a star. And just as suddenly we needed to decide how to handle his new status. We found many light and easy teachable moments, like encouraging him to find ways of giving credit to all of the other players who fed him the ball.

In his senior year, the entire school looked to Jonathan and his team to go beyond what he and they had done the year before. However, early in the season it became apparent that the talented supporting cast from his junior year would not be matched his senior year. With each game the frustration of disappointing play, not scoring, and losing games became greater and greater. In one game it boiled over when Jonathan walked off the field in frustration during the game. This time the teachable moment felt heavy and hard and was filled with angry tears. Finding the courage to face the team, digging in and locating enough humility to ask forgiveness, and unearthing the endurance to press on when life was "just not fair" offered choice opportunities for teachable moments. This fun, then not so fun experience presented a prime occasion for informal discipleship.

Either we capture or miss these teachable moments depending on our awareness that they exist and our alertness to God's message in them. We can capitalize on these informal discipling opportunities when we become aware of what our kids need from us in order to be "In Their Lives." What do they need from us?

Accept them. Sometimes children in general and teenagers in particular can be hard to love. Parents tend to attach expressions of love to their children's behavior. So we say something like, "As long as you follow the rules, stay out of trouble, do what I say, then . . ." Then we tend to accept them. But when they break a rule, fail, have a bad attitude, or otherwise screw up (which they do a lot), we tend to withdraw our acceptance. Our children sense it when we become cool and distant.

The message our kids would like to deliver to us is, "Please look beyond my everyday failures, imperfections, and messes and accept me for who I am." Didn't you want someone to offer that message to you as a teenager? We can communicate a message of acceptance to them that undergirds our teachable moments: "Failing or succeeding, winning or losing, loving or hateful, with good or bad behavior, I love you and accept you as you are, now and forever—period." This statement does not negate discipline, rebuke, or correction. It simply shouts out to our kids over the loud and ever-present noise of rejection in their lives, "I accept you because I love you."

Affirm them. Rejection rains on our kids' hearts every day. Teachers, bullies, coaches, and even friends throw out hurtful hailstones of sarcasm and cynicism. Frederick Buechner says that in adolescence we become "scorekeepers of pain."[5] Often kids fight back the pain with sarcasm and cynicism, applying it like morphine. Using that kind of medicine both dulls the senses and becomes addictive.[6] With negatives pouring down on everyone, it follows that kids respond to sarcasm and cynicism with more sarcasm and cynicism. Caught up in the negative, our kids' hearts become numb with resentment, bitterness, and anger. At a heart level we *must* help our kids face the pain of rejection.

Instead of raining down more negatives, we have the opportunity to pour positives on them! Instead of saying, as dads are prone to do, "I don't know what the question is, but the answer is 'no,'" we need to say yes as often as we can. Think about counterbalancing every negative they receive with at least seven positives.

Don't give up on them. Parents who do their best to raise their children to love God have no ironclad guarantees. Our children may or may not choose God's direction. If not, then our worst fears become realized. When that happens, like the father of the prodigal son, we wait. My good friends Bill and Kitti Murray experienced that anguishing wait. In *A Long Way Off* Kitti writes:

> There is an agony in waiting known only by parents who have gazed down the long road that led their child away from home. They wait in hope that this road will lead them back, yet how does one find peace for the moment in long days of anticipation?[7]

Kids who rebel, perhaps getting into serious trouble with drugs or alcohol or struggling through a long-term problem with no end in sight, are harder to love, and the teachable moments can become teachable months or teachable years. In these difficult and chaotic circumstances home becomes the anchor where "in spite of" love embraces a struggling child and communicates, "We will not give up on you!"

Listen to them. With so many distractions pulling at us, we struggle to listen to our kids. One teenager commented about how his dad listens to him: "You know what I am? I'm a comma. When I talk to my dad, he'll say something, and then when I start to talk, he makes a comma. He doesn't interrupt me, but when I'm finished talking, he starts in right where he left off. It's as if I didn't say anything."[8]

By learning to actively listen to our kids we pave the way to move beyond surface communication to interacting on a heart level. Try asking questions like these to move the conversation from one level of depth to another:

- *Clichés.* "How are you?"
- *Facts.* "What did you eat for lunch?"
- *Ideas.* "What do you think about that?"
- *Feelings.* "How do you feel when that happens?"
- *Intimacy.* "What makes you feel that way?"

Then listen!

Make friends with our kids' friends. When our own kids hit adolescence and begin to think of us as "so uncool," we can continue to "be there" by deciding to become friends with our kids' friends. That means we hang out with them, spend time with them, and feed them. (Feeding is the answer to almost all teenage dilemmas!) As for my approach, I attended almost all of their games and some practices. Often after a game we met at Athens Pizza—parents, kids, the whole family. I took our group on a water skiing retreat, and two of the guys drove a Wave Runner into the dock! Talk about a teachable moment! We played basketball with some inner-city kids in downtown Atlanta. We spent a week at a conference in Washington, D.C. with twenty thousand other kids. I took them on a mission trip to Romania. Those guys became my friends. And so did my son!

Author Thomas Merton summarized informal discipling: "In the end it is personal relationships that save everything." Yes, a personal relationship will save us and them from missing countless precious teachable moments that informally encourage them to grow in their relationship with Jesus. What other investment can we make that will pay such huge dividends?

> "In the end it is personal relationships that save everything" (Thomas Merton).

The "Urge by Discipling" Account

Leroy Eims wrote a book entitled *The Lost Art of Disciple Making*. Jesus' Great Commission—*. . . go and make disciples of all nations . . .* (Matthew 28:19)—has gotten lost in the shuffle of church programs and frenetic family activities. The loss of this art has caused untold damage to the church and its families. This loss has left parents with "no path to run on" in order to spiritually invest in their children. Discovering formal disciple-making offers us a path that leads our children toward their maturity. Let's take up this "Toward Their Maturity" investment motto with a view toward rediscovering the lost art of disciple-making.

The apostle Paul knew the art of disciple-making. We see that clearly when he uses the word *urging* in the family-friendly verses of 1 Thessalonians 2:11-12. *Urging* carries a strong sense of spiritual authority, meaning "to solemnly charge." It implies to press, appeal, implore, plead, insist, and advise. This word challenges us to exercise our spiritual authority by adding formally discipling our children to informally discipling them. *Formal discipleship* means that we create a *platform* to spiritually invest in our kids and their friends—*structured meetings where kids discover transforming messages.*

> Formal discipleship: structured meetings where kids discover transforming messages.

By meeting together regularly as a discipleship group, each person receives consistent spiritual input that can transform his or her thinking, attitudes, and behavior as the Holy Spirit does His work. A real, live, adult Christian models love for Jesus and engages the group in conversation about it. As they interact with God's Word, kids verbalize their insights. They learn to pray in front of their peers, expressing their needs and then trusting God together to meet those needs. They discover their identity and purpose in Christ. In their journey with Jesus, they hold each other accountable. They develop compassion for their friends who do not know Jesus, becoming servant-leaders to those same friends. This kind of platform does not exist for our kids and their friends outside of a *formal disciple-making relationship.*

> **We equip our kids to experience life-change and to become life-changers.**

When we *formally disciple* our kids and their friends, we join with the Holy Spirit and our kids to move them "Toward Their Maturity." In the process we *equip them to experience life-change and to become life-changers.* By doing this we move toward two important investment goals:

1. *Life-change.* We invest in them so that they encounter Jesus Christ who transforms their lives.
2. *Life-changers.* We invest in them so that they can equip others to encounter Jesus who then transforms their lives.

In the context of Paul's discipling relationship with the Thessalonians, he explains how to implement formal disciple-making:

> *And we also thank God continually because, when you received the word of God, which you heard from us, you accepted it not as the word of men, but as it actually is, the word of God, which is at work in you who believe.*
>
> 1 THESSALONIANS 2:13

Notice the simple outline for discipling our kids and their friends.

- PRAY. And we also thank God continually . . .
- LEARN. . . . you received the word of God . . .
- APPLY. . . . you accepted it not as the word of men, but as it actually is, the word of God . . .
- CHANGE. . . . at work in you who believe . . .

Following this outline with our kids makes sense if we understand the *discipling dynamics* behind it. Finding out more about how Paul made disciples will help us disciple our kids. Let's look at a portion of a letter he wrote to one of his disciples, Timothy, with instructions on discipling his friends.

> You then, my son, be strong in the grace that is in Christ Jesus. And the things you have heard me say in the presence of many witnesses entrust to reliable men who will also be qualified to teach others.
>
> 2 TIMOTHY 2:1-2

We can use the important practical elements of making disciples that emerge from these verses with our kids and their friends.

Be Strong in . . . Grace

Most kids think that following Jesus means taking the ten things you like to do the most and stop doing them and taking the ten things you like to do the least and start doing them. But disciple-making doesn't focus on rules and religion but rather on a relationship with Jesus.

We want to communicate to our kids an attitude of grace. We have defined grace as God's supernatural ability working in us through the cross and the resurrection (see Chapter 5).

Gracefully we stop appealing to our kids to change from the outside in, and we start appealing to them to invite Jesus to change them from the inside out. He does the changing—by His grace!

Invest in Relationships

When Paul writes to Timothy he uses the words *you* and *me*. It's clear they have a personal relationship. We may shy away from this "discipleship thing," knowing we are not the apostle Paul and may make mistakes. I made many mistakes, and so will you. Like the kid who wanted to join the Jewish synagogue after attending my first discipleship group! Today that kid, Lee Grady, is one of my best friends and the editor of one of the largest Christian magazines in the world. He overcame my blunders and came to Christ, and we have enjoyed a significant discipling relationship for years. As with Lee and me, our growing relationship with our kids and their friends will cover those mistakes. We can relax in the relationships and invest.

In the context of grace, relationships provide the connection that causes disciple-making to work.

Enter a Partnership

When we disciple another person, we enter into a partnership. That's what the apostle Paul has in mind when he uses the word *entrust*. We *entrust* ourselves to a partnership with the Holy Spirit, our kids, and their friends. It works like my safety-deposit box at the bank. I can only take out my valuables when both the bank and I insert our keys. Discipling our children functions like that. When we enter into each other's lives, that turns the key that opens the box to the person, power, character, and compassion of Christ in us. In this partnership we discover who Christ is in us.

We enter into a sacred partnership with our kids and their friends to open the riches of Christ inside of us.

Live in Reality

Experienced disciple-makers like the apostle Paul know that we lead from weakness, not strength. He had that in mind with the phrase *in the presence of many witnesses.* Those witnesses had seen him in many real-life situations—when he felt tired, frustrated, lost his temper, or spoke harshly. No kidding—the apostle Paul! When we let kids see our flaws, they realize that we live life as regular guys and gals just like they are and struggle like they do. Living authentically with our kids makes us much better leaders with them.

Disciple-making only becomes authentic in real-life situations.

Locate Reliable Kids

We think our kids should be reliable. After all, Paul instructed Timothy to entrust what he had been taught to *reliable men.* Certainly we want that kind of kid to disciple. They show up every week prepared. They memorize their verses, witness to their friends, and never struggle with lust. But since no kid like that exists on Planet Earth, including our kids, we have a problem. So who, then, *do* we disciple? Regular kids, flawed kids, our kids, and their friends.

Disciple-making means investing in presently unreliable people until they become reliable.

Reproduce by Multiplying

Years from now what will happen to the kids we disciple today? When kids goof off, crack jokes, and don't pay attention, we can lose sight of our vision for discipling them pretty quickly. Yet we will remain highly motivated when we realize that the Lord will do through us what He did through the apostle Paul. He describes four generations of disciples in 2 Timothy 2:2—Paul, Timothy, *reliable men*, and *others*. That multiplying process changed the world! Amazingly, we know Christ today because of what Paul did here! See how that worked out in the chart below. Reading Paul's letters closely, we see names of people whom he discipled and who then discipled others. Take note of Paul's reproducing impact.

The Apostle Paul's Multiplication of Disciples

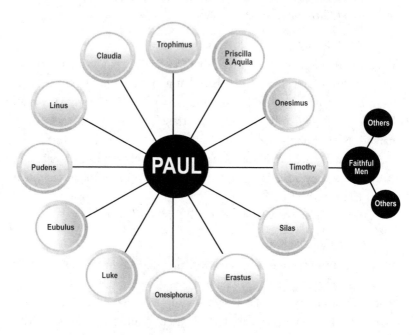

We have the privilege of joining God in His multiplying process—with our kids and their friends. Considering the math of the following diagram, envision the amazing power of multiplying disciples and how God will use your disciple-making efforts! It doesn't get any better than that!

Multiply by Making Disciples

Adding Believers	Multiplying Disciple-makers
If each kid we disciple adds one kid to our group(s) each year over the next six years, we will experience this result.	But if we equip our kids to disciple others each year, then over the next six years we will experience this result.
$1 + 1 = 2$	$1 + 1 = 2$
$2 + 2 = 4$	$2 \times 2 = 4$
$4 + 4 = 8$	$4 \times 4 = 16$
$8 + 8 = 16$	$16 \times 16 = 256$
$16 + 16 = 32$	$256 \times 256 = 65,536$
$32 + 32 = 64$	$65,536 \times 65,536 = 4,294,967,296$ (nearly two-thirds of the world's population!)

Reproducing disciples by multiplication is God's way of fulfilling the Great Commission!

On the morning of Carol's death, when I stepped out of the hospital elevator, Trent Walters and Rodney Anderson greeted me. They had come home from college and had stayed at the hospital all night, praying for Carol and our family. Seeing them, I felt overwhelmed with emotion and deep gratitude. Even in my sadness I realized at that moment that the investment of those four years of discipling that group of guys had paid off—for them and for me.

Today four of the five guys in my discipleship group love the Lord with all their hearts. Trent travels around the world doing evangelism and equipping leaders (and maybe still bounces his head on ceilings). Rodney serves on the staff of a church as a youth and worship pastor. Tim faithfully serves as a leader in his church. My son Jonathan helps lead a church planting team in Berkeley, California.

When we invest in our kids and our kids' friends by praying for, relating to, and discipling them, we will receive *our hope, our joy . . . the crown in which we will glory* (1 Thessalonians 2:19)—the return on our investment both in this life and in the life to come. If we pour fuel on God's fire by making disciples of our kids and their friends, we join His ever-expanding combustion of multiplying disciples.

Taking Action

Prayerfully consider this once-in-a-lifetime investment opportunity to disciple your kids and your kids' friends, then make a decision about pursuing it. If you decide to go for it, write out a one-page Plan of Action with the steps you will take to make this a reality. (To guide you, read through "The Practical Steps to Discipling Your Kids and Their Friends" in Appendix 3 on pages 253-256.)

Penetrating Questions

1. Reflecting on 1 Thessalonians 2:19, do you view your kids and their friends as a long-term investment? Make a list of the potential dividends.

2. Understanding from 1 Thessalonians 1:2-3 that you must make the "To My Knees" investment first, what specific actions will you take to deepen your own prayer life and to pray for your kids and their friends?

3. Meditating on 1 Thessalonians 2:8, how do you relate that verse to your kids and their friends? What specific *informal discipleship* actions do you need to take to get "In Their Lives"?

4. Considering the word *urging* in 1 Thessalonians 2:11-12, how do you understand your role of having spiritual authority to urge your kids to experience life-change and become life-changers?

5. Reviewing the "Toward Their Maturity" ideas built on 1 Thessalonians 2:13 and 2 Timothy 2:1-2, what platform will you build to *formally disciple* your kids and their friends? Be specific.

6. What five practical steps will you take to begin a discipleship group with your kids and their friends? (Use "The Practical Steps to Discipling Your Kids and Their Friends" in Appendix 3 on pages 253-256 as a guide.)

7. In one sentence what is your vision for making disciples of your kids and their friends?

Fresh Ideas

• Using the phrases of 1 Thessalonians 2:19, close your eyes and picture your kids. Let God speak to you as you imagine what they will be like in ten years and in eternity.

- Begin your day by using "To My Knees" in prayer for your children. Decide what specific forms that prayer will take.

- Take specific action this week to get "In Their Lives." Consider taking each child out this week just to talk—asking questions and actively listening.

- Move toward your kids rather than away from them by inviting their friends to your home to feed them.

- Design your specific plan for moving your kids "Toward Their Maturity" by making disciples of your kids and their friends. Write out specific, practical steps with details, using what you discovered in this chapter. (See "The Practical Steps to Discipling Your Kids and Their Friends" in Appendix 3 on pages 253-256 as a guide.)

Further Reading

Robert Coleman, *The Master Plan of Evangelism* (Grand Rapids, MI: Fleming H. Revell, 1963). This classic text will show you the specific plan Jesus followed to develop His disciples.

Leroy Eims, *The Lost Art of Disciple Making* (Grand Rapids, MI: Zondervan, 1978). This masterpiece will give you practical, biblical instruction on how to disciple another person.

Spread a Wildfire in and Through Our Kids

By fueling our own fire and then dispensing that fuel to our kids, we intensify God's fire inside of them. As we discipline them, guide them to discover their unique destiny, lead them through disappointing experiences, motivate them to pursue a greater vision, and release them to change the world, then their fire for God spreads like wildfire.

11

Fan the Flame with Discipline

*How do we equip our children to move from dependence
to independence?*

The Great Late Night Tomato Fight turned into a night-mare adventure for my fourteen-year-old son, Scott. Entering into his first experience with this annual church youth event, he discovered that the older guys battled the younger ones to see who could smash each other with the most tomatoes. (The redeeming value of this event has yet to be determined.) As a first-timer and taking this event seriously, Scott dressed in dark clothes and blackened his face with charcoal. He and his buddies drove in a pickup truck to the Farmer's Market to plan their strategy and gather an extra supply of tomatoes.

After being out for the evening, Carol and I arrived home to one of the two calls parents fear: "Your child has been in an accident" or "Your child is under arrest." In this case the officer said to me, "Mr. St. Clair, your son is under arrest."

Confused, we asked, "What for?"

"Stealing property."

"Surely some mistake has been made," we replied.

"Is your son's name Scott St. Clair?" he asked.

"Yes, but surely there's some mistake."

He cut in, "Is your son's name . . ." We got the idea.

When I arrived at the police station, our son's criminal activity unfolded. Earlier, while picking up the tomatoes, half of the guys went into the store, and half of them stayed in the truck. The ones in the truck talked strategy. They decided that they would build a barricade so the college guys could not get to them. About that time they spotted a big crate in the trash pit. *The perfect barricade*, they thought. So they put it in the truck. Moments later five security officers—yes, five—came over to arrest them. They took them to the security office, charged them with stealing, took their pictures, fingerprinted them, tape-recorded their confessions, and called their parents.

They had a very frightened fourteen-year-old on their hands! When Scott and I got home, he told us the entire story and concluded by saying, "When they took my picture, I knew I would go to jail. I saw my future going down the drain."

The next day Scott and I went back over to the Farmer's Market and straightened out the mess. The security officers had obviously overreacted. True, Scott and his friends should not have taken the crate without asking. And Scott's parents should have had more oversight of that situation.

Blindsided by the situation (after all, it was a church event), we had not set the limits of discipline needed to care for our son properly. As our children had gotten older, we needed an updated and defined discipline plan but did not have one. We set out to discover that discipline plan.

Quickly we found out that discipline usually gets a bad rap. The growing number of discipline issues and the divided viewpoints among parenting experts confuse almost all parents including us. But we also learned that discipline is doable! It begins with and builds on what we have learned in this book so far. For example, let's connect discipline and disciple-making. If you spell discipline—d-i-s-c-i-p-l-i-n-e, you can see the word d-i-s-c-i-p-l-e in there. From my experience I have found that parents who do not *disciple* their kids almost always have difficult *discipline* issues. However, when we do *disciple* our kids, the number of *discipline* issues and the magnitude and intensity of them decrease dramatically. Disciple-making gives us a context for discipline.

Disciple-making gives us a context for discipline.

Discipline in the context of discipling puts parents on the right road that can move our kids *from dependence to independence.* That discipline applied by us fans the flame in our kids, causing them to live out their love for God with obedience, responsibility, and freedom.

Discipline moves our kids from dependence to independence.

In the Driveway

Before we set out on the discipline road and "set the speed limits" with our kids, we need to pause in the driveway and make sure we know our destination. Personally, knowing my destination does not fit my normal mode of operation. I get in the car and go, and then later I ask the question, "Where am I going?" I get lost a lot! Since our kids hold so much more importance than a brief trip in the car, I recommend that we know our discipline destination before we begin. We can pinpoint it with this question: *How do we discipline our kids so we equip them to move from dependence to independence?*

This vivid picture illustrates how we can view moving our kids from dependence to independence: Birds build their nest on our front porch every spring. I watch with fascination as the baby birds, their mouths wide-open and turned upward, wait for their father to bring worms and for their mother to feed them. "Oh, how cute," we always say. The picture of the baby birds naturally corresponds to our young children.

But as our children get older and grow into adolescence, the picture changes. The cute little birdies grow up, scramble up the side of the nest, and with their weak little legs and fragile bodies try to jump out of the nest. The picture sometimes turns to a scene of intense danger. (Visualize middle school!) What if they jump and can't fly? The father and mother bird let their babies jump and flap their wings. If the young ones aren't yet able to fly, the parents swoop down and grab the babies with their strong talons. They protect them from crashing to the ground while at the same time teaching them to fly. Since flying is what birds are made for, they'll best experience freedom by getting out of the nest!

The bird family picture captures the dilemma of parental discipline as our children grow older. When do we face the danger, take away the limits, and let them jump off the side of the nest and fly on their own? And when do we swoop down to rescue them? During adolescence, more than any other period of their lives, we need a high level of awareness about our kids, their needs, and our ability to know when to let go and when to rescue. We fly continually between the nest and the ground using the instrument of discipline to equip our children as they move from dependence to independence.

Sitting in the driveway (or on the side of the nest, if you will) and considering how to move our kids from dependence to independence can cause us to panic. Intuitively we know the danger of helping our kids learn how to fly.

When our children start trying to jump out of the nest, exerting some independence, we fear that they will get into the wrong crowd or participate in harmful activities. Our fear of this often drives us to clamp down on them. When we panic, we cannot act with a cool head or with a steady hand. Fear responses do not equip our kids to move from dependence to independence, nor will they take our kids to the destination of freedom.

Love, however, overcomes fear. The Bible tells us not to fear 365 times, once for each day of the year. We need God's encouragement not to fear because fear haunts all of us. For example, consider this promise from God to us that can move us beyond our fear:

There is no fear in love. But perfect love drives out fear, because fear has to do with punishment. The one who fears is not made perfect in love.
1 JOHN 4:18

God's love coming through us blasts past our fears and zooms toward our kids.[1] Moving past our fear frees us to love our kids with God's love and to make the daily discipline decisions that equip them well. Right now, sitting in the driveway before going anywhere, will you ask God to motivate you to discipline your children by love, not fear?

Oh, yes, one more thing before we go—a quick glance to see what kind of road we will travel to our destination.

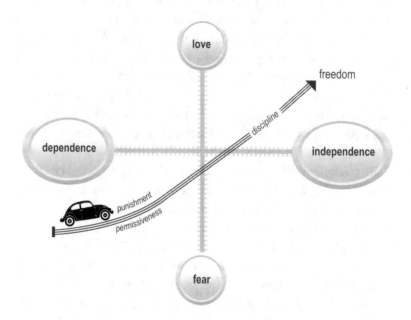

In the Ditch

Once we get going we want to drive onto the road of discipline. But before we go far, we will find that the discipline road has dangerous, fear-based ditches of *punishment* on one side and *permissiveness* on the other. Parents who misunderstand discipline can easily drive themselves into either one of these ditches.

The Punishment Ditch. Fear for our children's well-being drives us into this ditch. Yes, our children's welfare deserves much consideration, but our fear causes us to try to overcontrol their behavior. When parents do this, teenagers feel the true definition of punishment: a penalty imposed on an offender for a crime. When we parent from punishment, we emphasize the power of the authority, the consequences of the "crime," and the problem person, not the problem itself. For example, we might say, "I told you to come home on time. Since you didn't, you're grounded. Don't be so stupid next time."

Treating our kids like criminals will cause them to feel like and eventually act like criminals. To get out of the punishment ditch, try to identify the specific fear(s) that put you there, and ask God to bring in the tow truck of His unconditional love to pull you out.

The Permissiveness Ditch. We can lose control and drive into the permissive ditch in many ways—fatigue, illness, giving up, etc. But often, fear of our children's rejecting us steers us quickly into this ditch. Certainly we want to become friends with our children, as emphasized in several chapters of this book, but an unhealthy fear causes us to work too hard at possessing their friendship. Fearful insecurity leads parents to tolerate unacceptable and unbridled behavior. Lack of boundaries follows, creating emotional chaos inside a teenager's life and behavioral chaos inside the home. When we parent from permissiveness, we de-emphasize authority and consequences and then naturally set aside clearly defined boundaries. This comes across as a lack of concern for the child involved. For example, we might say, "Look, I don't care. You can come home whenever you want. Whatever you do doesn't matter to me."

Rooted in our own insecurity, permissiveness creates a double-sided insecurity in our kids. First, they have no idea where the boundaries are, and, second, they feel disrespected by us because they think we don't care. Their insecurity about themselves then leads them to a lack of respect for themselves and other people. To pull out of the ditch of permissiveness, pinpoint the specific fear that drove you there, and ask God to bring in His tow truck of disciplined love to get you out.[2]

Many parents find themselves in one of these two ditches. But we don't have to stay there. When driving, if I steer my car into a ditch, I will never get out of that ditch and back on the road if I never admit having driven into the ditch in the first place. Honestly acknowledging that we have driven our car into the ditch of punishment or permissiveness offers the quickest possible solution for driving back onto the road.

With a Road Map

With punishment and permissiveness behind us, let's look at the details of our road map that will take us to our freedom destination.

A classic description of discipline in Hebrews 12:7-11 lets us see down the road before we arrive there.

Endure hardship as discipline; God is treating you as sons. For what son is not disciplined by his father? If you are not disciplined (and everyone undergoes discipline), then you are illegitimate children and not true sons. Moreover, we have all had human fathers who disciplined us and we respected them for it. How much more should we submit to the Father of our spirits and live! Our fathers disciplined us for a little while as they thought best; but God disciplines us for our good, that we may share in his holiness. No discipline seems pleasant at the time, but painful. Later on, however, it produces a harvest of righteousness and peace for those who have been trained by it.

From this passage we can visualize how we follow the road of discipline to the destination of freedom.

• The Lord uses difficult circumstances to discipline us (v. 7).

• All fathers discipline their children (v. 7).

• Without discipline we feel like illegitimate children (v. 8).

• Disciplining our children produces respect (v. 9).

• Discipline only works if we submit to our Heavenly Father (v. 9).

• God disciplines us for our good—to make us holy (v. 10).

• No discipline is pleasant but painful (v. 11).

• Discipline results in *a harvest of righteousness*—children rightly related to God who therefore think rightly and behave rightly (v. 11).

• Discipline results in *peace*—harmony in your home now and in your children's homes in the future (v. 11).

Discipline comes from the very heart of God.

Discipline comes from the very heart of God. A loving God disciplines us and our children for our good. He uses us parents to carry out His discipline in our kids. Only those trained in discipline receive the wonderful benefits of *a harvest of righteousness* and *peace*. When we grasp God's discipline plan, not only can we deal with the discomfort of applying discipline, but beyond that we enter into it with great enthusiasm.

To highlight the value of staying on the road of discipline as explained in God's Word, let's compare it to the two parenting approaches that can drive us into a ditch.

Contrast in Parenting Approaches

	PUNISHMENT	DISCIPLINE	PERMISSIVENESS
PURPOSE:	Take control	Promote growth	Avoid rejection
FOCUS:	Penalty	Future correct attitude	No boundaries
PARENT'S ATTITUDE:	Anger / hostility	Loving concern	Apathy
RESULTING BEHAVIOR:	Rebellion	Respect / obedience	Disrespect
RESULTING EMOTION:	Fear / guilt	Security / love	Insecurity

Now that we know where to go, how do we get there?

On the Road

We can drive down the road with confidence when we know the road will take us exactly where we want to go. This good definition of discipline takes us down that road:

Discipline: external control that when removed leads to internal self-control.

Discipline: external control that when removed leads to internal self-control.

A book with an illogical title describes the seeming contradiction of our discipline definition and the practical discipline challenge that we face: *Hold Me While You Let Me Go*.[3] In other words, "Apply external control to my life, and then gradually remove it so I can run my own life." Although our kids would not say it quite that way, that defines what they need and want.

Our kids say, "Hold me." If only they could understand the enormity of that statement: "feed and clothe me," "protect me from my brother (and other dangerous influences)," "provide activity and transportation for me," "pay for college," and on the list goes. We know the necessity of the *Hold Me* discipline role because when we leave them unsupervised

176

and without restraint, chaos reigns, and our kids either injure or get injured.

But also our kids say, "Let me go." Over an eighteen-year period we want to launch our kids out of the nest so they can fly. Flying lessons take time, energy, and huge amounts of know-how. We must understand the importance of *While You Let Me Go* discipline because through it our kids become self-aware, skilled, competent, and responsible.

Hold Me While You Let Me Go discipline feels so overwhelming, like driving in rush-hour traffic on a fast-moving highway while guiding the steering wheel, pressing the gas pedal, and applying the brake as the kids wrestle in the backseat. We have our hands (and feet) full when applying *Hold Me While You Let Me Go* discipline.

But we can do it with two powerful words: *You decide.* Those words, offered at every possible opportunity and in safe settings, guide us through the *external control that when removed* part of our discipline definition. The use of those words begins with small kids, and the choices carry low risk, like picking out plaids or stripes for an outfit. *You decide.* As our kids grow a little older, we can offer them medium-risk decisions, like going to a party or not. *You decide.* The older they become, the greater the risks, perhaps whether or not they take a weekend trip with friends. *You decide.* The lowest- to the highest-risk decisions require communication and counsel. We can train them to make good *you decide* decisions *if we control the rate of independence by matching it to our child's maturity.*

Sometimes the risk of the *you decide* decision is too high: drinking, taking drugs, deepening an opposite-sex relationship with a nonbeliever, etc. If our children do not have the maturity to make the decision without endangering themselves, we must intervene and perhaps even get outside help.

If we decide not to allow our children to make independent decisions until they leave home, then when they do make decisions, they will choose poorly. Like a car with a faulty steering wheel, they will crash into a wall. How much better for them to hear the words *You decide* from loving and disciplined parents all along the way.[4]

Control the rate of independence by matching it to your child's maturity.

Within the Speed Limits

Picking up speed as we go down the discipline road, we must ask, *What's the speed limit?* Our kids want to know how fast they can go in the following areas and more.

• eating	• studies
• safety	• phone/Internet
• chores	• transportation
• TV	• curfew
• bedtime	• dating
• friends	• sex
• activities	• family time
• behavior	

We know the frustration of driving down the highway, seeing the speed limit sign, trying to follow it, but then it changes every three miles. In the spirit of keeping things simple for our kids, we do not want to see how *many* speed limits we can create but how *few*. Pick only one or two hot issues to address, and use the guidelines that follow.

Lying on the bed in Scott's room one night, he confided in me that he wanted to take out a girl. I knew this day would come sooner or later. I had hoped for later. Fourteen seemed very young, especially since the girl was sixteen! Immediately I gave him all the standard lines. "At fourteen you can go on group dates. When you turn sixteen you can double date. Once you reach eighteen you can single date." He started laughing, and as I kept talking he laughed so hard that he almost fell off the bed. I wasn't laughing. He said, "Dad, where do you find those rules in the Bible?" Stunned, I told him I would get back to him about that. When I thought about it, I had no basis for my directives except that I had heard other parents say those things. I had some serious homework to do. Over the next couple of weeks, with Carol's help, we set out to set up some guidelines for addressing dating and other dilemmas as well.

1. *Define it.* To define the guideline we tried to answer two questions:

• What is the speed limit exactly? (What boundaries do we need to set?)

- What happens if someone breaks the speed limit? (What consequences can be expected?)

We need to define the speed limit on the basis of principle, not opinion. To do that, we can search for a biblical principle, precedent, or illustration that can guide us, then draw up a brief but thorough proposal about the issue in writing. After that we can go over the proposal in written form with our kids.

2. *Give reasons for it.* Often parents don't give reasons when telling their children what they can and cannot do. Maybe you have had a conversation like this:

"Mom, can I go . . ."

"No!"

"Why not?"

"Because I said so! And besides, I'm your mother."

(Under his breath) "I thought I knew you from someplace." (Out loud) "Everybody else is going."

"If everybody else was jumping over the cliff, would you jump too?"

(Under his breath again) "With a mother like you, I'm considering it."

Teenagers, especially, question their parents' values and decisions. They may conform their *behavior* to the decision "because my parents told me to" but not their *hearts.* Knowing the principle and the practical reasons for the decision increases their motivation to apply it now and to make their own good decisions later.

3. *Discuss it.* How can we offer a principled guideline with reasons and then enter into a vigorous discussion without getting into an argument? Set aside a specific time to talk. Address any underlying tension and unresolved conflict, and ask forgiveness where needed. Talk through the proposal honestly and with respect, considering others' thoughts and feelings. Listen carefully. We must encourage our kids to express their opinions on the subject without fear of our negative response. With their input they gain ownership of the final decision. We need to keep the relationship, not the issue, as our top priority.

Come away from the discussion with a decision made! Follow that by communicating clearly to our teenagers where the discussion stops and the decision implementation begins. Parents have the final say!

After that follow through on the decision. Once we finish this definitive conversation, we execute the decision(s) utilizing our parental authority. After allowing some time to pass, we can set up a time with our teenagers to evaluate. Let them know that they can talk, but not argue, about this issue or any other issue at any appropriate time.

4. *Be on the same team.* Instead of constantly fighting and arguing over an issue, create a same-team environment. Instead of the issue becoming "us vs. them," focus on making it a "we" situation. The difference is crucial.

If we slant the initial conversation with our teenagers as a team approach, they will understand that we want to work together with them on a solution. The team approach minimizes conflict and creates a bond with our teenagers around the issue in question.

5. *Don't go overboard with it.* We can avoid going beyond what our teenagers can tolerate on this issue by using these reminders.

• Don't make too big a deal out of the issue, even if it has become a big deal.

• Use a low-key approach to keep the discussions amicable and relaxed.

• Look for what will motivate instead of irritate.

• Show them the bigger picture of desiring to move them from dependence to independence.

• Avoid discussing this in the presence of other people.

6. *Be consistent with it.* The responsibility for carrying out the agreement lies with our children, not us. We must emphasize that we will

not hound them or check up on them every day about their responsibility. If our children move beyond the limits of the agreement, then the responsibility for the consequences falls to them. Using this consistent approach will teach them the positive consequences for positive behavior and negative consequences for negative behavior. Taking away privileges and grounding them for a reasonable amount of time helps us remain consistent and aids them in becoming responsible.

If they have a legitimate problem fulfilling their responsibility or if they have a dispute about some part of the agreement, then listen and understand. Assist them in solving the problem. To do that, go back to the agreement. That will keep us out of the "I said . . . You said" syndrome.

Back on the bed with my son, Scott, about two weeks later, I had thought through the guidelines above, and I had "The Dating Agreement" in hand. Along the way much discussion had taken place between Carol and me, as well as some conversation with Scott. We had our pillows propped up on the back of the bed and were sitting beside each other. I told him, "Scott, I've worked on this because I love you and because of the importance of this issue for you. The way we handle this will make you a more disciplined person with more responsibility and more freedom. Let's go all the way through this together. Then we can go back and discuss each point. Will that work for you?" He agreed. I handed him the following document.

The Dating Agreement

1. I can have one date per week on either Friday or Saturday except on special occasions. Church youth group meetings and church group activities are not considered dates.

2. I will date only committed Christian girls.

3. I will date properly by calling the girl in plenty of time and inviting her to a specific place at a specific time.

4. I will be allowed to stay out until 11:00 P.M. If I am running late for any reason, I will call home. If I am late without cause, my curfew time will move back one half hour for the next week.

5. I will discuss each date with my parents beforehand, giving them all of the details (where I am going, when I will return, who I will be with, what is the purpose of the occasion).

6. If my parents don't know the girl very well, I will have my first date at home with them. My parents will determine that.

7. I will limit where I go on my dates. All parties will have adult chaperones. Rock concerts and private dances will not be allowed, but school-sponsored functions are acceptable. All movies will be selected upon my parents' approval and the guideline of Philippians 4:8.

8. If my date and I want to talk at the end of a date, we will do so either with the group or in the girl's living room. We will not remain in the car.

9. I will be able to double date when I complete the following project and go over it with my parents: Study all of the Scriptures on pages 150-152 of *Dating: Going Out in Style*,[5] and write a brief paragraph on each one. I will select the five most important ones to me and write a specific paragraph on each one.

10. I will determine what holding hands and kissing means to me. I will determine when I will hold hands or kiss a girl. I will go over that with my parents.

Some readers will say, "That is the most liberal document on dating I have ever read. How could he allow his fourteen-year-old son to date, especially an older woman, and to make matters worse, stay out until 11 P.M.?" Others will respond, "I can't believe he asked his son to do those hard projects. My child would never do that!" Either response is okay because that was *our* dating agreement, *not yours*. (By the way, we never used Scott's dating agreement with any of our other children. They needed their own.) Every child thinks and acts differently. My firstborn, highly conscientious son responded well because it appealed to what I knew would motivate him.

Interestingly, Scott agreed to every one of these points—except one. Can you guess which one? Try #6! Scott said, "Dad, I can't live with #6. That's embarrassing." I agreed, and we struck it from the agreement.

We experienced many positive results from this exercise.

First, we established our guidelines, so we had no need to argue about this issue every time it came up.

Second, we avoided the superficial "You can date when you are sixteen" argument by setting up a project that allowed Scott to prove his maturity to date by completing it. It took him over six months to complete those projects! By then he had moved well into his fifteenth year.

Third, the agreement gave us a concrete reference point. On several occasions Scott and I disagreed on a dating issue. "Let's go look at the agreement," we said. We did. Several times I had forgotten something in the agreement, and Scott caught me red-handed! He loved that. And a few times I got it right.

Fourth, we followed this agreement through high school. During those years we updated the agreement on occasion to fit Scott's age and maturity. For example, we adjusted the curfew times.

By his senior year he had proved himself so responsible to this agreement and in other areas of his life that we knew we could trust him totally to make wise decisions.

We had come a long way from "The Great Late Night Tomato Fight." Scott had traveled down the road from dependence to independence. Even with a few swerves and crashes, he had learned the "speed limits" along the way. We had no need for *external control* because over time he had demonstrated *internal self-control*. His response to discipline got him what he desired all along—freedom!

Traveling down the road of God's discipline, we can have great confidence that our kids will move from dependence to independence. As we gradually lessen our *external control* because our kids demonstrate *internal self-control*, they will learn to fly—freedom!

God's discipline through parents fans the flame in our kids' hearts and causes them to love God and experience the freedom He gives even more.

Taking Action

Determine one issue where discipline is needed with your child. Applying what you learned in this chapter, design a plan to address that issue. Begin by writing your definition of and guidelines for discipline, then draw up a specific agreement and discuss it with your child.

Penetrating Questions

1. How would you describe your approach to handling your children now—punishment, permissiveness, or discipline?

2. Do you make decisions about your children from fear? If so, how do you think that affects your child? (Discuss this question with your spouse.)

3. In conversation with your spouse, decide specifically what you need to do to change your disciplinary approach.

4. From what you discovered in this chapter, how do you define discipline? What purpose and goal does discipline have, and how will you pursue it?

5. What one discipline issue in your family would you describe as hot right now? Why?

6. What will you do to address that issue from what you learned in this chapter?

7. How do you think disciple-making with your kids and their friends can help you discipline your teenager?

Fresh Ideas

• Put the foundation under discipline by discipling your teenager *before* implementing a plan of discipline. Follow through on Chapter 10 *before* trying to apply this chapter. In the context of disciple-making our kids will move down the road of discipline much more quickly!

• When it appears that your child does something wrong, discern the real issue before passing judgment. This will help you apply discipline much more accurately.

• Write down all the rules your family has now, ask yourself why you have them, and see how many you can eliminate.

• Think of several low-risk decisions that you make for your kids now. Decide to turn the decision-making process toward them, and say, "You decide."

• Join a group of parents at your church who have children your age. Engage in conversation about how you will discipline your children.

Further Reading

James Dobson, *The New Dare to Discipline* (Wheaton, IL: Tyndale House, 1996). As the foremost authority on family and children, James Dobson provides penetrating and powerful insights into how to discipline our children.

Intensify the Heat with Destiny

*How do we inspire our kids to discover their
unique direction in life?*

Who am I? *Where am I going? How am I going to get there?*

The first time I ever asked those questions I had raised the window in my dorm room in college and leaned out the window. I inhaled a breath of fresh air. About six bodies lay strewn around the room, still asleep. They stunk up the place as a result of their rager the night before and their current stupor. With that scene I had reached my limit.

Back in high school everything I did had turned to gold. I led our school as president of the student body, played basketball well enough to make the All-State team, made good grades, dated any girl I chose, and had received a basketball scholarship for college. So why did I need to answer the questions above? They didn't matter to me.

When I arrived at college, though, all of the tangible successes of high school quickly faded, and I felt like a failure. A lowly freshman, I found myself in over my head. The first week of basketball I discovered that other players owned much bigger bodies than me, not to mention they played much better basketball. *Failure.*

In the classroom I received a 74 on my first history test—my major. I studied harder for the second test. I made a 47! *Failure.*

The girl I invited for Homecoming called the day before and gave me the shaft. *Failure.*

All of that piled on after the death of my grandmother, my closest adult friend, only days before I left for college.

The Saturday morning of Homecoming weekend, with feelings of disappointment, death, and failure looming over me—and alcohol-soaked bodies all around me—I opened the window for fresh air. And for the first time I asked myself:

> *Who am I?*
> *Where am I going?*
> *How am I going to get there?*

I had no answers.

From there, it took me a year to get a clue about a relationship with Jesus. Then for twenty more years I struggled with how Jesus' answers to the questions above applied to me. By then I had turned forty![1]

During those years of discovery, I had developed a passion for encouraging other people to ask and answer life's most important questions. I inflicted that passion on my son, Jonathan. I wanted him to discover at fourteen what I didn't see clearly until forty. I gave him a one-sentence assignment—to define his life direction, his mission. But he struggled with it. I did not ask for a treatise, just one sentence—no more words than fit on a T-shirt. Yet he had a hard time getting anything down on paper. At one point I had an "aha!" moment: At fourteen I could not have written that sentence either!

Why not? At fourteen neither one of us had the capacity to define our direction. I realized that in order to help Jonathan succeed at "the one sentence assignment," I needed to help him answer life's three most important questions first. Over time we pursued, and still pursue, answering those three questions. And eventually that led to successfully completing "the one sentence assignment":

My purpose in life is to love God with a heart of gratitude, a soul of obedience, and a mind of dependence on Him, and to love others as myself by serving.

Inspiring our kids to discover their unique life direction in life fits into the disciple-making process. And with each new discovery about life's three most important questions, the heat of our kids' passion for Jesus will intensify!

What Is Your Dash?

Why do all of us struggle to answer life's three most important questions?

I believe it's because God has created us for something much more in life, and getting our arms around that "something much more" often proves difficult. We're like paper clips. Lloyd's Bank of London followed a hundred thousand paper clips and observed that only 20,286 were used to hold papers together. The bank said 14,163 others were bent and twisted during telephone conversations, 19,143 were used as chips in card games, 7,200 clipped garments together, 5,434 became toothpicks or ear scratchers, 5,308 were converted into nail cleaners, and 3,916 cleaned pipes. The rest, about twenty-five thousand, fell ingloriously to the floor and were swept away.[2]

The original author of this illustration asked these pointed questions:

"How could something so neatly invented and so useful be so misused and, often, at least, seemingly wasted?"

"Are we picking teeth and cleaning nails when clearly God has made us for something much more?"

For parents and for our kids, these two questions hang heavily in the air. They beg for answers!

> **"Are we picking teeth and cleaning nails when clearly God has made us for something much more?"**

When I speak to students I try to answer those questions with another question: "What is your dash?" Students always stare at me blankly until I explain. In a cemetery every tombstone has two dates engraved on it—birth and death. In between those dates is a dash, representing what that person did from birth until death.

"What is your dash?" is a profound question. It creates an urgency to answer life's three most important questions.

> **When our children graduate from high school, one-fourth of their lives is gone!**

When our children graduate from high school, one fourth of their lives is gone! Five years later they will have made most of these life-changing decisions: college, career, lifelong friends, marriage partner.

Sobering! Our time on this earth faces severe limitations. The psalmist declared, *Each man's life is but a breath* (Psalm 39:5). Living within that truth applies a healthy pressure to our parenting style. Limited time exists for us and for our kids to discover our destiny and live out our dash. So the earlier we discover our destiny and pursue it, the longer we have to make our dash count!

We can answer "What is your dash?" by addressing life's three most important questions. Throughout the ages and across the globe, no barriers of race, gender, color, economic status, or religion have avoided these questions. God has put it in the heart of every person to ask them. And He alone holds the answers.

Who Am I?

This *destiny* question hinges on understanding one's *identity*. With teenagers, identity emerges as the most important matter in their lives. Yet they struggle intensely with how to answer the "Who am I?" question. My experience as a summer camp counselor in Maine illustrates the spirit of the struggle.

The vehicles transported us to the end of the road in the Maine woods. The counselors, including me, lifted the canoes off the racks and put three middle-school kids under each canoe, instructing them to carry the canoes to the water. Three scrawny guys, who already had backpacks and supplies to carry, hoisted a canoe over their heads and began to walk. Carrying these heavy canoes only a hundred yards might have worked, but they kept going . . . and going . . . and going. Unlike the Energizer Bunny, these "I haven't quite entered puberty yet" middle-schoolers got real tired real fast. They sweated profusely under the hot sun with their heads stuck underneath the heavy canoes. One kid stumbled over a root, and his canoe lurched forward. It rammed the canoe ahead, causing that canoe to ram the next one, and so on down the line. Canoes, paddles, gear, and kids with bruises and abrasions spread out along the trail. After much complaining, sweating, whining, falling, and not much walking, we finally arrived at the river. Needless to say, they let out a loud, "Waahoo!" when they dropped the canoes in the water. We enjoyed a refreshing swim. Then we put the gear on board, got in, pushed out into the current, and chilled.

Once in the water, those canoes moved swiftly down the river, dramatically increasing our speed with far less effort on our part. The switch from the woods to the river made the trip much more enjoyable!

This story shows us the dramatic difference between our kids' struggle to walk under the canoe without knowing their identity as opposed to swiftly traveling down the river when they do know their identity. Our kids cannot find their identity in the woods—"out of Christ"—but only on the river—"in Christ." So many adolescents struggle through life blindly, walking with the canoe over their heads. They exert incredible effort but don't get out of the woods. The river flows right beside them, but they don't know how to find it. When they don't reach the river, they decide that walking in the woods must be the only option.

Kids who don't know who they are create a false identity that helps them cope. They settle for less than who God created them to be. Simon Tugwell explains this phenomenon:

> And so . . . we either flee our own reality or manufacture a false self which is mostly admirable, mildly prepossessing, and superficially happy. We hide what we know or feel ourselves to be (which we assume to be unacceptable and unlovable) behind some kind of appearance which we hope will be more pleasing. We hide behind pretty faces, which we put on for the benefit of our public. And in time we may even come to forget that we are hiding, and think that our assumed pretty face is what we really look like.[3]

Sadly, that describes almost all teenagers I know. The end result of their efforts is exhaustion and frustration; they are bruised and scraped, wandering along the trail, still looking for the river.

How much better to get out of the woods and to put the canoe into the river!

When we guide our kids out of the woods of *self-identity* and into the river of *identity with Christ*, they not only find themselves but discover their destiny as well. That makes the ride so much more enjoyable.

This will happen as we take them through the disciple-making process. Along the way we enjoy the privilege of aiding them in answering the "Who am I?" question. How do we do that?

Let's visualize our children—and ourselves—as a triangle with each side representing a different but important facet of who we are.

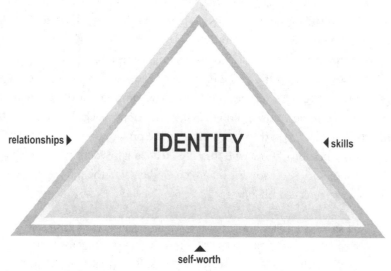

Who Am I?

relationships ▶   **IDENTITY**   ◀ skills

▲
self-worth

Relationships tend to define us. Our identity forms through family and friends and can lead us to a positive sense of self. But the downside of an identity based on relationships shows up when family and friends let us down, as inevitably they do. We may face the wounds that parents inflict, the rejection of a friend, a breakup with a boyfriend or girlfriend, a divorce. All of these and more cause the relationship side of the triangle to collapse at some point. When that happens, it causes our kids to think of themselves as neither lovely nor lovable. A feeling of worthlessness sets in.

Skills also give us a sense of identity. Most kids measure their value by their talents. No skills, no value. If they do have abilities, they long to perform and then gain the recognition for using those talents. Yet no matter what their skill level, someone somewhere achieves a higher plane of performance. When they fail a test, break a leg playing ball, or get fired from a job, they not only doubt their abilities but also feel like failures. They question who they are, concluding they have little value.

We can acknowledge the importance of relationships and skills in determining our identity, yet realize their limitations. At some point those two sides of the triangle will let us down.

Self-worth, the base of the triangle, therefore, plays the most significant role in answering the "Who am I?" question. The apostle Paul explains why.

> *It's in Christ that we find out who we are and what we are living for. Long before we first heard of Christ and got our hopes up, he had his eye on us, had designs on us for glorious living, part of the overall purpose he is working out in everything and everyone.*
>
> EPHESIANS 1:11-12, *THE MESSAGE*

With great delight God eagerly desires to show us our identity that leads to our destiny.

With great delight God eagerly desires to show us our identity that leads to our destiny. He designed us so that we cannot find our true selves unless we place ourselves *in Christ*. Ephesians 1:1-14 mentions *in Christ* or *in him* or similar expressions ten times. When we put our canoe *in Christ*, we discover not only the depths of who He is, but also who we are. *In him* we have every resource that He has (v. 3). We are chosen by Him (v. 4), adopted into His family (v. 5), forgiven (vv. 7-8), and included in His plans (vv. 9-10).[4] He is our identity! And in that identity we move toward our destiny. That changes everything!

To lead our kids out of the woods and into the river of their destiny meets their greatest need!

Where Am I Going?

Most students graduate from high school and even college without a clue to the *destination* question. They go blank on how to answer *where am I going?* Most can't seem to see what they really desire for their lives.

Yet once our kids put in with us on the river (*in Christ*), they begin to discover their destination. They find out that *Jesus' future destination for them begins right now!*

People ask young kids, "What are you going to be when you grow up?" They answer, "A fireman" or "an NBA star" or "a nurse." Then they go play like their future is now.

But by the time kids get to high school they have forgotten that. So when I ask high school students, "What do these have in common? Dating, friends, sex, parties, job, money, school," they look at me like a deer staring into the headlights and answer, "Nothing." Except for "It's fun, and my friends are doing it," most young people have not found the unifying theme that joins their present pursuits with their future. Their failure to see God's future plan in their present activities keeps those activities from having a *destination*.

By the time they enter college and then graduate, confusion reigns for the younger generation because they have mixed up finding a fulfilling career and a comfortable lifestyle with God's purposeful plan for them. They miss God's unifying theme that ties their future and their present together.

What unifying theme does bring our kids' present and future together? When we catch sight of God's future destination in the present, we must be careful lest in our excitement we jump up and turn over the boat! Three times in Ephesians 1:1-14 the apostle Paul uses the phrase *to the praise of his glory* or a variation (vv. 6, 12, and 14). In that phrase we find our unifying theme, Jesus' future destination that begins now: *to live to reflect God's glory.*

Our children's destination is to live to reflect God's glory.

In Ephesians 1:14 the apostle Paul explains that the Holy Spirit is *a deposit guaranteeing our inheritance.* A *deposit* signifies a pledge *now* that the rest of the money will be paid *later.* God has deposited the Holy Spirit in us *now* as a guarantee of the fullness of His glory that He will give us *later*. In the present we reflect God's future glory. Since we will spend eternity *living to reflect God's glory*, it only makes sense to get in plenty of practice now.

We have God's promise: God's glory is given to us now in the Holy Spirit now! When we grasp that *we live in the present to reflect God's future glory*, our entire perspective changes. There is no need to wait until we grow up or go to heaven to reach our destination. It belongs to us now!

To live to reflect God's glory brings our future in heaven into our present lifestyle. When someone asks our kids what they want to do when they grow up, they will not stutter but will say, "I want to live to reflect God's glory." Our kids will engage in their present activities—dating, friends, parties, job, money—with their future destination in mind: *to live to reflect God's glory*. When our kids think about what they want to do when they graduate from college, their careers will be secondary, and this unifying theme will be primary: *I want to live to reflect God's glory*.

When parents and kids adopt the unifying theme of *living to reflect God's glory*, then we can wake up in the morning, look in the mirror (bad hair and all), and know that every moment of that day we can be mirrors that brightly reflect the glory of the Lord (2 Corinthians 3:18). And as the Holy Spirit changes our thoughts, words, attitudes, actions, and habits, we become more and more like Him (2 Corinthians 3:18). When we help our kids grasp this, we will know we have the canoe headed in the right direction.

Speaking of a canoe headed in the right direction, check out this amazing boat story about a man who *lived to reflect God's glory* and definitely discovered God's destination for him.

Because Christopher Columbus took God's destination for his life seriously and pursued it, we have the privilege of living in America today. Probably you have never read this in school, but here is the real story of how he discovered America.

After Columbus's ships had been at sea much longer than anticipated, the crew was ready to mutiny. When they confronted him about turning back, Columbus prayed and then requested three more days to sail. Immediately the wind picked up, and the ships moved more swiftly than at any time before. On the evening of the third day they spotted land. He wrote in his journal later:

> It was the Lord who put it into my mind (I could feel His hand upon me) the fact that it would be possible to sail from here to the Indies. All who heard of my project rejected it with laughter, ridiculing me. There is no question that the inspiration was from the Holy Spirit, because He comforted me with rays of marvelous inspiration from the Holy Scriptures. . . . I am a most unworthy sinner but I have cried out to the Lord for grace and mercy, and they have covered me completely. I have found the sweetest consolation since I made it my whole purpose to enjoy His marvelous presence. For the execution of the journey to the Indies, I did not make use of intelligence, mathematics, or maps. It is simply the fulfillment of [prophecy].[5]

God's unique destination for us and our kids holds no less significance than God's destination for Christopher Columbus: *living to reflect God's glory.*

To point our kids down the river toward their ultimate destination launches them on life's greatest journey!

How Am I Going to Get There?

Parenting can get rather confusing. Dealing with the hundreds of daily concerns with our kids, we usually find the help we need. If they get sick, we go to the pediatrician. If they struggle in school, we find a tutor. If they desire to pursue soccer, we find them a good coach. But on life's weightier issues it's hard to know where to go for *direction.* Now that we know our kids have a destiny and a destination, we must ask the direction question: *How am I going to get there?*

Once we get the canoe into the river and moving toward its destination, we need a compass to help us navigate our direction. As we paddle on the river we find ourselves at various forks, all looking the same. How do we choose? With confusing options before us every day, we need a compass to guide us.

As always, God has provided a compass. He points us in a specific direction regarding His unique plan for each of our children's lives.

For we are God's workmanship, created in Christ Jesus to do good works, which God prepared in advance for us to do.

EPHESIANS 2:10

The word *workmanship* means "unique work of art"and always refers to a divine creation. [6] God has prepared all of our children for their own unique life purpose and direction. If our kids are *in Christ* and *living to reflect God's glory*, then they have the capacity to ask and answer, *How am I going to get there?*

God's compass contains nine destiny-deciders that will help our kids discover God's unique course for their lives.

Warning: These nine destiny-deciders are not designed to overwhelm you or to lengthen your to-do list. Quite the opposite. I put them here to give perspective on what your kids need over time and to give some specific tools to help you work on these in an age- and time-appropriate manner. Most kids will begin to think seriously about these issues during their junior year in high school, after taking the SAT test! That turns their focus toward the future. Disciple your younger kids through the "Moving Toward Maturity" series mentioned in Chapter 10, and then work on these destiny-deciders at the appropriate time. (Reach Out Youth Solutions can provide you with detailed instructions and specific, practical tools to apply each of these destiny-deciders with your kids. Go to www.reach-out.org for more information.)

1. Personality

What is your child's personality, and how can he or she know it?

Socrates said it well: "Know thyself." Our kids need to know themselves. Since our culture saturates us with everything selfish, many would think that the challenge to know ourselves is selfish. Not necessarily true. Jesus put knowing ourselves on a higher plane. He said, *Love the Lord your God . . . love your neighbor as yourself* (Matthew 22:37-39).

To know and love themselves, our kids need to understand their unique personalities.

A simple and enjoyable personality test will help you and your kids understand each other's personalities better. You can use the "Discovering Your Personality Survey."[7]

195

2. Spiritual Gifts

What are your child's spiritual gifts, and how can he or she use them?

What if I offer you a credit card with no spending limit? Astounding! Who has one of those? All of God's kids do. He has given us a credit card of spiritual gifts for the primary purpose of spending them on other people.

Using our spiritual gifts, we can offer the presence and power of Christ to any person in any situation.

Giving our children a spiritual gifts test such as "The Spiritual Gifts Survey" will help them understand, recognize, and then use their spiritual gifts.[8]

3. Abilities and Experiences

What are your child's abilities and experiences, and how can he or she maximize them?

Studies show that the average person possesses five hundred to seven hundred skills. Although God did not design our children to do everything—and they will never have some skills no matter how hard they try—they do have many unique abilities and life experiences. God wants to use those for His glory. Testing our children to determine their primary abilities and most significant experiences will allow them to engage in activities that will enhance their strengths and minimize their weaknesses.

"The Abilities and Experiences Survey" will help kids discover and pursue their unique abilities and experiences.[9]

4. Motivation

What motivates your child, and how does he or she give 100 percent?

An admirer of Teddy Roosevelt once said, "Mr. Roosevelt, you are a great man."

Mr. Roosevelt replied, "No, Teddy Roosevelt is a plain, ordinary man—highly motivated." High and healthy motivation among some in the younger generation runs in short supply these days.

Yet motivated kids pursue all of life with passion and enthusiasm. Whether our kids pursue photography, business, homemaking, friendships, or any one of a thousand other interests, true motivation says,

Whatever you do, work at it with all your heart, as working for the Lord, not for men (Colossians 3:23). Anything they do, they will put every ounce of energy into it for God's glory.

"The Motives and Motivations Test" will engage our kids in discovering why they do what they do, leading them toward greater motivation.[10]

5. Purpose

What is your child's life purpose, and how can he or she discover it?

Without purpose we function like the turnpike close to my childhood home in West Virginia—it starts nowhere and ends nowhere. Without purpose we're traveling but going nowhere. Probably 90 percent of the Christian students to whom I talk have no sense of purpose.

Purpose acts as a target. If we miss it, we miss the entire reason for our existence. Realizing its importance, we can work with our kids to discover their purpose by developing a one-sentence life purpose statement.

"The Purpose Discovery Exercise"—which I finally completed with my son Jonathan—will help your kids do just that.[11]

6. Values

What are your child's values, and how can he or she define them?

We live in a post-Christian era, which has created a values vacuum. Violence, drugs, alcohol, and teenage sex scream at us daily. Yet no one seems to know how to stop the slide down the slippery slope.

But we can stop the slide with our own kids. We can work with our children to identify their six core values and to begin to live by them. Then what they believe (values) will begin to match up to how they behave. The six core values will keep them on course when they feel pressure to behave otherwise.

"The Values Investigation" provides a simple, practical method to determine the six core values.[12]

7. Goals

What are your child's goals, and how can he or she reach them?

"I'm too busy." This intense complaint comes from every direction. One parent of three teenagers told me, "By the time we get to the weekend, my kids are so exhausted that they sleep half the day, then sit around staring into space. They are pooped from the pace." Someone has called that "the barrenness of busyness." The result is exhaustion from doing too many things that then rob us of doing God's best things.

Defining our goals assists us and our children in knowing why we do the things we do.

To delve into goal-setting in more depth, use "The Goal-Setting Exercise."[13]

8. Time

How much time does your child have, and how does he or she use it?

The average American who lives seventy years spends . . .

- twenty-three years sleeping
- nineteen years working
- nine years playing
- six years traveling
- six years eating
- four years being sick
- two years dressing
- one year attending church

In a flash our children will be grown, and quickly their lives in this world will be over. That is why they need to spend their time wisely.

To pursue helping your kids use their time more wisely, utilize the "Time Tool."[14]

9. Decisions

What decisions does your child need to make, and how will he or she make them?

Most children don't think about their decisions having consequences. We know better. We grasp the truth of this adage: *We make our decisions. Then our decisions make us.*

Poor decisions in adolescence can cripple the rest of a teenager's life. However, we can help our kids learn how to make wise decisions.

Use the "Decide" chart—an on-the-spot, decision-making plan for both major and minor decisions—with your kids.[15]

Pursuing these destiny-deciders results in integrity.

Integrity! That's the end result of pursuing these destiny-deciders with our kids. The word *integrity* comes from the math word *integer*, a whole number. As we help our children discover their unique life direction, their lives become more *integrated*. All of the various aspects of their lives add up to the whole.

Our job is to disciple our children, over time, through the process of understanding and implementing these destiny-deciders and allowing God to shape them into persons of integrity.

To guide our kids to navigate their own unique direction steers them along in life's great adventure!

Within our brief dash we face life's ultimate questions: *Who am I? Where am I going? How am I going to get there?* To answer these sizable questions requires significantly involved parents. Our kids need us to lead them out of the woods and onto the river of their *destiny*, point them down the river toward their ultimate *destination*, and guide them to navigate their own unique *direction*. Then complex questions discover clear answers. Destiny—*who am I?* I am *in Christ.* Destination—*where am I going?* I am going *to live to reflect God's glory.* Direction—*how am I going to get there?* I am going to find my unique mission in life guided by the *destiny-deciders.* Destiny. Destination. Direction. Our involvement in our kids' lives inspires them toward their unique destiny, destination, and direction. With each step along the way the heat in their hearts for Jesus intensifies!

Taking Action

Write out your plan to answer the questions *Who am I? Where am I going? How am I going to get there?* with your kids. Realizing that this is a long-term project, map this out over time, deciding when, where, and how you will pursue it. Then take one small step to start.

Penetrating Questions

1. If one of your children asks you to answer the *Who am I?* question, what will you say?

2. If one of your children asks you to answer the *Where am I going?* question, how will you answer?

3. If one of your children asks you the *How am I going to get there?* question, what response will you give?

4. How will you explain to your children what it means for their destiny to be *in Christ*?

5. How will you communicate to your kids their clear-cut destination: to live to reflect God's glory?

6. Of the nine destiny-deciders, on which ones do you need to work for yourself in order to teach them to your children?

7. What decisions do you need to make now in order to lead your children through the nine destiny-deciders over time?

Fresh Ideas

• Consider how to work through the information in this chapter as a long-term rather than a short-term project.

• Think about the age at which discussions about these issues will be meaningful for your kids. Then put a time frame on when you will pursue this before they graduate from high school.

• If you think your kids can handle these discussions now, decide when you will set up weekly conversations with your kids about these topics. Use this as an opportunity for long-term discipleship with your kids and their friends. Decide on a fun activity each week that will go along with your serious discussions. Determine the material you need by looking at the list in this chapter, and then order it from www.reach-out.org.

• Meet with a group of parents regularly to discuss how you can support each other in discipling your children.

Further Reading

Watchman Nee, *Sit, Walk, Stand* (Wheaton, IL: Tyndale House, 1977). This wonderful little volume on Ephesians will take you deeper into answering the three questions we addressed in this chapter.

13

Don't Let Disappointment Douse the Fire

How do we build our children's confidence in God when life lets them down?

"Dad, could I die?" Scott asked me pointedly.

In that moment I realized that indeed he could die.

Earlier in the weekend a sore throat and fever had not kept Scott from playing in his high school basketball tournament. His body handled the illness until Sunday night when his fever spiked. Early the next morning he cried out for us. Hurrying downstairs, we found him thrashing in his bed and writhing in pain. We rushed him to the hospital. As he walked through the door, he collapsed. An already bad day steadily got worse. The doctors put him on a respirator. They diagnosed him with a staph infection that resulted in double pneumonia. As the doctors hurriedly wheeled him down the hall, Scott asked the question, "Dad, could I die?"

Fear more than faith motivated me to invite some men from our church to come to the hospital to pray for Scott. We gathered around his bed. My athletic son, who only two days before had run up and down the basketball court, lay comatose in the bed with needles stuck in his body, each one leading to a bank of machines behind his bed. An eerie scene. Five men dressed in yellow hospital gowns and masks gathered around my son to pray for healing and for God's presence to calm our fears.

Then I tried to sleep. Anxious about Scott's condition, I got up early and wandered down the hospital hallway. The nurse greeted me with the words, "The difference in Scott's lungs between last night and this morning is like night and day. It's miraculous!"

Physically the Lord had delivered Scott from death in such a dramatic manner that the doctors later reviewed his case to try to figure out how such a striking change could take place so quickly. Spiritually Scott had an encounter with the Lord during the night. Later Scott explained how God's Real Presence had been with him during the night. That experience totally changed Scott's view of his relationship to the Lord. On both counts—physically and spiritually—God confirmed that His presence and power were working in this situation.

Yet we still had a long way to go. Even though God did a miracle that night to save Scott's life, my son spent eighteen days in the hospital in all. His weight dropped from 155 pounds to 127. On his sixteenth birthday I walked into his hospital room, and big tears began to stream down his face. With wide-open emotions he confided in me how frustrated he felt confined to that hospital bed.

He went on, "Dad, bear with me. I just need to pour my heart out to the Lord. 'Lord, I'm so frustrated. I'm sick of everybody telling me how sick I am. I want to get up and get out of here now. But, Lord, You are in charge of my life. You can do anything you want. You can make me well in five minutes or five years. I want to trust You whatever.'"

We held each other and cried.

The life-threatening crisis and those eighteen days in the hospital ranked highest on the list of "My Most Harrowing Parenting Experiences" up to that time. Even now when I think about it, I shudder.

> **No one can escape life's difficult and disappointing circumstances!**

No one can escape life's difficult and disappointing circumstances!

That certainly has proven true in our family—a variety of injuries and operations, the wreck (see Chapters 3–4), and the death of my wife and my kids' mother. Life is hard. Tough and painful circumstances can douse the fire for God in our kids' hearts. Instead of that outcome, how can those agonizing difficulties actually build our kids' confidence in God?

When the Bottom Drops Out

Have you ever carried a bag of groceries that somehow got wet on the bottom? Suddenly the bottom drops out, and the boxes, cans, and bottles scatter, break, and roll across the parking lot. Frustrated, we want to kick them—hard—and yell and get angry. And sometimes we do.

We parents would like everything to work out perfectly for our children. We long for them to be spared all hurt and heartache. When our kids are experiencing pain, fear rises up within us. But Jesus states clearly, *In this world you will have trouble* (John 16:33). At some time in life, the bottom of our bag (and their bags too) *will* drop out. What do we do to clean up the mess and salvage the valuable contents? What a strange answer Jesus gives: *Be of good cheer* (John 16:33, RSV).

"How can I do that when my life has just fallen apart?" we ask, maybe angrily. Amazingly, if we look to Him, He calms our confusion and gives us a clue: *I have overcome the world* (John 16:33). Underneath that little hint on how to handle life's troubles, we uncover God's deep and meaningful perspective on suffering. It's not about putting on a happy face when we feel we're dying inside. Rather, the phrase *be of good cheer* means "find comfort, take courage, have confidence." Notice in John 16:33 the contrast between *in me* (Jesus) and *in this world*. Facing difficult life circumstances *in this world* holds no hope. But *in Jesus* we can experience comfort, courage, and confidence.

Throughout the Bible suffering and pain play a major role in how God works in people's lives. Of course, suffering for its own sake is never good. We should do all we can to alleviate it in our lives and in the lives of others. But pain is important because it wakens us from the illusion that all is well with the world. In suffering we get a wake-up call reminding us that we live in a fallen world and need help from outside ourselves to heal the effects of our fallenness.[1]

C. S. Lewis has helped me see the value of suffering and pain in my life. He summarizes the place of pain profoundly:

> God whispers to us in our pleasures, speaks in our conscience, but shouts in our pains: it is His megaphone to rouse a deaf world.[2]

Lewis goes on to explain that we are mistaken if we think of this world as some sort of grand hotel where our purpose is to find unending pleasure. Instead, we can view the world as a training ground for eternity. "If you think of this world as a place intended simply for our happiness, you find it quite intolerable: think of it as a place of training and correction and it's not so bad."[3] He explains further that we view pain like the cat that sees the trip to the veterinarian as a terrifying and cruel event when it may be just what the cat needs to save its life. God uses the difficult circumstances in our lives and in our kids' lives to save us from ourselves, draw us to Jesus, and make us more like Him.

When the groceries lie scattered in the parking lot, Jesus brings the big, sturdy box of His powerful promises. Those promises are not some flimsy pie-in-the-sky paper bag that will break again but rather a well-built container to hold our pain and broken dreams. For example, this classic promise scoops up our difficult circumstances and holds them securely.

> And we know that in all things God works for the good of those who love him, who have been called according to his purpose.
>
> ROMANS 8:28

Not some glib phrase that we Christians use to excuse the impossible-to-explain events in our lives, this always-true promise provides believers with a perspective on life's disappointing events that actually builds confidence in God and in His purpose for us through them. If we look closely we can see God's purpose for our pain and suffering. Notice the next verse in Romans 8: *For those God foreknew he also predestined to be conformed to the likeness of his Son* (v. 29). Comfort and hope can come to us in life's disappointing experiences because all things do work together for God's good and our good. The Lord's vision for all of us, including our kids, is that we become like Jesus. Even at the cost of our discomfort, God uses disappointment, pain, and suffering to make us more like Him.

How do we enter into God's vision of finding purpose for our disappointments? As Henry Rojas explains, "The events and circumstances of our lives have no power over us. The power is in the meaning we attach to those events and circumstances."[4]

When some devastating event comes upon us, each person can choose either the positive or negative meanings of that event. In spite of devastating and disappointing circumstances experienced by all people in our fallen world, God still controls the world, our lives, and our children's lives. Alan Redpath expressed this perspective and summarized how it works with poetic power:

There is nothing
—no circumstance, no trouble, no testing—
that can ever touch me until,
first of all it has gone past God and past Christ,
right through to me.

If it has come that far,
it has come with great purpose
which I may not understand at the moment.
But as I refuse to become panicky,
as I lift up my eyes to Him
and accept it as coming from the throne of God
for some great purpose of blessing to my own heart,
no sorrow will ever disturb me,
no trial will ever disarm me,
no circumstances will cause me to fret,
for I shall rest in the joy of Who my Lord is.

So when the bottom drops out, God's promise still holds in spite of life's difficulties. Choosing the promise gives us positive power in even the most negative events. *Note: Depending on the depth of the difficulty, consider asking people to help you work through a painful problem—a pastor, youth pastor, professional counselor, and/or friends.* Instead of dousing the fire in our kids' hearts, tough, painful life situations actually can assure them that God is who He says He is and that He will do what He says He will do.

Where We Get Nailed to the Wall

God has many purposes in suffering, and one of them is to teach us, preferably early on, that He is God and we are not! Sooner or later God sees that it's time for us to be "nailed to the wall." He uses difficult circumstances and suffering to bring us into deeper dependence on Him and greater submission to Him.

Have you noticed that in today's culture nobody wants to submit to anybody? We hear comments like this all the time:

- "It's not fair."
- "You can't make me."
- "No, I will not."
- "I have my rights."
- "I'm not your slave."

That prevailing destructive attitude impedes teaching our children to experience God through dependence and submission.

In a self-saturated culture, going against the flow of selfishness proves daunting for us and our kids. When speaking to a group of kids, sometimes I pull out a twenty-dollar bill and ask them what they would do with it if I gave it to them. Inevitably the answers revolve around something like buying pizza or getting new clothes. Rarely does anyone mention giving it to a homeless person, to the church, to missions, or even to a friend. All children, left to themselves, will choose selfishly. Selfishness, if ignored, wrecks both the selfish person and those closely related to him or her. Suffering has a way of nailing that selfishness to the wall.

David, the yet-to-be-king of the Old Testament, certainly got nailed to the wall by difficult circumstances and survived to become a towering example for us and our kids.

The concept of being "nailed to the wall" probably originated during a very difficult experience in David's life. In 1 Samuel 18–24 we find this young man in the midst of incredible intrigue. Anger, jealousy, fear, manipulation, love and sex, in-laws, war—it doesn't get any hotter than this on the most dramatic soap opera!

This sad saga began with what seemed to be the best of experiences: King Saul began promoting David through the ranks of his army. David became successful and well-liked. The trouble began to brew after he returned from a victorious battle campaign. After the conquest, the crowds gathered for a celebration and chanted, *Saul has slain his thousands, and David his tens of thousands* (1 Samuel 18:7). Saul became jealous of David, and David's wonderful life began to unravel. Because Saul's heart was open for jealousy, an evil spirit danced in to torment him. And on an evening when David was playing his harp to comfort Saul, as he often did, Saul picked up a spear and hurled it at him. David sprinted out the door, became a fugitive, and started running for his life. He lost everything—except his relationship with God and his own character.

David had done nothing but good for Saul, but Saul came to hate him for no real reason. We will find, much to our amazement, that some people will not like our children. Like David, people will turn against them, throw "spears" at them, and try to "nail them to the wall." Maybe a teacher doesn't like them, so they get lower grades. A coach keeps them on the bench when they deserve to play. An older student spreads rumors about them, and they lose their reputations. A boss fires them, and they find themselves without jobs or money. Encounters like these *will* happen, and more than once. We need to prepare our children to deal with them.

Deep hurt can come to our kids in these situations. They want someone to blame. So they focus their anger either on the person who hurt them, on God, or on themselves. And don't be surprised if you get the brunt of their anger. With anger boiling inside, our kids lose confidence in everyone around them, including God. Like David, they try to run and hide.

David ran until he could run no more. With Saul still pursuing him, living like an animal in the back of a cave, Saul found him and again had him "nailed to the wall," so to speak.

Both my personal and parenting experience confirms that for both parents and children, sooner or later we will find ourselves with no place to run, no place to hide. Life has nailed us to the wall. At that point what do we do?

When We Go on a God Hunt

The way that David responded to his troubles provides a model for us and our kids on how to deal with our own painful problems. At this low point in his life, in the darkness of his difficulties and disappointments, he went on a God Hunt—seeking to find God and let Him handle his problem. Interestingly, David wrote Psalm 34 during the time when King Saul wanted him dead, a time that included David's hiding in a cave. As we take a peek into his deep thoughts in this Psalm, we see that he searched for God in the confidence that God alone could deal with his difficult circumstances.

David consciously took his eyes off the darkness of his circumstances and instead turned them toward the light of the Lord. He turned from lamenting his problems to praising God.

> I will extol the LORD at all times;
> his praise will always be on my lips.
> My soul will boast in the LORD;
> let the afflicted hear and rejoice.
> Glorify the LORD with me;
> let us exalt his name together.

PSALM 34:1-3

David's response to hardship and heartache was, *at all times and in all things I commit myself to continually praise the Lord.*

David draws on four different words for praise: *extol, praise, boast, exalt.* All have one basic thought behind them: *to acknowledge God's greatness and goodness.* David steps beyond the natural into the supernatural by honoring God for His greatness and goodness in bad times and in bad circumstances. That spirit of praise becomes contagious. When one person who is afflicted *boasts in the LORD*, others among *the afflicted hear and rejoice.* Then in concert they say with David, *Glorify the LORD with me; let us exalt his name together* (v. 3).

In the same way, how can we lead our kids to go on a God Hunt when painful problems arise? And in the process how can we build our kids' confidence in God to handle those problems?

For us and our kids to respond to our suffering the way David suggests, we must change the way we see it. When problems overwhelm us, we tend to lose perspective. We *glance* at God and *gaze* at the problem. But David reverses that outlook: *GLANCE at the problem and GAZE at God.*

Glance at the problem and gaze at God!

How did David change his perspective?

Elohim—The True and Mighty God

He encountered *Elohim,* "*The True and Mighty God.*" From his childhood he had built his confidence in *Elohim*—one of God's three primary names in the Old Testament. The foundation was laid in the years of solitude as he shepherded sheep. (This might buoy our spirits when our kids seem to go through "friendless" times.) The name *Elohim,* used 2,700 times in the Old Testament, expresses the One True God's greatness and power. Perhaps David's father, Jesse, pointed out the potent power of *Elohim.* Perhaps it was Jesse, or maybe Samuel, who taught David to *gaze* at the mighty acts of *Elohim* and to *glance* at his problems. With strong confidence in *Elohim* David, as a young man, found the courage to stand before the oppressive giant Goliath and defeat him.

> *You come against me with sword and spear and javelin, but I come against you in the name of the LORD Almighty, the God [Elohim] of the armies of Israel whom you have defied.*
>
> 1 SAMUEL 17:45

David's encounter as a teenager with *Elohim—The True and Mighty God,* the giant-killer, gave him confidence about where to turn in the cave.

When we go on a God Hunt and our kids experience the power of *Elohim—The True and Mighty God,* they, like David, will have the courage to take their eyes off the problem and gaze at God. Then inevitably, like David, they will *extol, praise, boast, glorify, and exalt* the Lord.

Although people come from various religious backgrounds that express praise and worship differently, almost all Christians fall into the same trap no matter what their background. We put worship in a Sunday morning box. We think of it as something we do at church when we sing.

As a result we rarely express praise outside of church. We need to get out of that box and make it an *at all times* experience (Psalm 34:1).

God, by His very nature, is *worthy of worship*. Worship ascribes worth to something. When we recognize God as our Highest Value, He becomes worth worship to us. And attention given to the *worth* of God becomes *worthwhile* for us. Praise outwardly expresses our inward worship—the worth we place on God.

Music is the language of teenagers. And praise is the language of God. Connect those two with an understanding of what it means to praise God in the midst of pain, and our kids will experience the worthwhile worship of *Elohim—The True and Mighty God*. Then when the difficult times come, when our children doubt if God exists or when they feel that He has let them down, they will still GLANCE at the problem and GAZE at God.

Jehovah—Present to Meet Every Need

Jehovah—Present to Meet Every Need—embraced David in the cave. That's another reason David changed his perspective. Knowing *Jehovah* intimately taught him to *glance* at the problem and *gaze* at God. In the cave, with his back to the wall, David had honest conversations with God and expressed his needs. God heard him, answered him, and met his needs.

> I sought the LORD [Jehovah], and he answered me;
> he delivered me from all my fears. . . .
> This poor man called, and the LORD [Jehovah] heard him;
> he saved him out of all his troubles.
>
> PSALM 34:4-6

The Old Testament writers use the name *Jehovah*, another of the primary names of God, 6,800 times. David had confidence in *Jehovah* (*Present to Meet Every Need*) in the cave because from his early years his father, Jesse, had given him many opportunities for *Jehovah* to meet his needs. Taking care of his father's sheep, David had built his certain trust in *Jehovah* when he faced down lions and bears. In the cave David *sought, looked, called*. And his years of trusting had taught him that *Jehovah heard, saved*, and *delivered*.

Our kids need that kind of confidence in *Jehovah* to face down their problems. They want to know certainly and to experience tangibly that *Jehovah* will meet their needs. *Jehovah*—whose name means *The One Who Is Present to Meet Every Need*—must have known that because He gave Himself names that address our every need.

- If we need *resources*, *Jehovah-Jireh* is our PROVIDER (Genesis 22:14; John 1:29; Philippians 4:19).

- If we need *healing*, *Jehovah-Rophe* is our HEALTH (Exodus 15:26).

- If we struggle with *defeat*, *Jehovah-Nissi* is our VICTORY (Exodus 17:15; John 12:32).

- If we are *anxious*, *Jehovah-Shalom* is our PEACE (Judges 6:23-24; Philippians 4:6-7).

- If we experience *injustice*, *Jehovah-Tsidkenu* is our RIGHTEOUSNESS/ JUSTICE (Jeremiah 23:5-6; 2 Corinthians 5:21).

- If we feel *lonely*, *Jehovah-Shamah* is PRESENT (Ezekiel 48:35; 1 Corinthians 3:16).

- If we feel *guilty*, *Jehovah M'Keddesh* is our SANCTIFIER (Leviticus 20:7-8; 1 Peter 1:15-16).

- If we face *decisions*, *Jehovah-Rohi* is our GUIDE (Psalm 23:1; John 10:27).

- If we encounter *danger*, *Jehovah-Sabaot* is our PROTECTOR (1 Samuel 1:3; 2 Thessalonians 3:3).

We take our kids on a God Hunt when we give *Jehovah* the opportunity to meet their needs. Often parents step in to rescue their kids from a problem when, really, *Jehovah* wants to be *Present to Meet Every Need*. And we can see from His names that certainly He has the capability to do that. If we go on a God Hunt with our kids, they will experience *Jehovah's* many-faceted personality. Their confidence in Him will soar, and they will become ready for the tough times.

Adonai—The Lord who Rules and Reigns

Adonai—The Lord Who Rules and Reigns—the third primary name of God in the Old Testament,[5] rooted out David's negative attitude against authority in the cave. David wanted to strike back at Saul, as we all do when we get cornered. He cut off the edge of Saul's robe. That's when God used the cave experience to show David more clearly who He is. David, by *glancing* at the problem of his disrespect for Saul's authority and *gazing* at *Adonai—the Lord Who Rules and Reigns*—changed his perspective on Saul's authority and then exclaimed with enthusiasm:

Taste and see that the LORD is good;
blessed is the man who takes refuge in him.
Fear the LORD, you his saints,
for those who fear him lack nothing.

PSALM 34:8-9

What the Lord did in David's struggle with Saul's authority illustrates how far the Lord will go to allow difficult experiences in our children's lives in order to draw them to Him. As parents we must cooperate with Him. If our children get into a David-like cave, God will use that painful experience to humble them until they can let go and let God. Everything inside of us wants to bail them out of tough situations. Giving in to that temptation short-circuits the humbling that eventually will cause them to call God *Adonai*—the Lord who wants to rule and reign over their lives.

Walking with our kids through their struggle to release control to the Lord presents us with one of our toughest parenting assignments. Yet we can release control of them because *Adonai* is *the Lord Who Rules and Reigns.*

One teenager's T-shirt summarized *Elohim, Jehovah, and Adonai* well: GOD RULZ!

God Rulz!

I watched all of my children go through their "nailed to the wall" experiences. God took my Katie through a terribly painful breaking process during her senior year in high school and her freshman year in college. She experienced deep disappointment when she tore her ACL ligament and when her boyfriend broke up with her. She hurt. She struggled. And my heart broke for her. However, in her distress God created an intimate reverence in her for Him. Katie wrote in her journal during her freshman year in college:

Lord, I do not understand why you have chosen to strip away all the different parts of my life. I have felt so hurt and so alone. But you have quieted my heart to hear your voice—describing your amazing love and grace. I have seen your character in your Word and through prayer. May I never forget what you have taught me. I want to be refined and to know that you are in control. I surrender all!

In Katie's difficulties God pressed her to *glance* at the problems and to *gaze* at Him. He built her confidence in Him, and in time she saw what He had in mind all along.

Richard Bailey, a youth leader friend, found out that my Katie wanted to attend Furman University in the fall. Richard told Karen, a young lady in Richard's youth group, about Katie. Karen planned to attend Furman in the fall and tucked Katie's name away.

Arriving on campus that first day, we walked with Katie across campus. Karen was headed for the campus picnic. As we walked along, we heard someone call out our name—"Hey, St. Clairs." Karen, passing by, overheard.

"St. Clair!" she squealed in freshman-girl fashion. "Are you Katie St. Clair?" The two girls hit it off, and at the picnic Karen introduced Katie to a freshman football player named Bart Garrett. Katie and Bart became friends too. And to make a long story very short, when they graduated they married!

David told us that God always comes through: *Fear the LORD, you his saints, for those who fear him lack nothing* (Psalm 34:9). Even in the most disappointing times, as Katie experienced, He uses our pain to show us more of Himself, and if that weren't enough, He makes sure that we *lack no good thing* (v. 10).

Go on a God Hunt!

Yes, life is hard! But the problems are no problem for God. So in preparation for when the bottom drops out and our kids get nailed to the wall, we can take them on a God Hunt where they will learn to have confidence in Him; where they *glance* at the problem and *gaze* at *Elohim—the True and Mighty God, Jehovah—the God Who Is Present to Meet Every Need,* and *Adonai—the Lord Who Rules and Reigns.* Then no disappointment that life brings can extinguish their fire for God. Quite the opposite—the fire in their hearts will burn hotter and hotter for Him.

Taking Action

Go on a God Hunt. Identify the most difficult experience your child faces. Find out when the bottom dropped out, where he or she got nailed to the wall, and how he or she perceived God in light of this situation. Talk this through in several one-on-one conversations asking variations of the question, "Where do you see God working in this situation?" Then, using the information you learned in this chapter, discuss what he/she needs in order to *glance* at the problem and *gaze* at God.

Penetrating Questions

1. In what way has the bottom dropped out for you and/or for each of your children?

2. Reflecting on John 16:33, Romans 8:28-29, and the Alan Redpath poem on page 205, how do you need to adjust your view of your life as it relates to suffering? What do you think God is doing through the difficulties you and your children face right now?

3. Considering what David went through that got him "nailed to the wall" (1 Samuel 18–24), how do you and your children identify with his difficulties? In the past how have you tried to solve your difficult situations?

4. Do you feel you've ever been nailed to the wall in the back of a cave with no place to turn but to God? If so, how? Did you or will you, like David, decide to go on a God Hunt?

5. On your God Hunt how will you and your kids *gaze* instead of *glance* at the power of *Elohim—the True and Mighty God*? What one specific action will you take to trust His power as you face your difficulties?

6. On your God Hunt how will you and your kids *gaze* instead of *glance* at the presence of *Jehovah—Present to Meet Every Need*? What one specific action will you take to pursue His presence in the midst of your problems?

7. On your God Hunt how will you and your kids *gaze* instead of *glance* at the authority of *Adonai—The Lord Who Rules and Reigns*? What one specific action will you take to release control to His authority in the midst of your struggles?

Fresh Ideas

• Begin the habit of journaling the God Hunt insights you discover with your kids. Later the journal will serve as a positive confidence-builder as you look back on how God has worked through various difficulties.

• Buy several CDs of praise music. Play them at home and in the car. If you have teenagers, buy the ones they prefer. After a song or two go on a God Hunt, asking your kids to recount one thing they learned about God from the song.

• Gather for a God Hunt Family Night regularly. Together memorize one verse each week of Psalm 34:1-9. Share personal insights on how you see God working through the difficulties.

Further Reading

Philip Yancey, *Where Is God When It Hurts?* (Grand Rapids, MI: Zondervan, 1990). This penetrating volume explains the role God plays in human suffering.

Glow in the Light of God's Vision

How do we motivate our kids to pursue God's dream for their lives?

During her thirteenth year Katie and I traveled to Minneapolis to attend a high school conference with about a thousand high school students. The first night we sat in the back corner of the hotel ballroom because students had filled all of the other seats. After we sat down, only a few seats remained around us. A couple of minutes later Bill and Vonette Bright, founders of Campus Crusade for Christ and two of my heroes, sat down beside us. In the first small-group prayer session, I peeked and saw Katie in a group of three with the Brights. My thirteen-year-old Katie held hands and prayed several times that night with Bill and Vonette Bright!

The rest of the week, when I was not speaking, Katie and I sat in that same back corner, and to our delight the Brights came to the same corner too. They gave Katie personal attention and encouraged her numerous times during the week. At thirteen she had no idea of the renown of the Brights, nor of their spiritual depth, influential leadership, and global impact. Yet as one who knew the Brights since playing on the Athletes in Action basketball team,[1] I listened with wonder to the precious prayers they prayed for Katie. Only the Lord knows the rubbing-off effect they had on her.

Later I told Katie the following story. Years before, young Bill and Vonette had written a document outlining their dreams for their future, expressing their desires for worldly gain and comfort. Then as they grew in their newfound relationship to Jesus, they decided to reassess their dreams in light of their faith. They wrote down things like "living holy lives," sharing as "effective witnesses for Christ," and "helping fulfill the Great Commission in this generation." Then they consecrated these priorities in the form of a "written contract" with the Lord. In this document they renounced their materialistic desires, surrendered their lives fully to Christ, and took on the status of "slaves" of Jesus Christ. Soon after that experience, Bill received the enormous vision for Campus Crusade for Christ. Today Campus Crusade operates as a multimillion-dollar ministry that takes the gospel to the world. Yet through the years the Brights never received more than a combined salary of $48,000 and never owned a house or car. They measured success not by worldly gain but by sacrifice in order to pursue God's vision.

> **Measure success not by self-gratification but by self-sacrifice.**

Carol and I desired that same Kingdom Dream view of success in our family and for our children. We hoped for that dream instead of success defined by the American Dream. The difference in the two dreams is that one *gives* and the other *gets*. We've had great hope that our children would measure their success not by self-gratification but by self-sacrifice; not by grasping for more but by God's vision for giving their lives away. We wanted them to have a serving lifestyle, even in a shopping-mall culture. As Oswald Chambers put it:

> We are not called to be successful in accordance with ordinary standards, but in accordance with the corn of wheat falling into the ground and dying, becoming in that way what it never could be if it were to abide alone.[2]

I hope you will embrace that same view of success for your children.

When we encourage them toward the Kingdom Dream, the fire inside them will glow in the light of God's vision for their lives. And in time they will change the world.

With the everyday pressure to pursue the American Dream, how can we clearly envision God's Kingdom Dream and then motivate our kids to see it and pursue it for themselves?

Take the Eye Exam

Think of seeing God's vision as comparable to taking an eye exam. The optometrist examines our eyes and then writes a prescription for glasses. When we put on our new glasses, we find ourselves no longer holding a piece of paper at arm's length!

Poor vision abounds. Just as many of us need glasses to read the newspaper, we need improved ability to see God's vision. Perhaps the greatest vision impairment for teenagers today comes from parents and adults in the church whom kids see as hypocrites. Those adults act one way at church and another way at home. When our kids see this, it breeds cynicism and blurs their vision of God and His vision for them. The breadth and severity of this blurred vision problem in the church today cannot be overemphasized.

God wants us and our kids to overcome this blurred vision problem and have 20/20 vision. So let's begin by taking an eye exam, looking at our own intentions concerning God's vision for us. By honestly and fully engaging in answering one question we can determine how well we see what God sees: *Am I willing to do whatever it takes to let God use my life to change the world for His glory?*

> **Am I willing to do whatever it takes to let God use my life and my children's lives to change the world for His glory?**

This question causes us to pause and examine our intentions—our desires, motives, goals, priorities. And in its answer we can receive the prescription that causes us to see God's vision for us 20/20.

When we face how our kids fit into the answer to this question, concealed intentions that we never knew existed become exposed. Let's apply the question to our kids: *Am I willing to do whatever it takes to let God use my children's lives to change the world for His glory?*

Over the years I have watched parents struggle with that question. It seems to raise three other questions. Answer them as part of the eye exam.

1. Do I want to control my children's futures by imposing my dream on their lives?

2. To what degree is my view of my children's success focused on the *getting* motive of the American Dream?

3. Will I release my children to pursue the *giving* motive of God's Kingdom Dream, no matter what that means or where it takes them?

These hard but intention-exposing questions determine how we envision our children's future and what we will do in the present to motivate them toward that future. When we examine our own motives and put on the glasses of God's desires, our vision quickly becomes 20/20. Then we can see to help our kids with their vision too.

See the Unseen

Vision is the ability to see that which is unseen as already seen so it can be seen.

To grasp this definition of vision think about an architect who sits at his drawing table until he envisions in his mind's eye the building that he will construct. Then he draws a sketch of the building on his computer. After that he designs every detail of that building—all before anyone pours a foundation or lays a brick! Only when he has done his work can the building begin. When the construction crew completes the building, then others can see and enjoy it. However, the architect has seen it all along. That's vision.

In the same way, God has a vision for us and for our children. This Grand Architect's sketch works the same for all of us. Yet once we see the big picture, then He will fill in all of the specific, personal details that make His vision for us uniquely different from His vision for everyone else. What "big picture" vision does God have for us and our kids?

The Westminster Confession states, "The chief end of man is to glorify God and enjoy him forever." However, author John Piper contends that the theologians who wrote this confession intended for it to say, "The chief end of man is to glorify God *by* enjoying him forever." That one word change transforms the way we see how God views us and His vision for us.

To Glorify God

Sure, people use the term, but who knows what it means or practically what to do with it? Let's find out from the writers of the Bible, who all seemed to see it so clearly: *God desires to glorify Himself in us.*

For example, Isaiah instructed God's people:

Arise, shine, for your light has come,
And the glory of the LORD rises upon you.
See, darkness covers the earth
And thick darkness is over the peoples,
But the LORD rises upon you
And his glory appears over you.
Nations will come to your light,
And kings to the brightness of your dawn.

ISAIAH 60:1-3

Furthermore, Jesus prayed to His Father:

I have given them the glory that you gave me, that they may be one as we are one: I in them and you in me.

JOHN 17:22-23

Also Paul the apostle invites us into God's glory:

He called you to this through our gospel, that you might share in the glory of our Lord Jesus Christ.

2 THESSALONIANS 2:14

By Enjoying Him Forever

Honestly, many individual Christians and churches experience very little enjoyment. If we do find enjoyment we tend to seek it for our own pleasure, not God's. We have pursued the American Dream, amassing things (and massive debt along with them). We entertain ourselves 24/7 trying to enjoy ourselves. All the while it has hardly crossed our minds that we can enjoy God.

To aid us in seeing how limited and unfulfilling is our American Dream view of pleasure, yet how vast and satisfying is God's Kingdom view of pleasure, read this sampling of verses.

From David:

Delight yourself in the LORD
and he will give you the desires of your heart.

PSALM 37:4

From Jesus:

I have told you this so that my joy may be in you and that your joy may be complete.

JOHN 15:11

From the apostle Paul:

Command those who are rich in this present world not to be arrogant nor to put their hope in wealth, which is so uncertain, but to put their hope in God, who richly provides us with everything for our enjoyment.

1 TIMOTHY 6:17

John Piper summarizes these delightful thoughts with his famous statement, "God is most glorified in us when we are most satisfied in him."[3]

Going along with Piper's statement, David offers an outrageous affirmation of God's desire for us to "enjoy him forever":

You open your hand and satisfy the desires of every living thing.

PSALM 145:16

Rarely have I heard anyone connect God's glory with our personal satisfaction—pleasure, delight, joy, enjoyment, fulfillment of desires. Yet once we make the connection that *we glorify God by finding our satisfaction in Him*, it's like putting on new glasses. We can see!

> **God's vision for us: to glorify God by finding our satisfaction in Him.**

When we see that, we will change how we view our lives and our children's lives, and we will enter into the enjoyment of what we now see!

Display the Design

Once we view our personal vision as glorifying God by finding our satisfaction in Him, that drives every other personal and family decision. This vision influences our use of time, money, and energy; our choices in entertainment, food, sports; it determines the jobs we take and the way we do them.

> **Ironically, we find the ultimate in personal pleasure as we pursue glorifying God.**

Many people perceive that anything to do with God means depriving ourselves of pleasure. Ironically, we find the ultimate in personal pleasure as we pursue glorifying God. That's because each aspect of our lives finds its proper place in the pursuit of God's personal vision for us.

But living out our vision doesn't just happen. Jesus worked with His disciples every day for three years before they fully understood His design and embraced it. That should encourage us! Like the disciples, in pursuing God's vision for us we will struggle and grow, and so will our kids. And also like the disciples, living out that vision will follow a patterned process, a design that usually unfolds like this:

Vision➜Action➜Cost➜Death➜Life➜Multiplication
The Vision Design:
Vision➜Action➜Cost➜Death➜Life➜Multiplication

Looking at how Jesus displayed the design of His vision of God's glory to His disciples will help us see how He wants to display that same design in us and in our kids.

223

Catch the Vision

Jesus gave His disciples a visual demonstration of His vision for them. In a teachable moment He said to Peter and Andrew, *Come, follow me, and I will make you fishers of men* (Matthew 4:19). Being fishermen, they could picture what Jesus meant. In Luke's version Jesus told them to let down their nets to catch some fish. Peter protested that they had fished all night and hadn't caught a thing. But when he relented and put the nets down, they caught so many fish that their nets almost broke! Then in seven brief words (in English anyway) Jesus verbally expressed the vision: *From now on you will catch men* (Luke 5:11). Through the visual of the fish the disciples caught the excitement of God's vision for them. They left everything and followed Jesus.

Look for visuals (people, places, events) that demonstrate God's glory, and put your kids in those environments.

Join the Action

Jesus' disciples watched Him fish for men when He preached, healed, and cast out demons. Then He gave them a shot at it and enabled them to do exactly what He did (Luke 9:1-2)! *So they set out and went from village to village, preaching the gospel and healing people everywhere* (Luke 9:6). They got in on the action.

Look for action-oriented ministry activities for your kids.

Describe the Cost

Once the disciples caught the vision and joined in the action, Jesus communicated the cost of pursuing the vision. *If anyone would come after me, he must deny himself and take up his cross daily and follow me. For whoever wants to save his life will lose it, but whoever loses his life for me will save it* (Luke 9:23-24). Jesus explained the cost of the vision quite clearly and often. The disciples embraced the cost to the best of their ability to understand it at the time.

Look for occasions for your kids to pay the price for following Jesus, giving them practice at making daily sacrifices.

Die to Personal Plans

Even though Peter made the great proclamation, *You are the Christ* (Matthew 16:16), later he denied that he knew Jesus. When a young girl charged him with being a friend of Jesus, he refused to identify himself with the Lord. After that happened three times he wept at his failure (Matthew 26:69-75). With that his personal plans and vision died.

Death never seems appealing, but painful. Yet when we grasp Jesus' words in John 12:24 we can see that pursuing God's vision hinges on dying to our own hopes and dreams: *I tell you the truth, unless a kernel of wheat falls to the ground and dies, it remains only a single seed. But if it dies, it produces many seeds.* Jesus placed the cross at the heart of the gospel and of victorious Christian living. It holds the key to vision. The apostle Paul explained clearly how this works.

> *I have been crucified with Christ and I no longer live, but Christ lives in me. The life I live in the body, I live by faith in the Son of God, who loved me and gave himself for me.*
>
> GALATIANS 2:20

Only when we die to ourselves can Jesus live in us and carry out His vision through us.

Look for times to talk to your kids about the cross, especially in their hurts and disappointments, and about how our vision (hopes and dreams) must die if Jesus' vision is to live in us. Memorize Galatians 2:20 together.

Impart Life

After Jesus' resurrection, the disciples experienced their own "resurrection." Jesus replaced their disappointment and discouragement over the death of their own vision with His vision for them. He breathed His life into them and filled them with the Holy Spirit (John 20:21-22). From then on they expressed the life of Jesus and the vision of Jesus through their lives to the glory of God.

Look for times to talk to your kids about how the resurrection (life and vision) always comes after the cross (disappointment and discouragement). Find examples of how life comes out of death. As they see this, God will show them more and more of His vision for them!

Multiply Influence

As Jesus' disciples walked through the vision process, they saw ever more clearly the display of His design for their lives. Then Jesus fulfilled His promise to them: *But you will receive power when the Holy Spirit comes on you; and you will be my witnesses in Jerusalem, and in all Judea and Samaria, and to the ends of the earth* (Acts 1:8). With the new power of God within them and upon them, they expressed the glory of God through their lives wherever they went and whatever they did. God multiplied their influence, and in a few brief years they changed the world!

Look at the longer view concerning your kids, pointing out to them that God takes them through the vision process to display His design to them. Then in due time He will multiply their influence for the greater glory of God to change the world.

To see an actual illustration of how displaying the design of God's vision works with our kids, let's pick up on Katie's story from the last chapter and follow it since her encounter with Bill and Vonette Bright. Her experiences show us that when God displays the design of His vision in our children, even with all of its difficulties, He knows what He is doing each step along the way.

I remember how Vonette Bright prayed a very endearing prayer for Katie's future husband. Katie's mom and I had prayed for her mate since before she was born. Three years after Vonette's prayer, Carol and I gave Katie a ruby ring for her sixteenth birthday with Proverbs 31:10 inscribed inside it: *A wife of noble character who can find? She is worth far more than rubies.* We presented her the ring as a challenge to purity until marriage. (Catch the vision.)

All worked well for a while because she avoided romantic relationships altogether. But during her junior year in high school a guy caught her eye, and they dated for over a year. They had to deal with all of the immature ups and downs of high school romances. (Join the action.)

During that romance Carol and I had several talks with her about how she viewed the future of the relationship. We told her that if she wanted God's special man for her, she would have to wait for him. (Describe the cost.)

Then one day at the beginning of her freshman year in college, she called home crying—her boyfriend had broken up with her, and she felt heartbroken. With the departure of her boyfriend, her vision of her future mate departed too. It lay dormant for two years. Katie continually faced the challenges of giving up her plans for God's plans, wondering if God would ever come through and whether or not she could find her satisfaction in God alone. (Die to personal plans.)

Then in her junior year of college she began to date Bart Garrett. Every indicator pointed to him as "the one." The next Christmas they got engaged. When he asked her to marry him, Bart wrote her a letter that he later had framed. "I have loved you as a friend. I have loved you as a companion. I have loved you as a sweetheart. And I will love you as my wife. . . . I will love you forever, till death do us part." (Impart life.)

Now three children grace their lives, and they work together leading a church in Berkeley, California. (Multiply influence.)

God took Katie through the vision process. Without going through it, she would not have died to the old vision (old boyfriend). Without the pain of dying to the old vision, she could not have entered into the exhilaration of the new vision (new boyfriend/future husband, kids, and multiplied ministry for the glory of God)!

All of our kids go through this process with their own unique sets of circumstances. As they do, God displays the design of His vision to them for His glory.

Discover the Vision

What can we do to prepare our children to discover their own unique vision of glorifying God by finding their satisfaction in Him? Jesus demonstrated the vision to His disciples by using four real-life encounters as models. An awareness of how Jesus focused and expanded the vision of His disciples can guide us to do the same with our kids.

Model #1: Loving (Matthew 9:35-38)

Jesus traveled through the cities and villages teaching, preaching, and healing. He felt the pain of hurting and broken people. He had *compassion* on them—gut-wrenching emotion over the plights of other persons. Jesus saw them as *harassed*—beaten up and abused, *helpless*—hurled down on the ground and not able to get up, *like sheep without a shepherd*—without purpose, direction, or proper care. His compassion for people led to action.

For our kids, expanding their compassion capacity will give them a heart-felt burden for the needs of other people. Involving them in deeds of compassion will increase their compassion for others.

227

Model #2: Serving (John 13:1-17)

When Jesus wanted to show His disciples *the full extent of His love,* He washed their feet. In Jesus' day people walked everywhere on sandy or muddy roads. Customarily in a home the host provided a servant at the door to clean the feet of guests, but in this case no one took that responsibility. Since the disciples may have seen this role as beneath them, Jesus took the water and the towel into a room full of proud hearts and stinky feet. After He washed their feet, He told them that just as He had washed their feet, He wanted them to wash each other's feet. Radical!

Creating a servant attitude in our kids' self-oriented world presents no small task. But by asking this simple question we can create an awareness of serving in our kids: "Whom will we serve today?" Then we can model serving and can invite our kids to serve alongside us.

Model #3: Caring (Luke 10:25-37)

When asked the question, *Who is my neighbor?* Jesus told the story of the Good Samaritan. A Jewish man was going from Jerusalem to Jericho alone. He traveled a dangerous road where thieves often beat up people, and this lot befell him. He was stripped, beaten, and left for dead. Two religious types—a preacher and a musician, sort of—passed by the man without helping him. Then a Samaritan, hated by the Jews, came along. This man took pity on the victim, bandaged his wounds, took him to an inn, and paid the bill. After Jesus' story, answering the question *Who is my neighbor?* was not that hard.

Teaching our kids that our neighbors include all persons we meet, whether or not we know them, expands their view of caring. God desires that we, like the Samaritan, go all-out to meet our neighbor's needs. When you, like the Good Samaritan, help meet the needs of someone you know, your kids will see this demonstrated.

Model #4: Telling (John 4:1-26)

Jesus, hot, tired, and thirsty, stopped at a well in Samaria. When a local woman came to draw water, He asked her for a drink. A conversation ensued in which Jesus communicated to her the good news about Himself. That not only led this woman to believe in Jesus, but also many others from her town believed.

Our kids need to boldly share their faith. We can help them by demonstrat-

ing faith-sharing for them and then teaching them to do it. Plan with your kids to identify three of their friends who need Jesus. Then apply the models above with those friends. After that, plan a sleepover or party at your house so they can communicate the gospel to their friends.[4]

Implementing these models will move us toward God's unique vision for our kids. We do not need to concern ourselves with doing this perfectly. We will experience a learning curve as we put vision into practice and help our kids do the same. Even our mistakes become opportunities to focus and to expand the vision. The mistake we do not want to make is to do nothing. So let's decide how we might apply at least one of these models with our kids and get going!

The American Dream of *getting* pales in comparison to the Kingdom Dream of *giving*. Once our kids see the vision of the Kingdom Dream, they will never desire to return to the other. It will lose its appeal because they will have set their eyes on *glorifying God by finding their satisfaction in Him*. Nothing else will matter but to pursue this vision. As we motivate our kids toward this vision and model it for them, they will find their unique expression of their own vision. The more the design of their vision unfolds and the discovery of their own vision is experienced, the more they will radiate the glow of Light from the fire in their hearts. Then God will use them to change the world!

Taking Action

Select one of the four ministry models, and put that model into action. Make your selection according to which one you think will increase the Kingdom vision in your family.

Penetrating Questions

1. How would you express the difference between the American Dream and the Kingdom Dream? Be specific.

2. How do you think God wants to use your life to change the world for His glory?

3. After answering the three "eye exam" questions on page 220, how do your intentions line up with God's desires for your kids? Can you say that you are totally motivated toward God's vision for your life? For your children's lives?

4. In what ways does the vision statement *to glorify God by finding our satisfaction in Him* express or not express your personal vision?

5. How has the "The Vision Design" process worked out in your life? Your kids' lives?

6. Which of the four models do you think will increase the vision of your family? Why?

7. From the model you picked, what specific plans do you have to implement it?

Fresh Ideas

• Draw up a contract like the one Bill and Vonette Bright wrote, expressing your desire to become a slave of Jesus Christ. Include some of the ideas from this chapter in that contract.

• Think about how you can enjoy God more. Write a paragraph, song, or other creative expression to God that conveys your enjoyment of Him.

• Involve your family in a body of believers where the worship is alive, Jesus and the Bible are talked about warmly, and ministry, not entertainment, guides the youth group. Even if it means changing churches, place your family in a healthy spiritual environment. Look for a way to get involved in the youth ministry and for places where your kids can deepen their understanding of God's vision for them.

• Consider taking some training to develop your ability to minister to others and to share your faith. Teach your children what you learn, and then practice it together.

• Write a one-sentence prayer asking God to accomplish His vision for your children's lives. Record the prayer on a card, and put it in a place that will remind you to pray it daily.

Further Reading

John Piper, *Desiring God* (Portland: Multnomah Press, 1986, revised and expanded edition 2003). This powerful book provides an in-depth study of what it means to glorify God.

Barry St. Clair, *Giving Away Your Faith*, Reach Out Youth Solutions. This practical book will help you develop the "telling" model. It guides kids on the wild adventure of overcoming their fears and taking the risk to boldly communicate Christ.

Barry St. Clair, *Influencing Your World*, Reach Out Youth Solutions. This book will help you and your kids develop the models of loving, serving, and caring. Through it your kids will grow as influential leaders through serving the needs of people around them.

Spread the Fire of God's Desire

How do we release our children to change the world?

After Scott's graduation from high school, I took him and eighteen of his friends on a mission trip to Romania soon after the fall of Communism. After flying all night, we arrived in Budapest, Hungary and hailed taxis to the train station. Arriving with thirty minutes to spare, we grabbed some food and then boarded the train along with hundreds of other people. Only then did we realize that we had tickets for the train itself, but no tickets for seats! The idea of train tickets without seats caught me by surprise! Picture twenty kids strewn out on the dirty floor of a full train, traveling across Hungary and Romania. Scary.

Then things got worse. Our team arrived at the Hungarian/Romanian border in the middle of the night. After Hungarian officials examined our passports, the Romanian officials, accompanied by soldiers, came on the train to do the same. The armed soldiers, looking dangerous and a bit tipsy, surrounded our team. One soldier wanted to know if we had an official letter of invitation. We did not. He scowled and told our team we faced "big trouble." I could tell the kids felt frightened. Me too! I had visions of having to call the kids' parents from a Romanian jail. Hoping to convince the officers that we belonged there officially, I gave them a flyer about our team. In their drunken state they laughed and asked us to autograph it as a souvenir. The tension eased.

Our little band of missionaries fell asleep thoroughly exhausted until we arrived in Sibiu, Romania. When we got off the train, our contacts were nowhere to be found. We spoke no Romanian, and apparently no one spoke English—until we met Eva. This young woman helped us connect with our contacts, and while we waited for them, all of us engaged her in conversation. The kids invited her to our meetings, and she asked if she could bring her mother and brother since her father had died six months earlier. Of course she could. Eventually our contacts arrived with transportation.

Soon our novice team tried their hand at doing ministry in a foreign country. They met people who did not speak their language, ate strange food, and slept in places unlike anywhere they had slept before. They smiled, cried, and got very tired as they talked to individuals, told their stories of how they came to know Jesus, sang songs, performed skits, and communicated the gospel to crowds of people. They embraced the Romanian young people and the culture. And the Romanian kids embraced them.

Eva, our friend from the train station, did come to our first meeting, and she told us afterward that she felt very loved by our team. She explained how she felt isolated, friendless, totally hopeless, and physically weak because she smoked too much.

"I must go," she finished. "I feel too guilty to stay here." But she *did* stay and asked scores of questions, not arguing but humbly inquiring about Christ. We talked to her about Jesus, but she said she needed time to think. Two nights later, after one of our meetings, she received Christ while talking with a girl on our team. Later we agreed that if only for Eva, the trip was worth it. But Eva became only one of scores of divine appointments for this green group of missionaries. God did a good work through them that continues to this day.

About half a million kids go on missions trips like that every summer. For some it's just a trip. But for many it's a yearning that God has put in their hearts to answer the practical side of the question we asked in the last chapter.

How does God want to use my life to change the world for His glory?

In the last chapter we explored personal vision; now let's delve into world vision. God has the world on His heart. Clearly He is changing the world. And He wants us and our kids to join Him. When we do this, the Lord will use the already hot flame in our kids' hearts to spread the fire of God's desire.

How does God plan to use us and our kids to change the world for His glory?

Get Out of the House

Toys and raisins cluttered the kitchen floor. Three kids from the neighborhood danced around the toys and stomped on the raisins. Puddles of melted Popsicles covered the counter. Ear-splitting squeals bounced off the walls. Six-year-old Ginny, along with her friends, hung on my legs and tugged on my pants. At the breaking point, I shouted, "Get out of the house!"

Probably that scenario has never happened in your home! But if perchance it has, you know the feeling. Surely God must feel like that sometimes in dealing with His children, especially overly comfortable children who just want to stay in the house.

Loudly and clearly God is saying to us and to our kids, "Get out of the house!" Yet more often than not, parents do not respond to God's communiqué. Naturally when we think about our kids leaving home, we tend to freak out because we want to hold on to our children. But supernaturally God says, "Get out of the house!" Let's stop here and get a reading on our "freak out level" by taking the "Get Out of the House/ Freak Out Survey" below.

On a scale of 1–10 respond to these statements with 1 as "agree" and 10 as "disagree":

• I don't like it when my kids take their faith too seriously.

1   2   3   4   5   6   7   8   9   10

• I don't want my kids to have to sacrifice the "nice things" that the American Dream offers.

1   2   3   4   5   6   7   8   9   10

• I do not get very involved in my kids' youth ministry activities.

1	2	3	4	5	6	7	8	9	10

• I am not engaged in actively discipling my kids.

1	2	3	4	5	6	7	8	9	10

• I tend to resent my kids having to raise financial support for missions trips.

1	2	3	4	5	6	7	8	9	10

• I won't let my kids go on an overseas missions trip because I fear for their safety.

1	2	3	4	5	6	7	8	9	10

• I shudder at the idea of my kids moving far away to become a minister or missionary.

1	2	3	4	5	6	7	8	9	10

How did you do? Did you notice that every sentence in the survey started with *I*? If your numbers tended to hang fairly close to the first letter of each sentence, then it's time to redirect *your* "get out of the house" desires toward *God's* "get out of the house" desires for your kids. If the numbers tended toward the high end, then I hope you will indeed follow through on releasing your children to change the world.

No doubt God wants us to release our children. He made that clear from the outset. At the beginning, in the book of Genesis, God made His first "get out of the house" statement to Abram/Abraham.

> *The LORD had said to Abram, "Leave your country, your people and your father's household and go to the land I will show you. I will make you into a great nation and I will bless you; I will make your name great, and you will be a blessing. I will bless those who bless you . . . and all peoples on earth will be blessed through you."*
>
> GENESIS 12:1-3

Leave, God said to Abram. Human nature causes us to think that we receive God's blessing by *holding on* to what we have. God knows that we receive His blessing by *letting go* of what we have. Our view versus God's view. I wonder which is correct? Hmmm. Everyone wants blessing. If we selfishly choose to hold on to our kids, thinking that pursuing that option leads to blessing, big mistake! Blessing never comes from holding on. If we unselfishly choose to let go, then we receive blessing. It just makes sense to select God's option.

God wants to bless us to be a blessing to our children.

In Abraham, God offers a particularly vivid illustration of how He applies His blessing through children. Abraham received the promise of blessing from God. But soon the same God tested him. The test? Giving up Abraham's only son! God told Abraham to go up on the mountain and sacrifice his son. That seems foolish to us! God *gave* him his son in the first place. What was He thinking? But to Abraham it didn't matter how God reached this conclusion. He obeyed (Genesis 22:1-11).

Abraham built an altar on the mountain and arranged the firewood. Then he bound Isaac and laid him on the altar. With the knife in Abraham's hand, ready to come down to slay his son, God stopped him, saying, *Now I know that you fear God, because you have not withheld from me your son, your only son* (v. 12). God gave Abraham a few minutes to get over the shock, then spoke to him a second time. *I swear by myself . . . that because you have done this and have not withheld your son, your only son, I will surely bless you . . . and through your offspring all nations on earth will be blessed, because you have obeyed me* (vv. 16-18).

No story can have more impact on parents than this one—except, of course, that of the Heavenly Father giving His one and only Son. More than anyone, God understood what He had asked Abraham to do. God poured out blessing on Abraham because he offered his son to God. He let go of his child!

What bearing does this story have on us? Just as astounding as God's blessing to Abraham is the blessing God desires to give to us. The apostle Paul, after summarizing the *blessed to be a blessing* promise, says, *So those who have faith are blessed along with Abraham, the man of faith* (Galatians 3:9). That's us!

Clearly, then, we can conclude that we, like Abraham, have been *blessed to be a blessing.*[1] God presents His blessing to us by the supreme example of a Father giving the gift of His Son. Jesus is the blessing! Once we receive the Father's gift of His Son, the blessing begins. Then it follows that we, like God and Abraham, are to offer our children as gifts. We let go of them, putting them on God's altar and presenting them to Him. That's how the blessing continues.

Soon after my son Scott turned two years old, one day he chose to waddle out the front door. He moved rapidly toward the street. About the time I saw him, a big bus rolled down the street in our direction. In sheer panic I made a dive for my little boy and pulled him back from the curb. Over the next few days the picture in my mind of Scott getting run over by that bus haunted my mind. Every free moment my mind ran to that thought. I hovered over Scott, thinking I could protect him.

A few mornings later I came across the Abraham/Isaac story while reading *The Pursuit of God* by A. W. Tozer. One line from the book gripped me: "He who possesses nothing owns everything." God spoke to me so clearly that I actually clutched my son in my arms, walked out into the yard, got on my knees, and offered him to God.

"He who possesses nothing owns everything" (A. W. Tozer).

Later the Lord reminded me of His promise that *because you have done this and have not withheld your son, your only son, I will surely bless you* (Genesis 22:16-17).

The next day that city bus changed routes and never came down our street again! I promise! As only God can do, He created a circumstance early in my parenting years that brought me to the place of letting go of my son. It wasn't the last time I had to let go. But I did learn through that first experience that I could trust God with my kids. And when I did, then, like Abraham, the blessing flowed. But for what purpose? As clearly as God spoke His promise to Abraham, he speaks to us: *Through your offspring all nations on earth will be blessed, because you have obeyed me* (Genesis 22:18).[2]

Catch a Glimpse of the World

Blessed to be a blessing! God spoke that message to Abram, and He continued to broadcast that message throughout the Bible. He declares that, as with Abram, He wants to give us His blessing, particularly through our children.

We see throughout the Bible this broad, sweeping picture of how God arranged for His blessing to flow. Like any good book, the Bible has an introduction, rising action, climax, falling action, and conclusion. In the introduction, Genesis 1–11, the drama is set up through describing God's nature, man's image, and sin's distortion. The rising action, Genesis 12—Malachi, explains redemption's story. The climax, the Gospels, highlights Jesus' cross and resurrection, the heart of which is summarized in John 3:16.

For God so loved the world that he gave his one and only Son, that whoever believes in him shall not perish but have eternal life.

The falling action includes most of the remainder of the New Testament, beginning with Acts 1:8.

But you will receive power when the Holy Spirit comes on you; and you will be my witnesses in Jerusalem, and in all Judea and Samaria, and to the ends of the earth.

In the Bible's conclusion we get to visualize what God had in mind all along by blessing us.

After this I looked and there before me was a great multitude that no one could count, from every nation, tribe, people and language, standing before the throne and in front of the Lamb.

REVELATION 7:9

Throughout the centuries God has operated on the *blessed to be a blessing* principle, leading to this grand finale. What a sight that will be!

This sweeping view from the beginning to the end shows clearly that the Bible proclaims the *blessing* message. We receive the blessing; then we offer that blessing to others, who then offer it to others. As a result more and more people enter into God's blessing. Awesome!

In this generation the Lord has accelerated His blessing activity. It seems as if He has decided to put the pedal to the metal so to speak. Parents, caught up in the day-to-day activities of raising our children, can easily become isolated from God's worldwide activity. But He desires for us to see what He is doing globally in order to build our confidence in what He can do through us and our kids locally. When we look beyond our little corner of the world, we can catch sight of a sweeping view of God's exploits around the world and then expose our children to God's global movement. Note only a few examples:

• On average, 178,000 people worldwide convert to follow Jesus Christ daily.

• In the People's Republic of China 28,000 people become believers every day. In 1950, when China closed to missionaries, there were one million believers. Today estimates approach 100 million believers.

• In Africa 20,000 conversions occur daily; 40 percent of Africa is said to be "Christian" now.

• In 1900 Korea was deemed impossible to penetrate. Today in Korea more than 40 percent of the population call themselves Christian.

• In Indonesia, the largest Islamic country in the world, at least a million people convert to Christ each year.

• More Muslims in Iran have come to Christ since 1980 than in the previous thousand years combined.

In A.D. 100 there were 360 non-Christians per true believer. Today the ratio is less than seven for every believer.[3] Follow this diagram to note the significant ratio change.

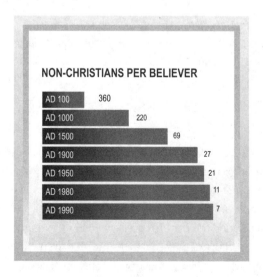

NON-CHRISTIANS PER BELIEVER

AD 100	360
AD 1000	220
AD 1500	69
AD 1900	27
AD 1950	21
AD 1980	11
AD 1990	7

Statistics like these get me fired up! Yet seeing it up close and personal is even more compelling. As a leader of a ministry that equips youth leaders around the globe, I see God's *blessed to be a blessing* plan in action consistently. In Russia, Ukraine, and other parts of Eastern Europe, in Cuba, Central America, Egypt, and all across Africa, our teams equip churches and youth leaders in Jesus-Focused Youth Ministry. In Africa, for example, people under twenty comprise about 65-70 percent of the population. We see a rising tide of interest in the church to reach the younger generation. Charles Juma, our leader in Kenya/Tanzania, recently reported, "I traveled to the most interior part of Kenya. I just stopped in Kisumu, speaking to numerous schools in the middle of nowhere. I have spoken to 87,000 students, and 26,000 have responded to Christ as Savior and Lord." Astonishing!

> **The Holy Spirit invisibly but actively works all the time in all places.**

Our ministry only plays a small part in the sweeping work of God around the world. Yet from seeing a tiny slice of God's global action, I have reached this conclusion: *the Holy Spirit invisibly but actively works all the time in all places.* He is doing so much more than even the most astute observers can document. And He uses people like us and our children to accomplish His work!

Join the Mission

From a quick survey of God's global movement, let's go one step further. Let's consider how to get involved in it. Once we lead our kids to get out of the house and catch a glimpse of the world, we need to take them somewhere. Not just anywhere, doing just anything, but rather going in God's direction and doing God's plan. What plan? As a follow-through to God's *blessed to be a blessing* plan, He desires to use all of our children to finish the task of fulfilling the Great Commission!

> **God wants to use our children to finish the task of fulfilling the Great Commission!**

Just as the last minutes of an exciting game take the most concentration, completing the Great Commission calls for asserting an intense two-minute drill. God wants to use us and our kids as time ticks down to the final buzzer.

Our families play a critical role in God's plan to finish His task. Even with our struggle to release our children, we can see from Genesis to Revelation that God's design and desire draw us to join His mission. And in it we can find deep satisfaction.

A Gallup survey found that Christians involved in changing their world here and abroad comprise 10 percent of the American population. These people feel satisfied with their lives far above the rest of the population. Yes, the Lord does desire for us *to glorify God by finding our satisfaction in Him.* And He designed us to do that by participating in His Great Commission task.

What does the Great Commission mission look like? Writer Robert Coleman offers this assessment: "When His [Jesus'] plan is reflected upon, the basic philosophy is so different from the modern church that its implications are nothing less than revolutionary."[4] Let's go back to the Source to see what Jesus had in mind about His mission.

> *Then Jesus came to them and said, "All authority in heaven and on earth has been given to me. Therefore go and make disciples of all nations, baptizing them in the name of the Father and of the Son and of the Holy Spirit, and teaching them to obey everything I have commanded you. And surely I am with you always, to the very end of the age."*
>
> MATTHEW 28:18-20[5]

As the shaft of a spear follows its tip, Jesus bids us to follow His Great Commission example and command. His disciples definitely followed the tip. They gave up their lives in pursuit of that mission. What motivated them? And what motivation draws us and our kids to do the same? What did Jesus have in mind?

• Jesus has *all authority in heaven and on earth.* Jesus has the absolute right to exercise power over all resources everywhere in the heavens (think universe) and earth (think the entire world). With the North Star, one of our closest stars, four hundred light years away, we get some small idea of how much authority He exercises. Jesus has what it takes to get the job done! And since He lives in us, He can get the job done through us!

• Jesus tells us where to go! He uses the phrase *as you go*, or we can say, *since you are going*... For parents that can mean, "Since you are going, go where your kids go." For our kids: "Since you are going to school anyway, go to your friends." Simply put, we go where Jesus leads us, and we do what He tells us to do. Then wherever we find ourselves, He will use us there.

• Jesus instructs us on what to do—*make disciples*. From Chapter 10 we know this means investing in Jesus-focused relationships with our kids and their friends. In time they become multiplying disciple-makers. That's important because . . .

• Jesus has His eyes fixed on *all nations*. In a world with over six billion people, three billion of them under twenty-five years old, and over 100 million people who have never heard Jesus' name, we have a huge task. However . . .

• Jesus promised us, *I am with you always*. With His presence and power living in us and working through us and our kids, we can have confidence that He will use us to do our small part in completing the task of fulfilling the Great Commission.

That brings us full circle. Since most of our children live in their own little worlds, what can we do to help them break out and begin to experience the Great Commission? How can we help them penetrate their culture to communicate Jesus to their friends at school and to people from other cultures? How can our children change the world by making a difference in their own little worlds and then gradually expand their worlds to include a vision for the whole world?

Take the Trip

An old gospel song begins, "I'm gonna take a trip in the good ole gospel ship." Jesus challenges us and our kids to take that vision-expanding trip!

> *But you will receive power when the Holy Spirit comes on you; and you will be my witnesses in Jerusalem, and in all Judea and Samaria, and to the ends of the earth.*
>
> ACTS 1:8

Jesus' words here move us from a Great Commission vision to Acts 1:8 action. What action? Our Acts 1:8 Strategy.

Action #1: Communicate to our kids: "Through *the power of the Holy Spirit*, God will use you to change your generation!" Without Jesus' power that statement looks foolish, but with it this challenge to our kids becomes a motivating reality.

Action #2: Carry out Jesus' four models of ministry as *witnesses*. As *witnesses* we can begin by implementing with our kids the plans from Jesus' four models of ministry in the last chapter—loving, serving, caring, and telling.

Action #3: Confirm the destination and the stops along the way— *Jerusalem . . . Judea . . . Samaria . . . the ends of the earth.*

• *Jerusalem*—the neighborhood, friends, and our kids' friends.

• *Judea*—work and our kids' schools.

• *Samaria*—other cultures and people groups, outside our comfort zone.

• *The ends of the earth*—another country that represents the vast majority of the world's population, yet has almost none of its resources.

Implementing our Acts 1:8 Strategy moves us down the road on our Great Commission trip!

What an adventure! On the Great Commission trip, boring does not exist!

On the Great Commission trip, boring does not exist!

For example, my kids, their friends, and I traveled by bus on the final leg of another trip into Romania. Previous experience told me that crossing the border would be a nightmare. About three miles from the border, the traffic backed up. Not one truck or car was moving forward. My co-leader and I walked to the border station to determine the holdup, only to find that the border guards had taken three hours off to watch the Romania/Ireland soccer match! Not one single person manned the border booths!

Knowing our tight schedule, we hurried back to the bus and asked the kids to pray. Five minutes later, suddenly, without the bus driver understanding one word of our English prayer, he turned the bus around on the small two-lane road with a steep embankment that dropped off on each side. Then he drove against the traffic with cars veering out of his way. He then headed his huge bus across an open field. Kids bounced and screamed the whole way. Finally we drove onto a small road that we traveled for about ten miles, arriving at another border crossing, a small one that apparently few knew about. Not one vehicle stood in the way of our crossing the border. Our team went through without a hitch. Kids were shouting and thanking God for a direct answer to prayer and one exciting bus ride! And that was just the first day!

Each day I watched my kids and their friends *love, serve, care, and tell.* They witnessed for Christ and led Romanian teenagers to know Him. One day I stood on a street corner watching my teenage son Jonathan lead a Romanian student to follow Jesus. As a parent nothing else quite measures up to that thrill! And our kids came home with their luggage full of Great Commission adventures.

> **Our kids come home with their luggage full of Great Commission adventures.**

From such adventures, God will fire up our kids' hearts for more *loving, serving, caring, and telling.* They will have gotten out of the house, caught a glimpse of the world, joined the mission, and taken the trip, all of which will lead them to do their part to change the world.

Stand in Awe

But will our kids pursue Jesus and His strategy once they're out of the house and on their own—the ultimate test of the validity of this book? Every person and situation plays out differently, but I offer this final illustration of encouragement as we bring our *Parent Fuel* journey to a close.

From the street corner in Romania as a high school student fast forward to my son Jonathan's freshman year in college. He joined a fraternity that year, a test of his relationship with and resolve about Jesus. Like all college freshmen he had his struggles, yet he lived out his faith. As a result he experienced some persecution in the fraternity, which fueled his fire even more. Instead of backing down, he responded with this e-mail when given the required assignment to submit a report entitled "What I Regard As Most Important in My Life." I quote Jonathan's response in part:

> In order to give you a better insight on my life, it is imperative that I share with you about the three most important things in my life: family, friends and faith.
>
> . . . Most important is my faith in Jesus Christ. I believe that all men are sinful and separated from God. Therefore, they cannot know and experience God's love and plan for their lives. . . . I believe that Jesus Christ is God's only provision for man's sin. I believe that we must individually receive Jesus Christ as Savior and Lord to know and experience God's love and plan for our lives. . . . Apart from Jesus Christ I am nothing. I believe that Jesus Christ lives in me and that my sins are forgiven. I believe that I am a child of God. I believe that I have received eternal life with God in heaven. I believe I can experience that abundant life right now.
>
> These three most important facets of my life are my identity. Without them I am not Jonathan Barry St. Clair.

Jonathan then sent his assigned paper to the entire fraternity.

Back then when I read that e-mail the first time, I realized that on his own, out of the house and without the input of his parents, Jonathan, the kid who had grown into an adult, had become a God-lover, a Christ-follower, a still-growing but maturing disciple, a God-glorifier with a deep desire to change the world. Knowing that about him and my other kids has caused me to *stand in awe* at God's gracious involvement in their lives and to sit back and enjoy watching the fire of God's desire burn in and spread through them.

Now as I read Jonathan's e-mail I realize that it offers a fitting end to this book. In the first chapter the college student who wrote that e-mail ran away from home as a ten-year-old. How quickly those years flew by! Looking back, the span of time to fuel the fire inside my kids seems so brief. In spite of many mistakes and by God's grace, the *loving God with all your heart* spark in them ignited into a flaming fire. And it will be so with your kids!

Close this book with confidence. When we pour our parent fuel on our kids' *love God with all your heart* spark, in time God ignites that spark into a fire inside our kids!

Taking Action

Make the decision to release your children to change the world. Then, using what you learned in this chapter, map out your route to get out of the house, catch a glimpse of the world, join the mission, and take a trip—a detailed Acts 1:8 Strategy.

Penetrating Questions

1. How did you rate yourself on the "Get Out of the House/Freak Out Survey"?

2. Do you think that God put you on this earth so you can be *blessed to be a blessing*? Why or why not?

3. What does the story of Abraham releasing his son Isaac to God mean to you as it relates to your releasing your children to God?

4. When you hear statistics and stories about the Holy Spirit's activity around the world, how do you respond? Why?

5. How do you react when you read the Great Commission in Matthew 28:18-20? How do you relate it to yourself? To your kids?

6. How can you help your kids break out of their own little worlds? What does your family's Acts 1:8 Strategy look like?

7. What benefits do you see for yourself, your family, and your children by implementing your Acts 1:8 Strategy?

Fresh Ideas

- Place this prayer where you will be reminded to pray it often: "Lord, I release my children to you. Use them to change the world."

- With your spouse draw two pictures. (No artistic skills needed.) 1: Your expectations of your children's future. 2: God's desires for your children's future. Frankly discuss how those two pictures differ. Then write a one-paragraph reflection on why you find it hard to release your children to God and what steps you will take to release them to Him.

- With your family read Genesis 12:1-3, then brainstorm a list of at least ten ways God has blessed you. Next make a list of ten ways you can bless others. Do this often with your family.

- Sit in your children's rooms for thirty minutes each, looking at what you see there. Make a list of what appears to be important to them. Of those things, what hinders each one from following Jesus? What encourages him/her to follow Jesus?

- In conversation with your child, choose one friend who needs Jesus. Use one or all four of Jesus' models to love, serve, care for, and tell that friend.
- Plan a night to write your testimonies as a family, then share them with each other.
- With your child, pray about and plan a missions trip you will take together in the next year.
- Read out loud a missionary book with your family at the evening meal, before bed, traveling in the car, or on vacation. I recommend the movie/book combination of *End of the Spear* and *Through Gates of Splendor* by Elisabeth Elliot.[6] The movie and the documentary tell the powerful story of five missionaries martyred by the Auca Indians in 1956.

Further Reading

Patrick Johnstone, *Operation World* (Grand Rapids, MI: Zondervan, 2001); www.gmi.org/ ow. This book provides a compilation of information on each country in the world and how to pray for each country.

John Piper, *Let the Nations Be Glad* (Grand Rapids, MI: Baker, 2003). This popular volume gives a challenge to pursue God's missionary plan for the world.

Barry St. Clair, *Leading Edge Climber's Guide*, Reach Out Youth Solutions. This training manual equips your kids for a cross-cultural trip. Focusing on seven leadership qualities of Jesus, it prepares your kids to discover these seven qualities of Jesus and then apply them on a mission trip.

Appendix 1:
Heart Helpers

*Create in me a clean heart, O God,
and put a new and right spirit within me.*
PSALM 51:10, RSV

After reading John Flavel's *Keeping the Heart,* I created six debris-cleaning tools, heart helpers if you like. These can assist us and our kids in cleaning up our hearts.

Heart Helpers

1. *Search.* Be honest. Our willingness to search ourselves shows that God's spring is flowing in our hearts. Pray Psalm 139:23-24 back to God.

2. *Turn.* Often looking inside ourselves causes us pain! Our pride wants to hide the pain. But humility says, "Lord, I uncover my hurt, my pain, my wound, my sin." Reflect on Isaiah 57:15 to see how God wants us to turn from our pride and turn to Him in humility.

3. *Agree.* To turn away from ourselves and to God, we simply agree with Him about the way He sees us. Turning Psalm 51:10 and 1 John 1:9 into prayer will lead us into agreement with God.

4. *Vow.* If we struggle with a wound, sin, or pain that we find particularly hard to resolve, we can make a vow to God and count on Him to enable us to fulfill it. For example, God has made a vow (promise) to us that we *can do everything through him who gives [us] strength* (Philippians 4:13). Because He made that vow to us, we can express that vow back to Him: "Lord, I can do all things through You who gives me strength."

5. *Stay alert.* Once God cleans the debris from our hearts, He wants

to keep them clean. We can keep clean hearts by staying alert to discover and stifle any wrong passion/desire/sin before it gets out of control. According to Ephesians 1:18-23, we can do that by not keeping our eyes on the passions/desires but on the Source of our life.

6. *Enjoy.* When we choose *the path of life*, we get to enjoy the results (Psalm 16:11): *Fill me with joy in your presence and with eternal pleasures at your right hand* (Psalm 16:11). Life doesn't get any better than that—on this earth or in eternity!

Appendix 2:
Time Alone with God

PRAYING FOR MY KIDS

(Child's Name)

DATE	NEED	ANSWER

PRAYER ACTION 𝒵

Date:

PRAISE: Write down one expression of praise.

THANKSGIVING: Write down what you are most thankful for today.

CONFESSION: Write down any sin(s) you need to confess.

PETITION: Write down one need you have in your life today.

INTERCESSION: Write the names of people you are praying for today and a phrase that expresses your prayer for each person.

BIBLE RESPONSE 📖

Date:

PASSAGE:

TITLE:

KEY VERSE:

SUMMARY / OUTLINE:

PERSONAL APPLICATION:

Appendix 3:
The Practical Steps to Discipling Your Kids and Their Friends[1]

When I equip parents to disciple their kids, I like to ask, "Can you read?" Making disciples is that simple. Often church stuff gets way too complicated. But God has an amazing knack for putting the cookies on the lower shelf for people like me.

To get started follow these clear-cut, practical steps.

1. *Pray.* This step serves as a reminder that without God's presence and power we don't accomplish anything of eternal value. Invite the presence and power of God into everything you do. (See the first section of Chapter 10 for practical applications.)

2. *Challenge.* Some parents fear inviting their own kids to join them in the disciple-making adventure. That's understandable, but that kind of fear doesn't come from God. You may think of many reasons why your child would not want to do this. Resist those thoughts.

When I first asked Jonathan to take the discipleship challenge, he resisted. Like most kids, he didn't want his dad around his friends. I pressed the issue, asking him to experiment with this for six weeks. He agreed. When I challenged him, with my Bible open to Matthew 4:19, I looked him in the eyes and said, "Jonathan, I see God's potential in you. He has such a great purpose for your life. I want to help you discover how to follow Jesus and to fish for men. That's why I want to start this group." You can use the same verse and the same words.

3. *Select.* With Jonathan on the team, I invited him to help me recruit

his friends. I asked him who he thought had a desire to grow spiritually. He gave me good feedback.

Jonathan and I went together to meet with each person individually. This gave Jonathan some ownership of and leadership with the group. I gave the same personal challenge to each of the other guys as I gave it to Jonathan. You can do the same.

4. *Commit.* Once I had challenged each person individually, we met as a group. In a relaxed atmosphere I discussed the following issues:

• *The cost:* "We will meet one hour every Tuesday at 6:45 A.M. I am asking you to pay a price, so to speak, to join this group. I don't anticipate too many conflicts. If you commit, you will need to attend every week and go to sleep a little earlier on Monday nights."

• *The benefit:* "This group will help you become a man of God. You will move toward maturity in Christ and will become a leader who helps others know Christ."

• *The commitment:* "Take this book. It will guide us each week. As part of the commitment, you must come prepared. Turn to page 11 in *Following Jesus* so we can understand clearly our commitments to each other." I asked different ones to read each point. I repeated this two more times, so they got the seriousness of their commitment. Then I had all of us sign each other's book on page 11 as a pledge of our commitment to the group and to each other.

• *The price:* I also charged them for the book. This helped them realize that becoming part of the group would cost them something.

5. *Prepare.* Prior to the first group meeting several actions need to occur for you and the kids to come prepared.

• View the group as a long-term process—you will disciple your child the rest of your life! Hopefully you will work with this particular group over the next few years.

• Use the materials with the long-term process in view. In the "Moving Toward Maturity" series five books of ten weeks each will take you on a stair-step course of maturing your group in Christ. Each book builds on the previous one.

Following Jesus builds a solid foundation for a life-changing relationship with Christ and for becoming a disciple of Christ.

Spending Time Alone with God deepens each person's relationship with Jesus by teaching how to spend time with Him.

Making Jesus Lord challenges each person to obey Jesus and to give Him control in day-to-day issues.

Giving Away Your Faith guides each person into the wild adventure of overcoming his or her fears and taking the risk to boldly communicate Christ.

Influencing Your World shows the group members that they can become influential leaders through serving the needs of the people around them.

Three additional books will supplement the discipling process. The *Moving Toward Maturity Leader's Guide* is particularly vital for you as the group leader. That guide gives you everything you need to lead a lively and life-changing discipleship group. The book contains the leader's material for the five books in the series.

Time Alone with God Notebook gives each person the practical tools for guiding him or her in a daily adventure with God.

Getting Started helps new believers successfully begin their walk with Christ.

Going through these books will take two-plus years. If you begin while your kids attend middle school and they finish in two years, they can begin to disciple a younger group of kids—multiplying disciple-makers.

• Order *Following Jesus* and the *Moving Toward Maturity Leader's Guide* online at www.reach-out.org. You will want to get your own copy of *Following Jesus*. Go through it just like the kids go through their books.

• Decide with the group the time, place, length of meeting, and size of the group. Ideal is from four to eight kids. Each book takes at least ten weeks to complete.

6. *Lead.* The success of the group depends not so much on the curriculum but on the way you lead. Build the relationships. Keep them focused. Follow these guidelines to structure the group.

• Focus. Begin each meeting reminding them of the purpose of the group. Memorize Matthew 4:19, and say it to each other weekly.

• Review. For the first two weeks, go over the commitments on page

11 of *Following Jesus*. Remind them to come prepared. Each week ask them to review one specific insight that God taught them the previous week and one way they applied that insight.

• Pray. After reminding them of their purpose, divide them into prayer triplets. Keep them in the same groups for several weeks, then switch. If the group doesn't divide exactly in threes, pray in twos.

• Discuss. Spend at least thirty to forty minutes going through the material related to the book. When they raise topics outside the discussion, engage them, but do not get derailed. Discuss those topics later. At the same time encourage them to talk. Resist the temptation to lecture or do all the talking.

• Share. Save time each week to talk about the personal issues and questions they raise. At first the conversation will be surface, but as the group grows closer they will openly discuss their issues. If time becomes a problem, invite them to your house to continue.

• Involve. Early in the group involve them in doing some ministry outside the group—meeting a need at their school, going to the inner city, doing a local missions project, or taking a missions trip overseas.

As you follow these steps, the Lord will use you with your kids and their friends in ways you cannot even imagine now!

These steps may be reproduced and used without obtaining permission from the author or publisher.

Other Resources by Barry St. Clair

To Encourage Parents

Life Happens: Help Your Teenager Get Ready
Talking to Your Kids About Love, Sex and Dating

To Pray with Passion

An Awesome Way to Pray Student Guide
An Awesome Way to Pray Leader's Guide

To Equip Youth Leaders

Jesus-Focused Youth Ministry

To Train Adult Volunteers

Building Leaders (3-book set)
    A Personal Walk with Jesus Christ
    A Vision for Life and Ministry
    Essential Tools for Leading Students

To Disciple Students

Moving Toward Maturity (8-book set plus 6 CDs)
    Following Jesus
    Spending Time Alone with God
    Making Jesus Lord
    Giving Away Your Faith
    Influencing Your World
    Moving Toward Maturity Leader's Guide
    Getting Started
    Time Alone with God Notebook

Jesus No Equal Set
> *Jesus No Equal*
> *Jesus No Equal Journal*

Leading Edge Trip Climbers Guide
> *Equipping Student Leaders on a Cross-cultural Trip*

Life Happens: Get Ready

To Reach Out to Students

Penetrating the Campus
Taking Your Campus for Christ
The Magnet Effect

Notes

Chapter 1: Wanted: Fire-Builders—Perfection Not Required for This Job
1. Jonathan has approved the use of this story here.
2. See Tim Kimmel, *Grace-Based Parenting* (Nashville: W Publishing Group, 2004), p. 8.

Chapter 3: Dry Out the Firewood: Gain New Purpose for Old Pain
1. Neil T. Anderson, *Victory Over the Darkness* (Ventura, CA: Regal Books, 2000), p. 50.

Chapter 4: Dry More Firewood: Gain More New Purpose for Old Pain
1. Used by permission of Interdev Partnership Associates, Edmund, WA; www.interdev.org.
2. Adapted from Neil T. Anderson, *Victory Over the Darkness* (Ventura, CA: Regal Books, 2000), pp. 203-205.

Chapter 5: Create a Draft: Open the Door and Let Grace Blow In
1. I am not promoting permissiveness with our children. I will address permissiveness in Chapter 11.
2. Religion is man working his way up to God. Grace is God coming down to man.
3. We find the apostle Paul's explanation of legalism specifically in Galatians 2:15-16; 3:1-3, 12-13, 22-23.
4. We discover the apostle Paul's reasoning for grace in Galatians 2:20-21; 5:1, 13, 16-18, 22-25.
5. We will discuss freedom further in Chapter 11.
6. See Chapter 11.
7. When our kids showed an interest and started asking questions, we used a simple tool to explain the gospel to them. See Further Reading at the end of this chapter and Chapter 15 for more information and resources.
8. We will discuss these later in the book. In fact, from here on each chapter will offer you both the causes and effects that result from throwing the grace door open wider and wider.

Chapter 6: Stir Up the Fire by Relating to Our Kids
1. Juliet Schor, *Born to Buy: The Commercialized Child and the New Consumer Culture* (New York: Scribner, 2004), p. 21.
2. Richard Halicks, "Products to Sell, Money to Be Made," *The Atlanta Journal-Constitution*, August 22, 2004.
3. Quoted in Josh McDowell, *The Disconnected Generation* (Nashville: Thomas Nelson, 2000), p. 10, as quoted in Barbara Kantrowitz and Pat Wingert, "How Well Do You Know Your Kid?" *Newsweek*, May 5, 1999, pp. 38-39.
4. Josh McDowell, *Beyond Belief* (Wheaton, IL: Tyndale House, 2002), p. 81.
5. George Barna, *Real Teens* (Ventura, CA: Regal, 2001), p. 68.
6. Ibid., p. 72.
7. Reach Out Youth Solutions, with its *Jesus-Focused Youth Ministry*, addresses these issues and offers a solution through applying the message and methods of Jesus to youth ministry. Through this relational disciple-making process, youth leaders, parents, students, and churches reconnect with kids to lead them to experience life-change and to become life-changers. See www.reach-out.org.
8. Barna, *Real Teens*, p. 124.

Notes

9. For starters see Genesis 12:2-3; Deuteronomy 6:4-7; Malachi 4:2-6; Matthew 18:3-6; 19:4-6; 21:15-16.
10. Chapter 10 covers this subject extensively.
11. Benny Proffitt, *Charting the Course* (Franklin, TN: Scribe Publishers, 2005), pp. 14-15.

Chapter 7: Burn Away the Junk to Find the Heart of Gold

1. To learn more about the heart with your kids, you can look up a few of the references in a standard concordance, about seventy-five verses, and discuss one verse per week.
2. John Eldredge and Brent Curtis, *The Sacred Romance* (Nashville: Thomas Nelson, 1997), p. 3. Several of the above-mentioned and after-mentioned ideas on the heart came from this book.
3. Ibid., pp. 5, 6, 10.
4. John Flavel, *Keeping the Heart* (Morgan, PA: Soli Deo Gloria Publications, 1998), p. 22.
5. Ibid., p. 4.
6. Quoted in Eldredge and Curtis, *The Sacred Romance,* p. 71.
7. Some of these thoughts about "The Biggest Lie" come from ibid., pp. 76, 78.
8. Flavel, *Keeping the Heart,* p. 2.

Chapter 8: Build a Fire That Blazes with Intimacy

1. Genesis 1:27, Galatians 3:26-28, and other passages confirm this statement. In Galatians 3:28 "one" means related to and equal with each other.

Chapter 9: Feed the Fire with Communication

1. See the previous chapter.

Chapter 10: Pour Fuel on the Fire by Making Disciples

1. In a tool I developed entitled *Jesus-Focused Youth Ministry,* you will find a comprehensive approach to how Jesus made disciples. This training tool for youth leaders has 118 pages of insights and nine hours of training on audio CDs. You can order *Jesus-Focused Youth Ministry* through www.reach-out.org.
2. Soon after I became a believer, I began to keep a Time Alone with God Notebook. I structured it around the prayer themes of praise, thanksgiving, confession, petition, and intercession. You will find the Petition page to pray specifically for your kids on page 249 in Appendix 2. You can order your own *Time Alone with God Notebook* from www.reach-out.org.
3. To order the complete *Time Alone with God Notebook* go to www.reach-out.org.
4. Josh McDowell, *Beyond Belief* (Wheaton, IL: Tyndale House, 2002), p. 81.
5. Steve Merritt, "Sneaking Past Your Kids' Cynicism," *Group Magazine*, September/October 2001, p. 51.
6. Ibid.
7. Kitti Murray, *A Long Way Off* (Nashville: Broadman & Holman, 2004), back cover.
8. John Maxwell, *Breakthrough Parenting* (Colorado Springs: Focus on the Family, 1996), p. 45.

Chapter 11: Fan the Flame with Discipline

1. Review Chapter 8 as a reminder of how God's love coming through us to our kids really works.
2. Sometimes we need outside help to pinpoint the causes and solutions. Seek the input of a counselor if you feel you cannot get out of the punishment or permissive ditch by yourself.
3. Rich Wilkerson, *Hold Me While You Let Me* Go (Eugene, OR: Harvest House, 1983).
4. The "You Decide" idea came from Dean Merrill, "You Decide," *Focus on the Family* magazine, October 1996, pp. 6-7.
5. Barry St. Clair and Bill Jones, *Dating: Going Out in Style* (Colorado Springs: Victor Books, 1993).

Chapter 12: Intensify the Heat with Destiny

1. I put those discoveries into book form for teenagers and parents, hoping to save them years of time in realizing their own unique destiny. Some of the material for this chapter came from those books: *Life Happens: Get Ready,* and *Life Happens: Help Your Teenager Get Ready*.
2. See www.brunningonline.net/simon/blog/archives/2003_01.html.

Notes

3. Simon Tugwell, *The Beatitudes: Soundings in Christian Tradition* (Springfield, IL: Templegate Publishers, 1996), quoted by Brennan Manning, *Abba's Child* (Colorado Springs: NavPress, 1994), p. 18.
4. Literally hundreds of promises in the Bible like these provide us with identifying characteristics telling us who we are in *Christ*.
5. Peter Marshall, Jr. and David Manuel, *The Light and the Glory* (Grand Rapids, MI: Revell, 1977), p. 17.
6. See Fritz Reinecker and Cleon L. Rogers, *Linguistic Key to the Greek New Testament* (Grand Rapids, MI: Zondervan, 1980), p. 525.
7. Order "Discovering Your Personality Survey" from www.reach-out.org.
8. Order "The Spiritual Gifts Survey" at www.reach-out.org.
9. Order "The Abilities and Experiences Survey" at www.reach-out.org.
10. Order "The Motives and Motivations Test" at www.reach-out.org.
11. Order "The Purpose Discovery Exercise" from www.reach-out.org.
12. Order "The Values Investigation" at www.reach-out.org.
13. Order "The Goal-Setting Exercise" from www.reach-out.org.
14. To order "Time Tool" contact www.reach-out.org.
15. Order the "Decide" chart from www.reach-out.org.

Chapter 13: Don't Let Disappointment Douse the Fire

1. See Terry Glaspey, *C. S. Lewis: His Life and Thought* (Edison, NJ: Inspirational Press, 1996), p. 85.
2. C. S. Lewis, *The Problem of Pain* (New York: Macmillan, 1972), p. 93.
3. C. S. Lewis, *God in the Dock: Essays on Theology and Ethics* (Grand Rapids, MI: Eerdmans, 1970), p. 29.
4. Henry Rojas serves as Director of Spiritual Growth Services at Remuda Ranch in Wickenburg, Arizona, a Christian recovery facility for adolescent girls with eating disorders. Henry was the original Phoenix Suns gorilla mascot. This comment came from a message he delivered.
5. *Adonai* appears throughout the Old Testament as one of God's names. Although it does not appear in Psalm 34 specifically, the meaning of the name *the Lord* in Psalm 34 is similar to that of *Adonai*. David uses military imagery (v. 7) to capture the idea that the Lord rules and reigns.

Chapter 14: Glow in the Light of God's Vision

1. Athletes in Action is a ministry of Campus Crusade for Christ.
2. From Oswald Chambers, *He Shall Glorify Me*, quoted in David McCasland, *Abandoned to God* (Grand Rapids, MI: Discovery House Publishers, 1993), p. 207.
3. Article on Christian Hedonism; http://www.desiringgod.org/ResourceLibrary/Articles/ByDate/1995/1538_Christian_Hedonism/.
4. In the disciple-making process you can guide your kids through learning to share their faith by going through *Giving Away Your Faith*. Order at www.reach-out.org.

Chapter 15: Spread the Fire of God's Desire

1. Certainly this biblical concept of blessing stands in stark contrast to the "Name it, claim it—health, wealth, and prosperity" messages proclaimed by many today.
2. This promise to Abraham in Genesis 22:18 becomes our promise through faith in Christ. See Romans 4, especially verses 13, 16, 18-25 and Galatians 3:6-9, 29.
3. Statistics are from the Lausanne Statistical Task Force, quoted from Dave Livermore, *Serving with Eyes Wide Open* (Grand Rapids, MI: Baker Books, 2006), pp. 33-34.
4. Robert Coleman, *The Master Plan of Evangelism* (Grand Rapids, MI: Revell, 1963), p. 19.
5. The Great Commission is repeated in each of the Gospels and in Acts—Matthew 28:18-20; Mark 16:15; Luke 24:45-49; John 20:21-22; Acts 1:8.
6. Elisabeth Elliot, *Through Gates of Splendor*, 25th anniversary edition (Wheaton, IL: Tyndale House, 2005).

Scripture Index

4:13	247
4:19	211

Colossians

1:8	117
3:23	102, 197

1 Thessalonians

1:1-2	152
2:6-7, 11-12	151
2:7, 11	30
2:8	154
2:11-12	158
2:12	151
2:13	159
2:19	163
2:19-20	150
5:19	30

2 Thessalonians

2:14	221
3:3	211

1 Timothy

6:17	222

2 Timothy

2:1-2	160
2:2	162
2:15	94

Hebrews

4:12	94, 102
12:7	175
12:7-11	174
12:8	175
12:9	175
12:10	175
12:11	175

1 Peter

1:15-16	211
2:24	52
3:15	102

1 John

1:9	247
4:18	172

Revelation

7:9	237
12:10-11	59

General Index

Dr. Barry St. Clair's twenty-eight years of marriage, raising four children, the death of his first wife, his experience as a single parent, remarriage, blending a family and being a grandfather of eight makes his perspective in *Parent Fuel* real-life and compelling.

For more than thirty years Barry has been on the cutting edge of youth ministry—nationally and globally—as founder and president of Reach Out Youth Solutions. Barry speaks to, writes for, and equips youth leaders, parents, and students to influence as many teens as possible to follow Jesus.

Barry has authored over twenty-five books, played basketball for the third-ranked team in the nation, and has run the Boston Marathon. Barry and his wife Lawanna live in Atlanta, Georgia.